Deborah was raised in a very rural farming area of Pennsylvania by extremely abusive parents. While the phrase 'extremely abusive' tends to indicate physical abuses, today, we have come to understand the deeper levels of abuse that verbal and neglectful parental behaviors can inflict. Deborah survived them all. This book goes on to describe the behaviors Deborah grew into that both preserved her and nearly destroyed her at the same time.

I want to dedicate this book to my EMDR therapist. She embodies all the strength and determination necessary to conquer the challenges life throws at professional women and she does it all with grace and finesse. There are no words adequate enough to express my gratitude for her help and dedication to my recovery.

Spots on a Leopard
EMDR Saved My Life

By Deborah Susan

AUSTIN MACAULEY PUBLISHERS™

London • Cambridge • New York • Sharjah

Ordering Information:
Quantity sales: special discounts are available on quantity purchases by corporations, associations, and others. For details, contact the publisher at the address below.

Publiser's Cataloging-in-Publication data
Susan, Deborah
Spots on a Leopard

ISBN 9781641826327 (Paperback)
ISBN 9781641826334 (Hardback)
ISBN 9781641826341 (Kindle e-book)
ISBN 9781645364566 (ePub e-book)

Library of Congress Control Number: 2019935775

The main category of the book — Biography & Autobiography / General

www.austinmacauley.com/us

First Published (2019)
Austin Macauley Publishers LLC
40 Wall Street, 28th Floor
New York, NY 10005
USA

mail-usa@austinmacauley.com
+1 (646) 5125767

Loretta Zwaan – without her help to copy-type the first seven chapters, that were written in 1996 into an electronic word document (and that were only in hard copy at the time), this book would have never been published.

Table of Contents

Prelude
EMDR Saved My Life!

I asked my therapist, the most recent of so many, if we might be trying to change the spots on a leopard by trying to heal behaviors that were ingrained within me from infancy. And she replied, *"You can change these spots because they were never yours to begin with! You were raised by leopards and they projected these spots onto you. And now, we will proceed to define and remove them, one by one!"* That was the day that finally changed my life. I was 62 years old at the time…

As an actual true story, you will see how I endured severe isolation, abuse, and neglect from childhood and throughout most of my adult life. My survival was accomplished by the use of paperback psychology combined with a deep-seated faith in prayer.

I suggest that you get real comfortable before you continue on. Grab a cup of your favorite warm drink, put your feet up, and consider this the longest letter you've ever read. And that is what this book is meant to be. Read it as if it were a letter to yourself from someone you know a little more than an acquaintance; however, a little less than a friend. *(Note: all names have been changed to protect both the guilty and the innocent.)*

I suffered the realities that schizophrenics only imagine and, yet, carried on a seemingly normal life as those around me would have verified, if asked. Yet, they too witnessed some of the 'crazy' behavior.

Had I not lived it myself, I would not believe anyone could have carried on any semblance of a functional, productive life with all the 'baggage' I carried.

However, the boom and bust rollercoaster results of my life do bear witness to the inner struggles. I was never fortunate enough to have anyone around me at any time who actually provided stability or knew me well enough so that, when I went into the self-destructive behaviors, they could stop me and say, "Hey, this isn't you" and, therefore, give me a shot at stopping it. That is, until at age 61 my one and only daughter did just that and I finally found a therapists that actually provided healing techniques.

Otherwise, the people around me were always too happy to write me off as crazy, a waste of time, or a loser, until I reached a point where I just never let anyone stay in my life long enough to write me off.

I do have to acknowledge the self-help writers who became my best friends during most of the time of my life covered in this publication. They are listed at the back and I am so thankful for them even today.

These people could have just lived their successful lives in private and they could have kept it all for themselves. Yet, because they *did* take the time to share what they learned, people like myself survived and did not become the most recent suicide statistic.

In fact, each and every therapist I worked with – and there were quite a few – commented on how I should have become a drug addict, a prostitute, and/or at least homeless. Yet, had it not been for the publications I clung to with all my might, surely and truly I would not have survived it.

And so, I feel that it's my turn to give back. It's my turn to write it out so others can read it and see themselves. Maybe there will be one thing in these pages that will assist you in putting one foot in front of the other tomorrow, and to just hold on enough to carry on into the next new day.

In one of my darkest hours, I bargained with God. We agreed that I would write out the entire process of my suicide. I would write down the most recent events that led up to it. I would also write the note to inform others that my death was intentional and by my own hand.

Then, I would package it all up neatly in an envelope, with the farewell note clipped to the envelope, and I would wait one more day. If I got up the next morning feeling the same way, I was permitted to go through with it and I had God's forgiveness.

And today, I am so, so very glad I waited that one more day!

Perhaps this will give you the courage to finally reach out to a therapist and get the help you deserve as a living human being on this earth. Find an EMDR Therapist in your area. Please do it.

Because tomorrow may just be the first day of change that will adjust your path enough to shift you from going nowhere to getting somewhere, and you have to be there for that. Don't let yourself miss your own success!

Chapter One
The Formative Years

I was born in 1953 and raised in a farming community just outside the booming metropolis of Reading Pennsylvania. Yes, this is the one and the same Reading that appears as a railroad in the Monopoly board game or, at least, the one I am familiar with. And the area I speak of that was just outside of that city; if you've seen the movie 'Deliverance' with Burt Reynolds as 'Lewis', then you've seen some of my relatives in the woods as extras in the movie.

Well, okay, so they were not actually my relatives but they sure looked like them!

Being the first of three, and a successful pregnancy after a previous miscarriage, there was a great deal of pressure to be everything my parents anticipated. Yet, I had already failed miserably by being born female.

My father came from the harsh, backwoods, German (Pennsylvania Dutch) autocratic, old-school way of thinking that men are the king of the castle and women were put on earth to serve men according to their every desire. He firmly believed that firstborn females were destined to serve the family as housekeeper, babysitter, farm hand, and extra-curricular sex partner for all the blood relative males in the family. My dad had 9 brothers.

My mother strongly opposed this perspective and, therefore, I was spared the lattermost responsibility. However, while being spared that wound, I suffered being positioned in the family as the scapegoat.

You see, in those days, they did not yet know about lactose intolerance in people, much less in babies. Due to this condition that was diagnosed only in my 40s, I was what was commonly known then as a colic baby – one that cries all the time.

Since the doctors could not find anything physically wrong with me, I was diagnosed as 'spoiled'. Well, you tell two new parents – one with just an 8th grade education, and the other with a full high school diploma that put her at the top of the food chain in her own eyes – that their baby is spoiled; what do you think they'd do about that? Quite simply, they would focus on depriving that child of anything positive, loving, kind – anything that would perpetuate the spoiled condition.

And what was the sign that the spoiled condition was rectified? There wasn't one! That was my label and that's all there was to it.

My parents would get into a heated discussion and it would not take long before dad was out the door and gone somewhere. He'd stay away for hours and Mom would throw incredible temper-like tantrums.

She'd continue on with the argument, playing both sides of it. And amazingly enough, she'd always lose these arguments. By the time Dad returned, she'd just voice the conclusions she came to and he'd agree. Then she'd huff and puff around the trailer (we lived in a mobile home on a couple acres of land until I was twelve. Then dad built the house on the property right beside the trailer and the trailer was hauled away), saying, "I knew it, I knew you'd say that." But Dad rarely said anything. She carried the fight for both of them. I often wondered if he knew that.

Sometimes the rage would carry on into the next day and drain Mom of so much energy that the slightest thing would set her off into one of her spanking rampages. She'd beat me until I'd pee in my pants, then she'd beat me some more for that.

I can still feel the desperate fear and panic that would wash over me whenever Mom started getting irritated, because I knew that sooner or later I'd be in for it. She'd always find a way to take it out on me. And I suppose, in a way, it was Dad's way of punishing us both for not conforming to his preconceived notion of a woman's place.

It seemed like a normal routine to me to have Dad gone all day at work and then fall asleep at six o'clock in front of the TV. Mom would take 'nerve pills' every morning, drink a pot or two of coffee during the day, and then wonder why she couldn't sleep at night. Needless to say, she was not a morning person.

To everyone else, my dad had a heart of gold and could not do enough for others. The common bond between my parents, besides disciplining this spoiled child of theirs, was the church.

It was an Evangelical Christian Church 'filled with the spirit'. To this day, I have to wonder what 'spirit' that church was actually filled with. They preached fire and brimstone and that the fastest way to heaven was to give the most money.

The majority of the congregation was struggling just to make ends meet and yet, the preacher got a new Cadillac every other year. And the congregation accepted that as the way it should be and rejoiced, vicariously living the pleasures of every new indulgence the preacher came up with.

The spankings in the church were always administered by Dad and were accompanied with a great deal of shaming phrases repeated throughout the ordeal. These performances were applauded by the congregation, because they all knew just how awful and sinful children could be and, by gosh, they were not going to end up facing their creator someday having to answer for sparing the rod! No sirree. They had scripture to back them up on this one, and that's all they needed to justify their actions.

They also had scripture that instructed that knowledge was evil and that women were the instigators of evil. After all, was it not *Eve* who ate of the tree of '*Knowledge*'?

I still cannot believe how many years I spent believing that the tree was the tree of knowledge alone rather than the tree of knowledge of good and evil.

Naturally then, when my aptitude tests demonstrated an unmistakable ability for learning – and I was encouraged by my elementary school guidance counselor to go into the college prep course as I entered Junior High School – I was severely beaten and promptly informed that I was a farmer's daughter and that was all I'd ever be.

My parents said that if they'd known I was doing grade eight math in grade six, they would have gone to the school and knocked some sense into that know-it-all teacher too.

When the guidance counselor called my parents to invite them to come to school, to see the test results and where I was on the aptitude curve chart, my mother huffed over the phone and said, "You people think you know so much from one little test. No one is going to tell me how to raise my own child. She's my flesh and blood and I know what's best for her, not you." And she promptly hung up the phone before the guidance counselor could respond to say that it wasn't just one test. It had been my progress throughout all of my elementary schooling.

I remember that day as if it was yesterday. I recall consciously checking out both emotionally and mentally and I never came back. From that day on, no matter what my parents said, I did not believe them. I hated them that day for the first time and from then on.

Problem with that is, that I did not learn anything further from that point on. My grades plummeted. I no longer cared about anything and that severely handicapped me as I entered the world later, at age 18; totally naïve and unprepared.

Looking back now, I realize that a great deal of my parents' behavior was due to their own shame of not having enough money to 'keep up with the Joneses', so-to-speak. The thought of having to pay tuition for a college degree was way beyond their means. And to have to inquire about alternative solutions, such as student loans or scholarships, not only challenged their pride, but also threatened their standing in the church community. Knowledge was evil and the preacher could not get his next new Cadillac if the parishioners were spending money on educating the kids.

Another very important procedure in my parents' repertoire of childrearing techniques included a full report to anyone who would listen about all of my failings, misbehavior, and wild, unrealistic expectation for my own future.

The audience members included complete strangers in the grocery store line (especially if they commented something nice about me), gas station attendants (who didn't even notice I was in the car), along with the regular family members, neighbors, and fellow church attendees.

And let me tell you, everyone was very willing to assist these poor, unfortunate people handle this troublesome adolescent.

Consequently, I was not allowed to ever participate in any after-school activities. I have yet to see a high school football or basketball game. The church taught that anything outside of sitting in the pews and serving the preacher was sinful.

My parents gained such a momentum of projecting my sinfulness that I was not even allowed to participate in any church social events either. Rather, I had to sit in a chair, in my Sunday best, and just watch the others play volleyball or bean bag toss. I was told that this was to ensure that my parents knew where I was and what I was doing at all times.

It was truly like living under a microscope, and every move I made was so enormously magnified to clearly expose the deep evils within my motives and my behavior.

Years later, my brother, who was fourteen years younger than myself, did finally demonstrate what a bad kid was really like. He got into drugs, abused alcohol, and drained my dad's retirement by repeatedly crashing brand new vehicles. Amazingly, my brother was never hurt in any of the accidents.

And what was so confusing and frustrating to me at the time was that my dad was *not* a farmer. He was an entrepreneur way ahead of his time. He decided, one day, to invest in a truck with a boom and bucket on it. You've probably seen them used by electric companies to work on overhead wires. In farming areas, they are better known as 'cherry pickers', as they were used for just that.

Anyway, he got one of these and ended up making a small fortune, all by himself, painting exterior buildings in the summer. He'd do inside work in the winter, also painting and hanging wallpaper.

My dad would stand on the top of a 12-foot ladder on one foot, with the other foot holding the wallpaper against the wall, while he smoothed it from the very top with a big brush. He was an acrobat!

People hired him just to watch him work. He earned the title 'Flying Dutchman' and eventually my parents really did live well; until my brother drained them of nearly every dime!

By being so ridiculously strict, all my parents accomplished was keeping me naive and inexperienced. They withheld and denied opportunity so much that my view of the world was way more idealistic than the typical teen. I spent all my time between the ages of twelve and eighteen fantasizing about being free and being able to do what I want, yet never realizing that I didn't know what I wanted! How could I?

I would sit for hours and stare out of the window at the street across the field and watch the occasional car drive by, recognizable only by the two headlights in the dark. (We lived on an acre of land in rural, rural, Wernersville, Pennsylvania and occupied a mobile home until I was twelve.)

The isolation was maddening to my mother. Our closest neighbor was on the acre next to ours, also in a mobile home; but they were rarely home. The farm, across the dirt road which led into our little homestead, was about a quarter mile down in the valley. Norman, the youngest boy of a family of five, was eight years older than me and his sister, Martha, was two years older than myself.

Martha had started to visit us on the occasional afternoon the summer I turned fifteen. My mom was grateful for the company, and I saw it as a relief Godsend, since that was the third summer I had been confined to my own yard for the duration of the summer. The only things I was given to do were to clean my room and mow the grass. Mind you, I mowed an acre of it with a walking mower, so it did take some time. But I was not offered library books or encouraged to learn anything. I had begged to take piano lessons, but my mom just mocked me saying that music took talent and that I certainly did not have any of that. She said that my enthusiasm would last two weeks and then she'd have to nag me to keep it up. And besides, she said they had no money for piano lessons. That was the normal routine speech given any time I showed interest in anything other than housework or watching TV.

I remember the hate I used to feel during those speeches. Then my feelings would move to guilt and, finally, to shame. Today, I look back and think what a waste of precious time my youth was. I also realize that it was due to this stifling, deprived experience that I lived so fast and so furious when I was finally released from this concentration camp that I was forced to call home.

During the summers between my fifth and eleventh years, I had been privileged to visit my grandparents (my mom's parents) for two weeks on the estate where they were caretakers. That place was heaven on earth! There were acres and acres of apple orchards. An evergreen forest surrounded a manmade lily pond that had two of the biggest weeping willow trees you would have ever seen; one on each side of the pond!

My grandfather was the groundskeeper and he kept the grounds immaculate. He groomed the rock gardens and the rose gardens to perfection. Even at my earliest recollection of that place, I can still remember appreciating it from the bottom of my heart. I used to escape from all the pain and confusion there. I would run and laugh and catch a glimpse of what happiness must have been like for 'normal' kids in 'normal' families.

I had a secret here at this place. Whenever I'd go to the garden alone, I'd meet a special being there. I could never tell if it was a man or a woman. They always spoke to me in a whisper and they used to always let me do whatever I wanted to do. Sometimes they would let me dance like a ballerina. Other times, I would sing with a choir and I could feel my voice come from way down deep inside me. Sometimes, I was allowed to talk to the animals and my favorite friend was a beautiful black, gray and white German Shepherd. He taught me how to sniff the air and to feel the impulses inside me when I got close to someone to decide whether that person had good intentions or bad ones. He was also very alone, like me, and so I played with him the most. He warned me once not to ever let anyone take my freedom away. I had no idea what he meant at the time. I just giggled like little girls do when he told me that, and wrestled him to the ground.

The squirrels taught me to climb. The groundhog talked about saving up for long winters and was very scheduled about everything. The birds were too busy, and that was okay, since I couldn't fly anyway.

We would play and run and sing and dance until I was so exhausted I would just have to lie down and rest. And every single time, either my grandfather or grandmother would come and find me asleep. When I'd tell them about my latest adventure in the garden, they'd just say that I dreamed it. But I knew I had not dreamed it – it really happened. And I was really sure I had not dreamed it when, one day, the grownups were talking about someone having spotted a lone wolf roaming around the area. They said he was black, gray, and white, and that when they tried to catch him, he got away. I was glad he got away but sorry that

I'd never see him again. (And I never did see him again; not even in my dreams!)

Another very consistent pattern was that the minute my parents figured out that I was having too much fun, it was always put to a stop immediately. Alas, upon a visit one summer evening (after my two-week (parole) vacation to the estate for that year), my grandmother stood up to my parents for the first time. Mom had been going on and on, again, about how much trouble I was and how bad her nerves were because of me. My grandmother stopped her and said that she (my mother) did not know what a bad kid was. My grandmother went on to say that I was a delight to have around and that they enjoyed me so much. And it was true. I always helped 'Pop Pop' weed the garden and I would ask if 'Gramies' would bake with me. Gramies never turned me down and we always had a wonderful time.

Well, needless to say, that was the last summer I spent with my grandparents. Although, I am sure the images of that guidance counselor calling were still fresh in my parents' minds too, as that had just happened as well. Having two adults stand up for me, one right after the other, was just way too much for them to handle. And I knew how my parents loved to take things away from me, and I could feel them actually feed on my pain and suffering. They would draw strength from it and they would bond during it, because then they did not have to be at each other's throats. The two of them could finally agree on something – punishing me. So, I became the one that could do no right, and that did not change in their minds, no matter what happened or what anyone else said.

And the reason I know how well they bonded over punishing me for sure is, because I heard every word they said about it. My parents spoke a second language called Pennsylvania Dutch. It is a dialect containing a cross mixture of German and Dutch. I understood that language perfectly from the time I was two years old.

One day that I remember specifically, when my parents were speaking this language, I responded and demonstrated that I understood. Their reaction was so negative and so severe that I decided right then and there to never respond again when they spoke that language. Like I said, I was only two at the time, and yet, I distinctly remember making a conscious decision to never reveal that I understood. So I heard things that kids should not hear; truly, for their own good. The things my parents said to my face were bad enough, but the things they said (seemingly to each other) behind my back were excruciatingly painful then and unbelievable to me now, as I look back. I also heard gossip about other people and situations that were way over my head at the time, and certainly not appropriate for my age.

And looking back now (as a parent myself) – on one hand, I still shake my head and wonder how anyone could be so cruel to their own child. Then, on the other hand, I met a five-year-old child recently who made my skin crawl the minute he walked into the room. There was an energy around him that made me want to just smack him up against a wall. I have never reacted to a child like that in my life. The harder I tried to be comforting and pleasant to this kid, the more artificial I sounded to myself. So, I suppose if I were a child like him, it's no wonder my parents hated me.

Anyway, back to the neighbors from the farm in the valley – Martha and Norman. Now, don't fall asleep on me here, this is a good part…

Martha hung around with us enough to actually create a fun atmosphere around our place. She'd come up from the valley below, enjoy our view that stretched on for hundreds of miles, and we'd play scrabble or cards around the picnic table all afternoon.

That particular year, my dad had a lot of extra work and ended up going back to work after supper. He was an entrepreneur painter. Coming from a farming background, he understood that it was necessary to 'make hay while the sun shines'. So, he earned the bulk of his yearly income in the summer when he could paint the outside of houses and farms. Daylight savings time also assisted in making the summer time more lucrative. During the winter, he had enough inside work, remodeling, painting, and hanging wallpaper, to get by.

So, one afternoon, Martha got the bright idea to invite herself and her brother to come up after dinner to play pinochle. It was necessary for the maximum enjoyment of the game to have four hands playing. Mom agreed to join us, and so a pattern began. It did not take long for Mom to become completely comfortable with the two of them. She even began to allow me to go visit

Martha on the farm on the occasional afternoon to help her with the chores so that we could all get back to our scrabble or card games.

My fifteenth birthday was much the same as all my other birthdays. My mom would invite her parents, her brother and sister, and their families over and we'd have a barbecue. The grand finale was them singing Happy Birthday to me so I could blow out the candles. I spent the day babysitting all my younger cousins so the adults could visit. And I was not allowed presents for my birthday because that would 'spoil' me. My grandparents would always give me something either just before my birthday or just after. My mom really disapproved of this and would always complain bitterly to them about it. For days later, she'd go on and on to my dad about how her own parents did not support her childrearing procedures.

But, this year, there was a new twist. Martha had invited me to come down to the farm for some cake she had baked. I was permitted to go because Martha had also mentioned that it was cherry-picking time and they needed extra help this particular year. It was customary for the adjacent farms to contribute the occasional bowl of cherries or blueberries to those of us who were not farming so that we could bake pies too. And, although my mom hated having me in the kitchen and had no desire to teach me anything other than doing dishes, she was an excellent cook and an even better baker. That woman could make a kitchen sing with aromas that I have yet to find anywhere else. Even her simple mashed potatoes were the best ever – or do all kids idealize their mother's cooking?

So, off I went to the farm the next morning to help pick cherries. It was Saturday so Norman was home from work and already out in the trees. We picked all day with only a short break to swallow some sandwiches Martha's mom brought out to us. Even though it was hard work, Martha and Norman kept it fun by talking, joking, and laughing the whole time. Norman was the funniest by telling stories about the people at his work. Norman was the first person I'd ever known (closely enough to have a real conversation with) who came from a farming background but had pursued a career in an office. He'd liken each member of the office staff to a different farm animal and then refer to them as such as he recounted incidents of conflict, misunderstandings, and typical group dynamic behavior. We'd laugh so hard that our sides ached more from the laughter than from the work. I guess what marveled us most was that these people in the office actually took themselves so seriously. From what I gathered, Norman offered a lighter side for that office and, I am sure, kept them all sane with his down-to-earth, common sense perspective on life.

You have to realize, too, that this was the first time I was involved in a group activity where I fit in, not only in my own eyes, but here, my opinion counted and I was not invisible to these people. Other than the time I had spent with my grandparents on the estate, I felt safe, for the first time, to really be me and express my true feelings and perspectives. Remember, too, that this was the third summer that I had not been able to be with my grandparents on the estate. So, this experience was really going to register as profound.

School, from junior high through high school, was just short of a nightmare for me. I was an outcast there too. My parents dressed me like a farm kid but sent me to the suburban junior and senior high school. The other students came from the upper-middle class professional families of the area. Pharmacists', lawyers', doctors', and teachers' kids attended this school. They all lived near the school and associated with each other after school. Many of them belonged to the same golf and country club. And here I was, bussed in from the farming community – a perfect target. They even used to throw rotten fruit at me on the bus. Once I ducked, just in time, as a rotten apple smashed against the metal frame of the bus window, leaving fragments of smelly apple in my hair and down my back. The ring of their laughter is still in my head. And if I cried, they just got worse.

Meantime, back on the farm, after we finished picking cherries, we went into the house for supper. Martha's mom had cooked a great meal of chicken and potatoes, and the best chocolate cake I'd ever tasted. Then Norman phoned my parents and asked if it was okay if I stayed to play some cards with his mom for a change and, to my amazement, they agreed! The condition of the agreement was that Norman would drive me home after the card game so I would not be walking home after dark.

I don't know what they were afraid of around there in the dark. We were miles away from civilization, and there were no wild animals in the area except the occasional deer roaming about. But, my parents' rules had nothing to do with reality, only power. Yet, in their mind, they were really doing what they thought was actually best for me, based on their background and the current teaching of the church they attended.

We left the house around seven-thirty. The 'lane' into the farm was unpaved and about half a mile long. At one point, it curved a bit so the house was out of sight and the main road was also not yet visible. This is where Norman stopped the car, twisted in his seat and just sat back against the car door and started asking me questions.

He asked me how old I was this birthday and I told him I was fifteen. He said he wished I was eighteen because then it would be okay for him to kiss me. I was shocked and physically pulled back a bit. I remembered what the wolf had told me, so I slowly and quietly took a deep, sniffing breath and tuned into the feelings I was having inside. I could hear my heart beating in my ears, but I felt calm and warm inside. At that point, Norman asked me what the matter was.

I twisted in my seat, sat back against the car door on my side, and said that I was just so surprised someone (let alone himself) would want to kiss me. I asked him how old he was and he said he was twenty-four. I didn't tell him but he seemed more like sixteen or eighteen to me.

Then he started telling me how pretty I was and that my smile lit up my entire face. He said I was fun and smart and that I should never let anyone tell me otherwise about myself. I remember looking into his eyes at that point and seeing real sincerity and compassion. I told him that no one had ever said anything nice to me before. He said he knew that. When I asked him how he knew that, he said he meant that he just suspected as much. Then he put the car back in gear and started driving out the lane, saying he'd better get me home before he got himself into trouble.

The conversation immediately switched back to the previous card game and projections as to when the next game would be, and where.

As he dropped me off, he told me to open my bedroom window when I got inside because he had to go find their dog after he dropped me off. So, I went straight to my bedroom and opened the window. The summer breeze was fresh and wonderful. A few minutes later I could plainly hear Norman whistling and calling for their dog, and he was *not* shouting!

At the time, I just chuckled and shrugged it off. I didn't get it then. *Now,* I realize that he was demonstrating how easily sounds carry in the country. If you sit out on your front porch without a radio or TV to occupy the immediate surroundings, you can hear conversations going on miles away on another front porch. No wonder these little communities were so 'close-knit'! No wonder everyone knew everyone else's business! Which means, everyone in the area knew about my mother's screaming temper tantrums. If I could hear Norman just calling for a dog, I am sure the entire community had to hear my mother's yelling. She rarely spoke in a tone much less than a yell.

But, like I said, at the time, I did not get what Norman was trying to demonstrate. I was too busy looking in the mirror at that point and realizing that I *was* pretty. I had beautiful wheat-blonde hair that fell just to my shoulders. My eyebrows and lashes were dark around my deep brown eyes. My lips were perfectly shaped, and my smile *did* light up my entire face. I also had that farmer girl's figure. We tend to develop early and fully in the country. The biggest difference about me was my long legs. In reality I was simply properly proportioned. However, because all the women in my family, and in that community, had short stubby legs; it made mine look abnormally long. This fact gave them yet another reason to make fun of me. I stood five feet, four inches at age twelve already; while none of the grown women in my community were taller than five feet, two inches. My grandmother was four feet, ten inches. My father was only five feet, nine inches!

My birthday is June 28, so the rest of the summer still lay ahead. Martha and Norman spent more and more time at my house and, finally, I was even allowed to go with them to the farmer's market on Saturday nights. The farmer's market where I come from offers everything from grains, fruits, and vegetables, to live bands playing the big band sounds. There was a dance floor comfortably occupied by expert waltzers. Fiddlers played for couples to 'jitter-bug', better known as 'Jive' and square dance. And this year, they even had a band playing some of the more popular 60s music. Remember, this was 1968.

The first time we visited the farmer's market, Norman said that I'd better hold his hand so I would not get lost. When I looked at him in my initial protest, thinking I was being treated like a kid, he winked, smiled at me, took my hand, and squeezed it gently. Martha looked at him warily and he gave her a raised eyebrow, defiant chin, questioning look, back. To that, she sighed a bit, said she'd meet us later at the car, and disappeared.

That set the pattern for our visits to the farmer's market. Norman and I tasted different foods. We'd judge the quality of the produce from different gardens. We'd check out the animals for sale. And, we'd listen to the music and really enjoy watching the dancers; but, we never danced 'cause neither one of us knew how. We simply had a good time together. I felt safe and as if I belonged there.

About the third or fourth visit to this market, Martha met up with some of her friends and decided to go out with them since one of her friends had brought her father's car. On the way home that night, Norman said that he missed having Martha in the car because, when Martha was in the car, I got to sit in the middle, right beside him. I just laughed and said, "Oh really, you like that, huh?"

Then he said, "If you were over here now, I could put my arm around you."

So, I just slid over and said, "Okay."

I will never forget the warm, safe, loving feeling I got when he held me that night. I took one of those sniffing breaths again and it felt so good. I snuggled into his chest and he started stroking my back and my hair. He said that I smelled so good and that holding me felt so good. Then he kissed the top of my head and rubbed his cheek gently across my hair as my face slowly turned up toward his, and our lips brushed.

Suddenly, he took the deepest breath that I have ever heard anyone take – either before or since – and said, "Whoa, stop now. We are going to have to keep it at holding hands for now." Then, he started pushing me away.

Naturally, I started feeling rejected and didn't know what I had done wrong. I was enjoying feeling appreciated and hearing such nice things being said to me from the first person other than my grandparents. So, I asked what I had done wrong and pouted a bit. He took my hand and said that I had done nothing wrong, nothing at all. He said that it was himself who had to remember where he was and who he was with.

So, I snuggled back into his chest, wrapped one arm around his middle, hugged him firmly, and said, "So, does that mean I can't do this?" Then I turned my head up, kissed his chin, and kissed his cheek. I brought my right hand up from his waist, slid my fingers up his neck to his left ear, kissed his other ear, and whispered, "And I can't do this?"

He grabbed my hand, which was caressing his hair by that time, and said, "Not while I'm driving!" And he was having trouble breathing.

So, I said, "Well, pull over then."

And he said, "Absolutely not; I am taking you straight home!"

At that precise moment, I got this flash in my mind of my father driving the car and us kids in the back seat having a typical sibling interaction of 'stop that', 'stay on your side', and 'leave me alone', until Dad would say, "Don't make me stop this car!"

And it made me giggle to think that now I was asking to have the car pulled over and the driver wouldn't. When Norman heard me giggle, he asked me what was so funny and I said, "Am I being naughty?"

He said, "Yes, you are and you know it."

So, I said, "Okay then," and just held his hand till we got to the top of our street, then I slid back over to the proper passenger's position and he dropped me off. I hopped out of the car, and when I turned and said good night, he just winked at me and smiled.

Needless to say, I floated around for the next two weeks. I didn't even notice that I'd not seen Norman or Martha that entire time. Martha finally showed up with a basket of green Granny Smith apples and said they'd been pretty busy. Mom took the apples and said that, if they need help, they should just say so and she'd send me down. Martha said any time would do, so I went back with her.

The garden was ready to be picked, apples were 'in' (as they say, to indicate that they are ready for harvest), and sweet corn was ready. I stayed on the farm for supper that night and Norman sat across from me and winked at me several times. After supper, we worked well into the night husking the corn to get it ready for canning.

That evening, when Norman drove me home, he stopped at that spot in the lane, put the car in park, and said he was going to kiss me good and proper if that was all right with me. I turned my entire body toward him and said, "Sure, if you really want to." With that, he reached down and pushed the front seat of that 1968 Chevrolet Impala back as far as it would go, and I am here to tell you that I have never been kissed like that ever since!

He took my face in his hands and paused a moment. He was calm and attentive as he stroked his thumbs across my lips. He looked me right in the eyes first, and then gently put his lips on mine for a short, affectionate moment. Then he pulled back, looked me in the eyes again, and somehow maneuvered me. I instinctively rolled over in his arms till he was holding me, cradled like a baby, and kissed me with a deep, sincere passion that I have never felt since. He held me so tight, so right, and it felt so natural and so perfect. We kissed and kissed until he started that heavy breathing again and then he said it was time to stop. I rolled back to my side of the car and then we noticed that the windows were completely fogged up. We laughed and laughed. And, as he pulled the seat back up, I started rolling down my window to let in some air. He started driving very slowly because we knew we could not pull into my driveway with the inside of the car all steamed up.

He reached over, took my hand, and said I could slide over beside him because he'd taken the long way around to my house to let the hot air out. I put my head on his shoulder and asked him if he loved me. He said, "Yeah, I think I do."

I popped up and looked at him as he kept his gaze fixed on the road and said, "Really? Me? You love *me?*"

With that, he pulled his neck in a bit, pinched his lips into a stretched smile, and nodded real fast. He stole a glance at me and then put one finger up to his lips to gesture 'Shhh'.

I pulled back to my side of the car and said, "I don't believe you. You are so much older than me. What about other women your age?"

"Oh right," he retorted, "like all the babes at work!" Then he made all the barnyard noises and we laughed and laughed. Then he said that we would go to the farmer's market that coming Saturday night and I was to point out anyone I could find who would be better for him.

And so, we did go to the market on Saturday, and he was right. What a bunch of cows (and I don't mean the four-legged kind). We had so much fun that Saturday! We were there all day, manning their table, selling vegetables and sweet corn. Sometimes, Norman would even say, "Oh, here comes a prospect." And I'd look up and there'd be a big-busted, robust woman with curlers in her hair. Another time, several girls walked up together and the best of the bunch was married.

Later, instead of walking around on the grounds like we always did before, we left right away and Norman drove us to a special secluded place between two fields. He pushed the seat back again and that night we didn't stop. We couldn't stop! And this time, the windows dripped as if it had rained inside!

Looking back on it, I have no idea how I knew what to do. It was so natural, so perfect. We had no inhibitions and he was so gentle and concerned about me.

I was fifteen then. I am over forty as I write this, and it wasn't until recently that I realized that this is the pure innocence and natural connection that I have been looking for in a relationship ever since.

Norman may have been twenty-four chronologically, but he was a simple farm boy inside. We were caught in a transition period in my area. We were in rural Pennsylvania during the late sixties. The culture there had a pattern of women getting married very young. My parents were so mixed up themselves. They were throwing me so many mixed signals. On one hand, I was attending this upper-class school; but on the other hand, I was not supposed to get too much education because education was a sin. I was supposed to be focused on getting married and having babies to make my parents look like good parents; but, I wasn't supposed to be interested in boys yet.

With all the mixed signals, plus I was so starved for love and attention, I suppose anything would have felt good. But I have relived that moment, and the many times after that first time, and it was truly wonderful and genuine.

We managed to conceal our affair until just before Thanksgiving that year. Sometimes, we would meet in the woods, or Norman would pick me up in the morning and drive me to school. Being driven to school was a real treat to me. It was such a relief to escape the harassment I faced on the bus. And we didn't always have sex when we were together. In fact, most of the time, we just talked and kissed.

Then one Friday night, just before Thanksgiving, I was babysitting my brother and sister and Norman came over. He had walked up from the farm and came to my house via the field beside us. Mom and Dad were supposed to be out till late, so I could not believe it when I heard them come in. It was a scene much like you'd see on one of today's sitcoms.

Norman rolled off the bed and slipped underneath just before my bedroom door flew open and the light flicked on with my mom now standing right beside the bed. She yelled, as she always did, "What are you doing? Sleeping? You're supposed to be babysitting!"

Of course, I jumped up to my feet, trying to straighten my clothes (which I did still have on, thankfully)! My confused and stunned behavior actually suited the situation. I started walking out of the room mumbling that I must have fallen asleep when I laid down with a headache. So, my mom slaps me behind the head and says, "Headache? I'll give you a headache! Now, go get your brother ready for bed."

As I walked through the living room, I saw these huge flakes of snow falling and said, "When did it start snowing?" Dad was in the kitchen standing and looking in the fridge. He said it had just started when the movie let out and that they decided to come home instead of visiting with their friends in case the roads got bad. The first snow of the season is always the worst on the roads.

I went and got my brother ready for bed faster than I ever had in my life! I tucked him in bed and dashed to my room. I could tell that Norman had escaped through the window, so I re-clipped the screen and closed the window as if nothing had happened.

The next morning, we saw that it hadn't snowed much at all. You could still see grass through the shallow layer of snow. Dad was puttering around outside, doing something around the yard.

After a while, he came in and said that there were footprints in the snow leading away from my bedroom window and into the field. He also said that he knew that the footprints were not made by women's shoes.

My younger sister was sitting at the kitchen table with me and Mom was at the sink. She spun around and the look of terror on her face would have been better suited to an announcement of murder. Then my sister pipes up and says that every time I babysit, Norman comes over and that we always go in my room together while she and my brother watch TV. My sister didn't see any reason for panic. She knew Norman was around a lot to play cards, so she thought she was comforting my parents with this information. Meantime, I was shocked to learn that she knew all along that Norman was coming to see me. I could not figure out how she knew since she was downstairs in the basement family room the entire time.

With that, my dad started towards the wall phone behind me and said I should get to my room because he didn't want to look at me.

The next thing that happened is my mom came into my room, sat down on the edge of the bed, and asked me what had happened. She seemed unusually calm and I started feeling that maybe I could actually talk to her. So, I started by saying that Norman loved me.

Well, she jumped up from that bed and backhanded me across the face so hard that I flipped over off the edge of the bed. Then she grabbed me and threw me onto the bed so that I bounced, and yelled, "Norman doesn't love you. Why would Norman love you? You're a skinny, long-legged, buck-toothed brat. What in the world would he want with you? My God, he's a man of the world. He works in an office and probably knows dozens of young women his own age. Grown women with a future to offer, not scrawny little brats like you. And quit your crying or I'll give you something to cry about!"

Then my dad walked in the door and said that he'd been talking to Martha on the phone. He said that Martha said that she knew that Norman and I held hands to walk around the farmer's market and that I'd admitted to her that Norman had kissed me. He asked me if that was all true. I said that it was true.

That was all Mom needed to hear. She started slapping me over and over and yelling, "Holding hands at the farmer's market; my God, everybody knows! What kind of parents do people think we are because of you?"

At that point, I started screaming, "Stop it, stop it!"

And Dad headed for the door saying that he was going to have a word with this guy.

Mom followed him to the kitchen and was saying, "He sat in this kitchen and played cards right in front of me and all the while he was having an affair with our fifteen-year-old daughter… that deceitful son-of-a-bitch. He's a twenty-four-year-old man; let him rot in jail. And Martha should've told us about this as soon as it started. I don't want to see her snot-nosed face around here either anymore, and you can tell her I said so. The neighbors probably think we condoned this. Oh my God, what a mess! I can't believe this! We'll never live this down either."

I had followed Mom to the kitchen, crying and saying that they didn't understand and it was not what they thought. Then Mom turned on me again as Dad went out the door, started pushing and shoving me back against the wall, then down the hall to my room again, yelling, "Get back to your room. You don't know what love is. All men want is sex and you'll learn that soon enough. Take it from me; once they get what they want, they don't care about you anymore. We'll see how much he thinks of you. We'll see what he has to say for himself." By this time, I was back in my room and she had pushed me until I was sitting on my bed. So then, it was time to pronounce sentencing.

She stood there with her hands on her hips huffing and puffing. She said, "So this is the example you want to set for your sister? Okay then, we'll set an example." Then she took a moment to bask in the glory of the powerful position she was experiencing before she said, "You are *so* grounded. You will go to school and to church and that's it! When you're in this house, unless you are doing your chores or eating a meal, you will be confined to this room. You will not talk to any of us in this house, and no Christmas for you this year. You can just sit in this room. After New Year's, we'll see. If you behave yourself between now and then, maybe by then we can get back to normal around here."

And that was it. My parents really prided themselves in being able to stick to their word. From that day until the day after New Year's Day, they did not talk to me, except to give me orders. And my brother and sister didn't talk to me at all either. They all made really obvious gestures of avoidance, and sometimes Dad would point his finger at me and make nodding gestures to my sister to impress upon her just how awful I really was. Then he'd whisper (purposely loud enough for me to hear him), "See what happens."

Once I tried to approach the subject with my mom and she just started her wild yelling. She went on and on, telling me how stupid I was to think anyone that age could be interested in me. She said I had been just practice for Norman, and that Norman was testing certain moves on me so he could feel more comfortable with whoever it was that he really wanted. She said she did not want to hear me mention it again. She said I was a total embarrassment to the entire family and that even my grandmother was completely disappointed and ashamed of me. She said if she could do it legally, she would have even kept me home from school.

Norman drove past me many times on his way to work as I was walking to the bus. Martha was usually in the car with him and they'd both turn their heads to the extreme other side to obviously avoid me.

The first three weeks of my solitary confinement sentence were the worst. The loneliness got louder and louder. I would waffle between laughing about it to crying so hard I'd nearly throw up. At one point, I decided that perhaps I should stop, look, and really listen to my parents. So, when I was in their company for meals and in the car back and forth to church, I really listened to them.

It did not take me long to decide that they were, in fact, the biggest assholes I knew. All they did was complain and find fault with everything and everyone. And all they did with one another was jockey for power. Every decision ended up with my mom asking, "Well, who's boss here," and Dad eventually giving in to whatever she wanted to do or have. It was impossible to respect them, no matter how hard I tried.

One night, I remember sitting in my room and thinking that I could accept that I was stupid to think that a man twenty-four years old could actually love me, but, what was I supposed to think? I sat there and realized that my parents only took things away and only identified what I did wrong. They never spelled out what I was supposed to do or be. If I asked questions, I was charged with 'talking back' and told that kids should be seen and not heard.

I sat there for the longest time and recalled all the things I had done that I was so proud of and reflected on their reactions to those times. I remembered bringing home a report card with all A's and B's and watching Mom stuff it in the kitchen drawer. They never mentioned that to the people in the grocery line. Instead, the report card with all Cs and Ds got center spot on the bulletin board.

Suddenly, I began to feel panicky inside. I felt fear, anger, hatred, guilt, relief, and anxiety all at once. I paced and paced around in my room, trying to stop the rushes of feelings. I stopped and talked out loud in a whisper to my reflection in the mirror. I said, "It's okay, just hold on and remember that, in a few short years, you will be old enough to leave this place and you'll never have to come back if you don't want to." I quickly got ready for bed while my feelings were calm. But as soon as I slid under the covers, the waves of mixed feelings and the sound of the yelling, the yelling, the yelling just would not stop echoing in my head. I could not stand it! Even if I covered my ears, it just kept going on and on and on until finally, I buried my face in my pillow and just screamed and screamed. My heart was broken. I did not want to believe that Norman was just using me and had no feelings for me either. I was so unbearably lonely and confused, and the pain inside was intolerable. All the feelings rolled into one huge pool of rage. I cried from the bottom of my feet that night.

Then, suddenly, the room filled with a moist, cool mist. There was a strange sizzling in my ears and it was as if I could hear soft music way in the distance. Then, I felt as if I was being picked up and cradled like a baby in huge arms. I could hear a soft voice saying that it would be all right. I could feel myself being pressed against a strong chest and held tight. I tried to see the face, but it was too far away, and my eyes were blurry with tears. I felt a peace come over me like I have never felt before or since. I fell asleep to a gentle rocking motion.

35

I woke up the next morning with singing in my heart. I felt a joy that made no sense, because I had nothing to be happy about. In fact, I was only halfway through my sentence, but, somehow, the rest of the following weeks were as if I was watching someone else go through them. I decided that I was just going to wait it out. I decided that time was really on *my* side. I decided I liked it alone and even after my sentence was over, I maintained the routine of retreating to my room. It got to the point where my parents finally came, actually dragged me out of my room by my hair into the family room, and forced me to watch TV with them.

I remember sitting with them in the family room, laughing inside, and taking off into my own dream world in my head. It was so neat to be totally free of them. I realized that they could not force me to think their way. I could be and do whatever I wanted in the world I had created. I remember thinking about how stupid I thought they were. There they were, so right and so perfect in their own eyes, and all they really were was two low-class farmers trying to live an upper-middle-class lifestyle. No one ever came to visit us; not even the church people. And it was not for lack of my parents inviting them. I realized that everything they accused me of really applied to themselves. At one point, I felt a twinge of remorse for them, but I quickly dispelled it because I decided that they did not deserve my feeling sorry for them.

Looking back, I can really see how, especially for young boys, one can be turned into a murderer or a rapist and the like. I can see how teenagers can judge their parents with only the standards the parents themselves provide. What did my parents think would happen to me as I was left alone for weeks on end? Did they think that righteousness and goodness would just come flooding in after listening to them put me down over and over again? Where was common sense on their part? They were supposed to be grown adults. In my eyes, there was nothing to be respectful of within my immediate surroundings. They were just big bullies.

Today, as a parent myself, I have taken great pains to ensure that the communication lines between my daughter and myself remain wide open. I share things with her that might surprise other parents. At the same time, I maintain a line of privacy between us as well.

My daughter and I have a level of friendship, but she is not my sorority sister. We express our feelings completely, and I have admitted when I was wrong and she was right when the occasion called for it. I firmly believe that you get out of a child exactly what you put into the child, consciously or unconsciously. And the teen years are the true demonstration of the kind of parenting a child has received... like it or not! If you do not like your teenager, take a long, honest account of yourself and your behavior as it was during their formative years. If you were, in fact, doing the best *you* could do, and the outcome is far less than you'd hoped, then, I suspect, that you are playing games with yourself. Unsavory peer groups cannot attract a truly grounded child who knows they are loved unconditionally in their family of origin!

Chapter Two
The Great Escape

By the time the following summer rolled around, my parents had enrolled me in summer school. It was the Bryland School of Cosmetology. I was going to be a hairdresser.

This private school was where I met my dearest and longest friend, Gale. This woman proved to be a stabilizing force for the tremendously trying years that followed. To this day, even though I've lost touch with her, I think of her often and wish her all the very best. I hope she is happy and healthy and living life to the fullest.

The church had loosened their view on women's roles in the economy and decided to allow us to become nurses, teachers, or hairdressers; but that was it. Anything beyond that was far too worldly. My mom decided that becoming a hairdresser was best for me because then I could have a shop in my home and raise kids at the same time. And the big plus was that I could do her hair, my sister's and brother's hair, and my grandmother's hair, and save them all lots of money, since they felt no obligation to pay me. But again, in spite of my mother's nattering, my grandmother always paid me to do her hair. She never concealed anything she did for me from my mother, but she did dare to defy my parent's harsh treatment repeatedly.

That was the year I'd also met a boy named Michael at school. He was willing to bear the ridicule of being seen with me. He stood up for me and life, for the latter part of grade nine took a turn for the better. Unfortunately, he was graduating that year and I was not looking forward to the repeated isolation I knew would result after he was no longer around to talk to.

I turned sixteen in the summer of '69 and my parents said I could date with a chaperone *and* the boy had to be willing to attend our church. I had confided in Michael about the previous year's sentence. He sympathized with me and, in turn, confided in me about his harsh family situation. Apparently, his father was an alcoholic and had treated his mother very badly.

We bonded quickly and, seemingly, deeply and vowed to provide for each other a loving and nurturing environment. We wrote our own rules because we did not believe in either of our parents' lifestyles. Naturally, our own rules not only permitted premarital sex; it demanded it. After all, we did not know any other way to be nurturing. Our relationship activities, therefore, revolved around scheming ways to find the time and place to have sex.

Michael and I were engaged the Christmas of '69. We planned to get married on August 7, 1971 – exactly two months after I graduated from high school. Michael had enlisted in the Army Reserves to avoid the draft. He left for boot camp right after the holidays, which was only a four-month assignment. It seemed like forever, but I waited dutifully. When he finally returned, he started working as a draftsman for a local architect. He also reported to the Army Reserve Camp near us for drills every other weekend and for an overnight camp one weekend every month for three years. The only way he'd see actual battle was if U.S. soil was invaded. We felt pretty safe. Our entire reason for living was just to get married and get on our own, away from both sets of parents. I literally counted the days.

One morning during Michael's four-month boot camp, I missed the school bus. I was seventeen years old and had my own driver's license. Mom had just learned to drive the year before me. I walked back home, and I'll never forget the horrified look on my mom's face when I stepped into the kitchen through the back door and said, "I missed the bus." You'd think I'd committed the most horrific crime. She started yelling about how stupid I was and how much trouble raising kids was. I composed myself and consciously decided to make an attempt to communicate with this raving lunatic who I was supposed to respect as my mother. I put on my kindest tone of voice and said, "Mother, please, I just missed the school bus for the first time in my entire school-bus-riding career; it is really no big deal. You can drive me, or I can drive myself this one time. I really do not want to miss school today."

Well, the rage that welled up in that woman was unbelievable! She dropped the armload of laundry that she was carryin', started slapping me, and yelling, "Don't you talk back to me! Who do you think you are talking to, and who do you think you are now?"

At first, I just assumed my usual stance of putting my arms up around my face to block some of the blows, and then something in me snapped. This time *my* rage welled up too. I remember grabbing both her wrists and looking her square in the eye as I was just short of touching noses with her.

You have to remember, too, that I stood five-foot-four, and what I lacked in weight, I made up for in youthful muscle tone. Mom was just barely five-foot-two.

I gritted my teeth, curled my lip, and started yelling back. I yelled, "Stop it, stop it, stop it, it's enough, right now!" By that time, I had spun her around and had her pinned to the wall by the back door. I could feel her fear now and her eyes were like saucers with shock. I remember I felt sorry for her, but I kept going anyway and yelled, "Stop hitting me, do you hear me? Stop hitting me now, and don't you *ever* hit me again! I'm bigger than you are now and I don't have to take this anymore." With that, I pulled her arms forward and then smashed them back up against the wall again and yelled, "Do you hear me? Answer me, answer me," I said.

Her lip started quivering and she started nodding her head 'yes' and I yelled, "And stop your sniveling and answer me." So, she mustered up enough voice to whisper, "Okay, okay, no more hitting." I immediately backed off and took a few moments to catch my breath. I was breathing as if I'd run ten miles. Mom just stood there looking at me as if she was seeing a ghost.

I composed myself again and said, "Look, it won't be long now till I'm married and out of your hair forever. Can we just make the best of these last years, please? I don't want to hurt you, but I don't want to be hit anymore either; is that so much to ask? It's just enough now."

I bent over, picked up the load of laundry, and said I'd take it down for her. Then I asked if she was going to drive me to school, or if I was driving myself. She said she'd take me. From that day on, our relationship to each other remained a bit distant… but she never hit me again!

Looking back on that now, I really think my mom had no idea where that reaction from me came from even though she always used some of those same phrases when she was beating me till I'd pee my pants. She'd expect this little kid to talk calmly while being attacked by this vicious monster that, moments before, was supposed to be the nurturing, caring mom.

Michael and I did marry right on schedule, even though I remember sitting out in the car the night before with my maid of honor and admitting that marrying Michael was not what I really wanted to do. I cried to her and said I did not know what else to do with my life. I was not in any financial position to move out on my own and I knew I just could not stay in my parent's place a moment longer than I had to. I felt that same panicky fluttering inside that I'd felt during my solitary confinement sentence. My maid of honor said that it was not too late to call it off. In fact, she really tried to encourage me to call it off. When she started to make too much sense, I just laughed it off and said it was probably just the traditional premarital cold feet.

I realize now that it was this circumstance that was the first time I consciously short-circuited my own intuition. Of course, I did not have the sophisticated perception at that time as I do now, looking back. But, I do remember that this was the first time I went against the feelings I had inside. Then again, this was the very first time I was making a decision for myself too. The thing was, I could not understand why the feelings were telling me not to get married because Mike and I had a very open and honest relationship. He knew everything about my home life and we both agreed that we wanted to provide a home life that was happy and all our own. We purposely paid close attention to birth control so that we could live our lives a bit before tying ourselves down with kids. Everything seemed to be in order.

My parents had to keep up their need for control, so they gave us an apartment building for a wedding present. Yes, you heard me, a five-suite apartment building just two blocks from the very center of the city of Reading.

This building was magnificent. Once upon a time this building was the home to a very prominent family. There were six white with gray, tan, and black veined marble stairs that started as wide as the house and narrowed as you reached the huge double dark oak doors with beveled, frosted glass. The doors were carved with amazing detail and opened to a small 3 feet deep and 6 feet wide entryway with two more doors, just as beautiful as the first, with beveled clear glass leading into the hallway.

There was a three-sided bay window to the right of the stairs that was part of the first floor front apartment. And that window was 3 feet deep. The outside was all red brick with concrete trim around the windows that was painted an off-white.

The floor in the entryway was all the same marble as the stairs and the marble came up on the walls to waist height on either side. Five mailboxes were on the wall to the left with an intercom buzzer to the right of the second set of doors.

Once inside the stairway to the left was breathtaking. The entire home had been finished with dark oak wood, the banister was 4 inches thick at the top. The spindles were carved like stretched out bowling pins with detail that looked similar to flower pedals curving toward the center at the top and base of each one. And trust me when I say they were tough to keep clean and dusted.

The stairs themselves were 4 feet wide with a 30-inch tapestry-style carpet going up the center of the stairs, and they creaked, only slightly, as you walked up and down. The ceiling on the first floor was 20 feet high and all the doors on the first floor were exactly the same detailed heavy dark oak with beveled glass and 10 feet high,

The hallway had the dark wood as panels on the walls up to waist height with a 2-inch ledge at the top. There was a flowered wallpaper on the walls from the wood paneling up to the ceiling.

The molding on the walls at the ceiling was 8 inches high and curved into the ceiling to make the join of the wall to ceiling look rounded rather than a sharp 90-degree angle. It was also very detailed dark oak in the hallway.

The first floor front apartment door was immediately to your right as you entered the hallway. The hallway was 7 feet wide and 18 feet to the doors to the first floor back apartment; which was where we were going to live.

When you entered our apartment you walked into a 12 x 15 foot living room. There was a dark green & black marble fireplace on the wall to your left. There was a grate in the bottom that opened into a dustbin in the basement, so you never had to sweep it out. You just had to sweep the corners into the open grate to clean it.

The mantel and the hearth were just beautiful. There are not enough adjectives to describe it.

The windows were 10 feet high and 3 feet wide and set in nearly 2 feet. I remember them well as I made the drapes for them.

All the wood trim in our apartment was painted white, including the inside of our entry door. That was disappointing to me even then as I really liked the dark wood.

The whole apartment was very bright. Our floor was a light oak hard wood. The living room led directly into the bedroom. That was awkward, I must say. We put beads up in the doorway leading through to the bedroom; however, we never did get the room divider that it needed to create a more private bedroom. So, it was like a studio or loft apartment in that regard.

Immediately to your right as you were through the bedroom was the bathroom. It was long and narrow. The same marble that graced the entryway was in this bathroom on the floor. Ceramic tile was on the walls up to waist height and the rest of the walls were painted white to the molding at the ceiling, which was also white.

Of course there was a claw foot huge free standing bathtub with a metal shower curtain all the way around it and a huge shower head with the typical white ceramic/steel faucet fixtures; including a separate faucet for hot and cold that were common when the house was initially renovated.

The sink was small and there was no vanity or any storage in there. However there was room for a freestanding storage unit right beside the sink that we did acquire immediately. The medicine cabinet was a good size and depth and there were stainless steel accessories attached to the wall between the mirror and sink for soap, cup, and toothbrushes.

The window in the bathroom was small and it opened out on a hinge at the top. There was a screen that had not been cleaned in a while, so that was addressed immediately and before we moved in.

Continuing on you entered the kitchen. Again, the same marble 'look' was on the floor; however it was as ceramic tiles with the typical grout necessary to use tiles. The kitchen sink looked like a sink that should be in a laundry room or shop area. It was a match for the bathtub with the wide rounded edges that you could reach under and feel the raw metal. It had the typical flat surface on each side with the water-draining grooves. The fixtures were the same as the bathroom. Yes, a whole separate faucet for hot and cold. It even had the curtain in front of it hiding two shelves for the things you keep under a sink.

The stove fit between two more huge windows. There was a door to a back area that was not a yard, but rather a short fenced concrete patio leading to the ally where the garbage bins were containing two huge silver metal trashcans with tight fitting lids.

There was a back room as well where Michael put a drafting table for work he'd bring home and we put a huge wooden wardrobe in there for our off season clothes.

We had a black cat named Tara and a canary named Caesar. And it was a Sylvester and Tweedy at times. But they got along for the most part.

I remember going in to see Michael working on his drafting to find Caesar sitting on his head while he worked. Caesar really loved the high ceilings and spent a lot of time at the top of those windows. Interestingly enough he never made a mess in the house! I used to comment on it all the time. I'd look behind the curtains, on the floors, furniture; and never found anything.

So, we collected rent instead of paying it. There was a mortgage, of course, and the building needed work inside, but that is just what Dad wanted. He loved his work and now he was in a financial position to start investing in fixer-uppers, and my husband represented the boy he didn't have as his first-born.

I have to say here that looking back through the eyes of a 'healing' adult, my parents really did think they were doing the best for me. And they did what they could with what they had to work with. They were not raised properly either. And that goes especially for my dad, as you'll learn later.

I was an ignorant young adult. If I had this opportunity now! The opportunity to have a five-suite apartment building to live in and collect rent, trust me when I say I'd be all over it!

My heart aches for what I threw away. It really does.

Anyway, back to the story:

Michael's parents gave us a new car and living room furniture. So, picture this: an 18-year-old hairdresser who brought home about $2,400 a month and a 21-year-old (very talented) draftsman who made over $4,000 a month at his day job, and another 500 to 1,000 on the side, driving a brand-new Ford Maverick (paid for), and living in a beautiful apartment in a building we owned where the other four apartments paid the mortgage and all the utilities and taxes for us, no kids of our own; and we were finally free of parental oppression in 1971. Can you guess what happened?

Michael's brother was in a rock band and was working very hard to make it big in the music industry. Meanwhile, he had all the necessary connections to act as if he had already made it big, and one of those acts included drugs.

Make no mistake, Michael and I had had our share of marijuana by that time, but we always limited it to that and booze. I just did not like the idea of letting myself get out of conscious control and I thought Michael agreed. Well, I now found out that he did agree with me as long as I was there, but he had been experimenting with acid (LSD) behind my back before we were married. So, now that this was his place too, he felt he had a right to do as he pleased. I decided not to argue because we had promised not to lay parent trips on each other.

Everything was going fine until just after Christmas, our first year of marriage. Dad came over and he and Mike went upstairs to start working on one of the apartments. It needed paint, wallpaper, and new carpet. The tenant had agreed to go stay with her sister for two weeks so we could renovate for her.

Dad would work most of the day and Mike and I would pitch in after hours. Dad and Mike did a terrific job in no time, and I was looking forward to the weekend to celebrate.

Michael came home that Friday night at his usual time and, for the first time, he had the evening paper with him. I always got home earlier and started supper. I commented on the paper and asked if we were going to the movies on our first weekend free and to ourselves after nearly a month.

He said that he didn't know and asked when supper would be ready. That was a strange and odd response as well. He always came and sat in the kitchen while I made supper and we'd talk.

I looked around the corner and saw him sitting in the living room behind the newspaper. So, I bounced in, stood in front of him with the paper blocking our view of each other, nudged his knees with mine, and said, "Hey, what's happening, buddy?"

Then the strangest thing happened. My dearest friend, my confidant, my husband, looked out around the paper for a moment with raised eyebrows, pursed lips, and stated, in a very authoritarian way, "I'm reading the paper and then I think I just want to watch TV tonight."

I struggled as panic gripped my gut and squeezed the air right out of me. My heart pounded in my head and my ears sizzled. This scene was all too familiar. This is exactly how my parents used to address my presence. I forced an insecure chuckle and said, "Awe, come on, quit foolin'…"

And before I could say any more, he folded the paper to one side and said sharply, "Now, knock it off. I said I'm reading the paper; quit your pesting and get supper finished." And then he just put the paper up again.

I just dropped to my knees in front of him and started crying. I begged him to please not do this to me. I reminded him of our promise to not pull parent 'crap' on each other. My entire body trembled from the inside out. All the rage and fear and frustration that I lived during my exile after the Norman episode poured through me.

Next thing I knew, Mike was standing over me, looking down his nose at me, and laughing. He said, "Your father said that this is exactly what you'd do just to have your own way. Well, I'm the head of this household and you'll do as I say."

I cried and screamed, "No… What are you saying? What are you doing? Stop this; this is not us! What happened?" And that's when he raised his hand towards me for the first time. He yelled at the top of his lungs, and I had never heard him yell anything before this.

"Stop your crying right now. I mean it, right now." I gasped and slid backward on my butt across the hard wood floor. I just held my breath and looked up at him in total disbelief as he continued with a version of a speech I used to hear over and over at home. "Things are going to be different around here from now on." He paced and occasionally pointed at me. "You complain and bitch constantly about how bad your parents are and look around you, look at what you have. Now, you want to drag me into your little game. Well, no more. You go and get supper done and then we are watching TV and you are going to settle yourself."

By now, my mouth was just hanging wide open in amazement. My mind was whirling. I couldn't think, I couldn't feel, I couldn't breathe. It was all just swimming round and round so fast that I couldn't fix on any one thing to say or feel. The next thing I knew, Mike had grabbed me by the back of my shirt collar, lifting and shoving me toward the kitchen, and snapped, "I said get moving *now…*"

I looked back to see him settle back into the armchair, jerk the paper into its upright position, and just continue to read. Who the hell was this guy?

My head kept spinning. My ears were sizzling and I could hear my parents going on and on. I could feel the slaps and bump as I'd hit the wall or the floor. I cupped my head in my hands and grasped my hair as I paced around the kitchen, saying that this couldn't be happening. I thought that I must be dreaming. My stomach was beginning to churn and my knees were like Jell-O. I sat down and put my head between my knees when I heard him yell, "I don't hear any pots and pans rattling. Do I have to come in there and knock some sense into you?"

Somehow, I jumped up and finished making supper. We ate and watched TV that night with him on one end of the sofa and me at the other. We didn't say a word to each other. I was afraid to talk and I guessed that I was supposed to be seen and not heard like it was with my parents. And so, the walls were established. We never went anywhere together anymore unless he made the plans and it was totally his idea. And I was right, he established that I was to speak only when spoken to, and he began using stronger and stronger drugs.

The first thing I did was have an affair. Before the next Christmas was upon us, I had moved out and was sharing an apartment with a girlfriend. My parents really freaked out over that. In fact, my father came to my place of employment and took my car away from me. The car I was driving was our second car, which was still in my mom's name. They had been planning to switch it over but had not gotten around to it yet.

At that point, I could see the setup. My parents *never* procrastinated about anything. The scene in the kitchen the day I confronted my mom about hitting me flashed across the back of my mind. This was the way they were getting back at me. This was why they did so much to support the marriage – so they could interfere with it and continue their domination over me! They were determined to mold me into whatever it was they thought I was supposed to be regardless if I was married or not.

With all the hate that I felt at that moment, I dare say, I feared myself. I am sure that if I had had higher levels of testosterone in my system at that moment, I would have been on the top of some building somewhere, shooting everybody and anybody that moved within range.

I refused to be manipulated back into a situation that I had waited and suffered to escape for so long. So, I hitchhiked home to my own place. And I continued to hitchhike back and forth to work rather than tell anyone at work what was going on. I also did not tell my parents that Mike was using strong drugs. They idolized him because he represented the son they did not have as their firstborn. He made their lives complete too, and they wanted him to be just like them. At the time, I just saw it as a no-win situation. I wasn't able to fight it. If I tried to fight, I'd just crumble into the beaten child again.

It was such a mixed up and confused state that I entered when confronted with conflict. On one hand I had such severe rage inside of me. However, if I tried to act on that rage, I'd collapse into the quivering, sniveling ball of useless flesh.

Finally, Mike did miss me enough to set up a meeting with me. Part of the agreement to meet included visiting my parents because they had told Mike that they had something they wanted to talk to us about. He picked me up at work and we went out for dinner. We did not really talk much because Mike said he wanted to hear what my parents had to say first.

When we arrived at my parent's place, I could not believe that my grandparents were there as well. I had always held onto the strength that at least my grandparents didn't think that I was such a bad apple. As I walked in, I actually felt a bit safer because they were there.

Looking back on it now, this whole meeting was set up much the same as an intervention for an alcoholic. And all I really wanted was to be free, to be myself without being abused and ridiculed for it. And I was the one *not* using drugs, *not* addicted to religion or anything else. Yet, I was the one they were determined to 'fix'.

Looking back it was exactly the same story as the Munsters. Remember that show? "The Adams Family" The one member that was not a monster; was considered the outcast. How much more could my life have mirrored that show at that time? Although, the show came along way after all this occurred. Don't mix the timeline…

At the same time, *(looking back)* I can appreciate where they were coming from. They were caught in the transition from farming to the industrial era. Dad had taken a giant step in not only switching from farming to painting contractor, but also by setting out on his own and introducing the use of hydraulic lift trucks in his industry.

My dad realized, very soon, that he was not going to be happy working for someone else, as farmers are very much their own bosses. He was driving home one day, after working for another painting contracting company, and wrestling with the idea of striking out on his own. He was trying to figure out a way that would enable one man to set up the necessary network of scaffolding used to provide access to an entire side of a barn or house for painting. He rounded a turn in the road and saw the electric company working on some overhead wires. They were using what was called a 'boom truck'. Dad had seen similar equipment used to pick cherries. It was a flatbed pickup truck with a hydraulic arm on it. The arm had a bucket-like platform on the end of it, just big enough to hold one man. There was a panel of controls in the bucket to enable the worker to maneuver the positioning wherever he needed it to do the job at hand. And that answered Dad's problem.

Even though everyone he talked to scoffed at the idea, and Mom was fit to be tied, he invested in having a truck designed specifically for himself, and he made a fortune with it. In a small town like ours, it quickly became the 'in thing to do', to hire my dad to paint the house or all the buildings on a farm. My dad was a very dutiful worker and did an expert job in a very reasonable amount of time. No hassles with unions, no typical tradesman disappearing acts. The customers were ecstatic and news traveled fast. He never had to advertise and he always had more work than he could handle. Although, he tried several times to hire help, they always failed to stay on – either because they felt Dad asked too much of them, or because Dad would fire them for slacking off.

My dad's dream was that he'd build up the company and eventually my brother would take it over. Well, my parents eventually got the chance to exercise their intervention procedures with my brother, all right. He did everything they accused me of, and more. He ended up draining my father's retirement resources and destroying my dad's business. But that's another story.

Back to the meeting at my parent's. This was when my parents told me one of the family secrets that was apparently only a secret to my generation. The secret was that my dad's father had murdered my dad's mother. Then he hung himself from the rafters in the homestead farmhouse basement. This had happened just after I turned one-year-old.

At the time, this was big news in the little farming community. My mom sobbed and sobbed as she recounted to me the shame and suffering they faced as a family in the community. She said that everyone avoided them for years because of it. My grandmother came over to me, took my hand, and said that she didn't think this was applicable to the current problems that Mike and I were having. At that, my mom yelled and said that she had invited her own parents to help do this, not to side against it. So my grandmother resumed her position on the other sofa.

By now, we were all crying, including my dad. My mom said that Dad was the one who found the mess three days after it had happened. She said it was a Saturday afternoon and that she and my dad had had an argument because Dad would not change my diapers. He said that changing diapers was women's work and stormed out like he always did during disagreements. Mom said that he ran home, as usual. But instead of finding his usual refuge, he found a mess far worse than a poopie diaper to clean up! Apparently, grampa (my dad's dad) had stuck a knife in grama's throat and bled her the same way you bleed a pig at slaughter. So, the entire kitchen was sprayed with blood. Finding that and a man hanging for three days was not a pretty or a very fragrant experience.

Dad said that his parents fought constantly and his dad used to beat his mother up so bad that sometimes she'd be in bed for two weeks straight until she healed enough to get up and work again. While she was laid up in bed, since she couldn't work, she had to perform extra service sexually.

Finally, I spoke up and said, "That's enough. I don't want to hear any more. Why are you telling us this now?" And my grandmother said that she wanted to know the same thing – she wanted to know what this all proved.

Then Dad got irritated, stood up, and paced the floor a bit. He said it proved that Mike and I could not possibly have anything as bad as that to live with. He said that if he, himself, and my mom could endure a marriage with all that to live down, then Mike and I had smooth sailing in comparison. And that the family had put up with enough shame and trouble and, therefore, they did not need the scandal of divorce to add to the gossip.

My grandmother just shook her head, rolled her eyes, and said, "Oh, for Pete's sake, that's not how you resolve problems – compare them to something worse and then get on with it. There is a lot better we would compare to. I thought we were going to ask the kids what was wrong and talk about their lives; not rehash yours."

At the same time, I was getting my coat on and saying that I had to get out of there. Mike was agreeing with me and getting his coat on too.

Mom stood up then and was obviously irritated as well. She cried to her own mom and said, "Oh sure, you never sympathized with what we went through even at the time; why should you now." Then she turned to us and said, "You two just think about what we said here tonight." And with that, Mike and I were out the door and driving down the street.

I just want to say here that they were right! They were absolutely right that we really had no problems of our own. However, we had NO tools to enable us to appreciate what we had. We were young and totally inexperienced and had had NO positive direction or training in financial matters, proper communication, or setting personal goals. We were just two kids that were finally out from under two of the most toxic families of origin anyone could imagine.

I just stared out the car window for the longest time. My head was spinning and my emotions were so mixed up. Mike never said a word the entire drive home (which was a good hour). Just before he dropped me off at my own apartment, I said that I had had no idea about any of the tragedy disclosed to us that evening and he just looked at me with a blank stare.

Two days later, I started waking up, every morning, very sick to my stomach. You guessed it; I was pregnant… and it was not my husband's baby! A week after I discovered I was pregnant, Mike called and we talked over the phone for hours. He said he was sorry for the way he had treated me. He admitted that my dad had put him up to treating me that way. Mike said that my dad told him that, unless the law was laid down right away with a wife, the wife becomes a nagging bitch like my mom. Mike said that my dad told him that my mom never appreciated what she had and what my dad had provided. He said my dad warned that the mistake he, himself, had made was not taking proper charge around the house right off the bat. My dad said that you couldn't be friends with your wife or they just take advantage of you. He said it wasn't necessary to go the extremes that his (Mikes's) dad did, but that the wife had to know who was boss or you'd fight about every decision for the rest of your married life.

Mike said that he realized he had blown it by being so harsh. He said he did not want to live without me and he would never hit me; and he had not actually hit me! Mike said that he had lived with enough fighting in the home as well and felt that we could make a home of harmony and understanding just like we'd planned on from the very beginning.

So there I was, pregnant with some other guy's baby, and all I wanted to do was go back to my husband, my very best friend, and make a go of my marriage. I thought if I told Mike that I was pregnant, it would ruin everything. He'd surely know it wasn't his since we had been apart more than four months. I paced the floor all night trying to figure out what to do. I finally decided to go to my dad. I thought since the big secret was out, maybe he'd be more receptive to me.

Boy, was I wrong! Dad just freaked out on me. He said I was no longer his problem and that any problems I had should be on Mike's shoulders now. When I tried to explain that I did not want to mess things up with this pregnancy, he just said that there should be no secrets between man and wife. I challenged him about all the money he kept hidden from Mom, and with that, he just said that I was not too big for him to still slap in the face if that is what I wanted.

I was devastated. I was trapped again. I could not go to Mike with this – I knew he'd never forgive me for being unfaithful. I saw only one way out – suicide! I went home and took every pill I could find. My roommate kept company with some of the best drug dealers in town. There were uppers, downers, acid, and black beauties – and I took them all.

I laid down on the bed and waited to feel them hit. As soon as my vision started to blur and my ears rang, I called Mike. I told him what I had done and why. I told him I loved him and that I was so sorry. I told him to find someone without a history like mine and to be happy.

The room started spinning and I could hear voices in the distance saying, "Here she comes, look out, here she comes."

The next thing I knew, I was opening my eyes in a hospital bed and a man looking very similar to Groucho Marx was standing beside my bed, looking at a clipboard.

A nurse was doing something with the covers of my bed and I saw that the side rails were up. The nurse walked over on the opposite side from Groucho and very compassionately said, "Well, hello! We thought we'd lost you," and started putting the sides of the bed down. I asked where I was and what time it was. The nurse started answering me but Groucho interrupted.

He told me he was a doctor of psychology. I immediately rolled away from him and said that I could not afford a shrink. Then I realized that I was bleeding as if I were menstruating. I told the nurse that I needed a pad and she brought me one right away from a drawer in the nightstand next to the bed. As she handed it to me, she said that it was a natural reaction for the body to get cycles mixed up after the ordeal it had just been through. I blurted out that I was sure I was pregnant, and asked, "In that case, what does this bleeding mean?" The nurse looked at Groucho and said she'd get another doctor to examine me.

They wheeled me out of intensive care and into the loony bin that same day. The doctor said that the fetus had apparently absorbed the majority of the drugs that I'd taken and that was what had saved my life. If there had been no fetus, I would have surely died. Further tests proved that the fetus was developing very abnormally and, under the circumstances, it was legal for them to remove it. They labeled the operation a 'D and C'. This explanation was delivered to both my father and my husband at the same time. Therefore, Mike found out that I was pregnant.

No one came in to see me until after the D and C, which was four days after my initial admittance. Then my dad came in, sat down beside my bed, and started going on and on about how much he cared for me and asked me why I had not come to him for help. Well, that did it. I just started screaming and throwing whatever I could get a hold of. I backed up to the wall next to my bed and yelled, "Get him out of here… get out, get out, get out!"

I can still feel the frustration and the confusion when I recall this experience. I felt as if I was surrounded by a magnetic field that held me at a certain distance from everyone no matter what I did. If I moved closer, they were repelled back and away from me. If I moved away from them, they were drawn nearer, but yet never came within that seemingly arm's-length, deep void, that surrounded me. It was as if they all just said whatever was appropriate for the moment and yet, it was never relative to the sequence of events.

I had gone to my father and asked for his help when I realized I was pregnant. I had told him everything and he had just brushed me off. Now, he was sitting in my hospital room acting as if he knew nothing about our conversation. But, of course, to the doctor who was just introduced to the situation, I looked like a lunatic, throwing things and shouting that my dad should get out of the room. Meantime, my dad just looked at the doctor with wide, innocent eyes, shrugged his shoulders, and said, "See, this is what we had to put up with." And that was a boldface lie! I had never thrown a temper tantrum, ever, in my life. My mom took up all the temper tantrum time. The hate and rage that filled me the moment my dad pulled that stunt in front of the doctor was indescribable.

They shuffled my dad out of the room and Groucho sat down on the chair my dad had been sitting on. I stood against the wall for a moment with my arms folded in front of me. Then the doctor said something to me that no one had ever said to me in my life. He said, "I want you to tell me what is going on. I want *you* to tell me what *you* think. I don't want to hear what you think anyone else thinks. I want to hear *your side of* the story."

Well, the floodgates opened! That poor doctor could not write fast enough in his little pocket notepad. I remember looking at him several times during the session and helping him catch up with what I'd said. I paced and talked and paced and talked. Then I paced and talked some more.

But I realize now that, as I recounted my life to this doctor, I went only so far back as Michael with my segment on relationships. I completely omitted the Norman episode. I omitted it not by conscious choice – I had actually wiped it clean out of my mind; just as if it had really not happened.

I stayed in the loony bin for a total of fourteen days. The doctor instructed that I was not to have any drugs. He said he was very pleased with my progress and that my speedy recovery was due to my willingness to talk about everything so openly.

He had Michael come in every evening for the last five days of my stay. He instructed us to talk about whether or not we wanted to get the marriage back on track and then left us alone for the first session to decide that. When we said we did want to stay together and make another go of it, he gave us some very good advice. He said that on one hand, it was simply a matter of a severe generation gap between my parents and myself. What complicated the issue was that our marriage was interwoven with my parents through the apartment building. He said that Michael and I needed to break free and make a life of our own. I still remember the last session, when that doctor looked me in the eye and told me that there was nothing wrong with me. He told me that I had a right to live my life the way I chose to now. He said that Michael and I were both adults and were allowed to try our wings, make our own mistakes, and create our own success.

Looking back, that was absolutely the best advice we could have been given – except for one thing. We had no ongoing support group to keep us on track. We didn't consciously realize that at the time; we were just too excited to have been given all this freedom all of a sudden.

Michael and I spent the night together in our own apartment that night, after I was released from the hospital. The next day was a Saturday. We got up and decided to pray for guidance. It was the first time he and I had ever really prayed together. Then, we ate breakfast and decided to take a drive to our favorite park. I packed a lunch and took a book and he grabbed the frisbee and a blanket.

We were not there very long, when we noticed a group of young people performing some sort of ritual about a hundred yards from us. We could tell they all had long hair and were dressed in typical jeans, shorts, and T-shirts; so they weren't Hare Krishnas. But it was obvious that it was some sort of religious thing that was going on.

Just then, the ice cream truck came by and Mike took off to get us some popsicles, leaving me alone on the blanket. The group broke up and it became obvious that the couple in the middle, who had been blocked from our view previously, was getting married. She was dressed in a full-length, cotton summer frock with a wreath of flowers on her head. She carried a bouquet of wildflowers and was barefoot. He wore a cotton robe that had designs on it that looked like a Persian rug over jeans and a white t-shirt. He was also barefoot. I concluded that these must be the flower child types that we'd heard so much about but had never really seen in person.

The group broke up and started fanning out in every direction. One fellow headed straight for me on my blanket. He was smiling a smile I had seen before, only during pot-smoking parties. My first instinct was to get up and run, but I was seemingly frozen in place. He just sauntered up, sat right down beside me on the blanket, and asked me what I was reading.

I showed him the cover of the book and to that, he produced a small Bible from behind his back. He asked me if I'd ever read the Bible and I thought to myself, *Oh no, Jesus freaks!* I was cringing inside and wishing that Mike would hurry up. I turned my head to look behind me where I thought I'd heard the ice cream truck stop, only to see that Mike had been cornered by one of these people while standing in line for ice cream.

As I turned my attention back to this fellow, he was saying something about looking for the right way to live our own lives. He was saying that many people our age were feeling lost and found that the standards our parents lived by really did not work for our generation. I asked him to repeat what he had just said and, without missing a breath, he said that the group he was with was called the Forever Family. All the people in the group were there to support each other in finding a way to live their lives the way they were initially intended to be lived by God.

I couldn't believe my ears. This was exactly what Michael and I had prayed for. We were not happy at the church we were attending. It was the same church my parents had taken me to since I was about eight.

When Michael was finally able to get back to our blanket, we asked if we could talk between ourselves in private about what they had told us. Michael and I compared notes and were both amazed. This really seemed like an answer to prayer and we thought it couldn't hurt to check it out a bit more. The two fellows that had been talking to us had each invited us to come back to the meeting place with them and find out more about the group. And so we did.

They were made up, primarily, of runaways, ex-drug addicts, and street people. There was one main leader of the group, a man by the name of Henry Pathe. Apparently, he was a nuclear physicist who set out to disprove God and ended up converting to the Christian faith.

Their funding came solely from the members themselves. Some worked at menial manual labor jobs, off and on, while most of them worked for Henry Pathe's company. His company rebuilt old vacuum cleaners and sold them door-to-door.

There was also a small percentage of the membership who came to Bible studies on a regular basis, held down regular jobs, and lived in single family dwellings in the suburbs. This suburban group donated food, clothing, and money on a regular basis as well.

They had a street ministry and actively sought out people with no direction or purpose in their life. They fed and clothed these people and gave them work. Then, when all the basic physical needs were in order, they focused on saving the souls of these seeming misfits. The organization was growing in leaps and bounds and they all seemed so genuine, loving, honest, and free.

Within two months, we were so involved with this group that we sold the apartment building and went to live in their commune. At this point, my parents disowned us both (as I am sure you can well imagine).

I advanced very quickly to a leadership position with this group because I had a very solid background in the Bible and no addictive problems. I thought Michael was following along very sincerely until, one afternoon, I noticed his pupils were dilated differently from one another. I knew what that meant – he was using LSD again. I was very upset and went to one of the elders immediately.

Without hesitation, they packed me up and sent me to Baltimore and Michael to Washington D.C. We were instructed that we were to live separately until Michael caught up to the same or greater level of commitment than myself. Otherwise, we were considered unequally yoked. They firmly believed in the traditional archetypal structure in which the male is the head or dominant figure and the female is to be submissive.

I was in the Baltimore commune no more than three weeks when I suddenly became head of it. The couple who was in charge when I got there, moved to Virginia to open a commune there. At the same time, the couple who was supposed to take over was held up due to the husband's job. Because of this position consequently being held by a female, there was quite a stir amongst the elders. You have to understand too, that when I say elders, I mean only seniority within the group. There were very few people older than twenty-four in this group.

I just did the job as I saw it needed doing. I had had no formal training for this position, but common sense seemed to suffice. Within two months, my commune was the wealthiest and growing the fastest. This really upset the young bucks who were basking in automatic kingship just because their genitals were placed externally. I soon found myself on a mission to prove that it did not matter, in the eyes of God, whether you were male or female. And my first exhibit was the success of the commune I had been in charge of for over four months.

Naturally, that evidence was written off to luck and/or momentum created by the previous leaders. I felt then that it didn't matter what they thought; I knew what I'd accomplished and God knew. And God was going to be my judge in the end anyway, not them. The funniest thing was, no matter how hard they tried, they could not get another couple to move to Baltimore to take the commune over from me. I ended up running it for nearly a year while Michael was in Washington, in another commune, trying to break his drug habit.

During that time, I remember my grandmother telling me that the group was good except for the fact that they promoted this male dominance thing. She also did not agree that they separated Michael and I. My grandmother said that God does not divide; especially not married couples. I'd also learned that the group had instructed some husbands to beat their wives into submission when the husbands thought it necessary. That really disturbed me.

Meanwhile, I was working on a very special Bible study that I felt was being given to me through divine inspiration. We were a full month away from one of our big convention meetings where Henry would enlighten us with all the wisdom God had bestowed upon him as the leader of our group. I was ready to give my Bible study and we had just enough meetings to conclude it before the convention.

You probably know what's coming. When we got to the convention and Henry started giving his Bible study, it was the exact same one that I had given, nearly word for word! And there was no way I could have confiscated the information because Henry lived in Lancaster, Pennsylvania, and I was in Baltimore, Maryland. The women in my group just started jumping up and down and singing, "Praise the Lord, we are equal. He does speak to us directly, just the same as he speaks to men!" The entire meeting was disrupted.

At first, I just buried my face in my hands and cried. I was so overcome with joy to think that God would have actually chosen me to demonstrate, so blatantly, exactly what His will really was. People were coming over to me, hugging me, and congratulating me. Oh and, by the way, the Bible study was on miracles! I felt like I was living one right then and there – until I looked up and saw Henry's face.

If looks could kill – a phrase I only then appreciated the true meaning of. For that split second that our eyes met, I witnessed all the evil that absolute power generates. I realized, in that instant, just exactly what I was up against, and I also realized that

I'd never win the battle. I could see the 'elders' behind Henry with their heads together, whispering to each other and occasionally glancing my way. I thought to myself, *Uh-oh, there's going to have to be a crucifixion; and guess who's in line for the honors!*

There was no way these guys were going to turn around now and admit they were wrong in beating their wives. There was no way that these guys, who had enjoyed total control, answered to no one except God himself, and basked in unchallenged authority, were going to turn around and live a democracy with beings they regarded no higher than animals in intelligence and ability. From their point of view, it was as absurd as if we women were instructed to inquire of the family dog before making decisions. There was no way generations of tradition would be turned around overnight. I ended up sticking around long enough to tell most of the women that it was just an impossible task to try and create change within. We either had to strike out on our own or just continue living as is.

Meanwhile, Michael had disappeared, and we all expected that he was using drugs again. I had no support group to create a commune of my own. I was then twenty-one and felt it was time to put some sort of career together. Our money from the sale of the apartment building was spent, and the money I was earning stocking shelves at Kreske's Five and Dime Store was not going to replenish my financial needs. So, I packed up and moved to Philadelphia. I must say, however, it was not an easy thing for me to do. I really had found comfort and acceptance with this group, for the first time in my life. I had also received counseling from the social workers who came to assist us in our drug and alcohol rehab programs. That was in 1973.

In 1996, I found a publication that was printed in 1985 entitled *Beyond Sex Roles,* by a theologian named Gilbert Bilezikian. In it, he accounted for all the Scripture that supported the equality of women in the church and in life, in general. I wonder what Bilezikian was doing in 1973? What is even more amazing, is that my grandmother had given me nearly the exact same Scriptures as he identified to support her theory of equality of women. Now, *she* was a lone voice in her day – smack in the middle of the Pennsylvania Bible belt with all the hellfire and brimstone preachers. *Wow*!

So, this chapter of my life brought me to a clearer understanding of my own personal autonomy. It gave me permission to cut the family ties and start re-raising myself.

I was also very confident, at this time, that God's hand was indeed on my life. I knew I was going to do something significant, somewhere, somehow. I just had to find that something.

Unfortunately, the task of re-raising myself and finding my purpose was not accompanied by the necessary set of tools. Therefore, I struck out on my own to employ the only means I had available to me. That means was 'trial and error'.

Chapter Three
Live and Let Live

I walked into Philadelphia with two suitcases and a purse. I got a furnished apartment within twenty-four hours of my arrival and that very next day, I was out on job interviews. I even knew all my neighbors within hours of arrival, and the fellow I was renting the apartment from also owned and operated the small hardware store on the main floor of my building; and, the little corner grocery store/deli on the next block.

In those days, I never dwelled on what might have been or worried whether or not I was doing the right thing. I just did what I thought had to be done, period.

There were several opportunities that were of interest to me. One of which was a stylist in one of the top hair salons downtown. I had a trial interview at two o'clock. That meant that I was to report to the salon and they would let me work on some of their clientele for the afternoon to see if I was good and fast enough to be part of their team.

Everything was in order. I had my license, my scissors, my standard regulation operator's uniform, and my special 'clinic' shoes. I was feeling pretty good about myself at this point.

I know I got on the trolley at the right place, but I did not get off the trolley at the right place. That was evident when I came up to street level and every building in sight was boarded up, newspapers and garbage littered the street, and the air had a damp, musty smell to it even though it was a clear, sunny mid-summer day.

I had to find the entrance to the subway going the opposite direction and it was not clearly within sight from where I was standing. I really should have just gone back down and continued on in the same direction until I was out of this area, but hindsight is always twenty-twenty.

Instead, I foolishly started walking down the street, hoping to see the entrance to the southbound subway. I didn't get half a block away from the corner, from where I started, when I was pulled into one of the boarded-up buildings and raped.

It was a bizarre experience. The skirt I was wearing was A-line and in those days, uniform skirts came to the knee so, no; I was not wearing a mini-skirt. It took this fellow no time at all to have me stripped from the waist, including my shoes. There was an old ripped mattress on the floor in the one room. He stuffed my pantyhose in my mouth and threw me on the mattress. He kept one foot on my diaphragm while he took his pants off. I thought he was going to break my ribs. I was crying and saying, "No, don't," as best as I could with a mouth full of pantyhose.

And he just kept yelling, "Shut up, I won't hurt you. This won't take long."

When he was on top of me, doing what he intended to do, I managed to reach into my purse and get ahold of my haircutting scissors. These scissors had two three-inch blades that came to a perfect point.

And by the way, those very same scissors are currently on my bathroom counter, by the sink; and I use those scissors to cut my bangs to this day.

I knew, at that moment, that I could kill this man if I could just get up enough nerve to shove those scissors into his temple. Then, I thought, *Suppose he catches me trying to kill him and turns the scissors on me!* He was busy enough for the moment that I knew I had to act right away or trust that he meant it when he said that he wouldn't hurt me.

Just then, I realized it was too late to use the scissors. He was finished. I pulled my hand out of my purse before he opened his eyes and laid really still. Then he just got up and left. He grabbed his pants and put them on in the hallway and walked out the door.

I listened for a moment and heard nothing except the noises from the street. I got up and very slowly walked out into the hallway and collected the rest of my clothes. I spotted a bathroom and it even had a roll of toilet paper in it. I cleaned up as best as I could and took the map out of my purse. I figured I was only about three or four blocks from where I was supposed to be for my interview. I still had enough time to get there because I had started out way ahead of time to give myself time to get lost, being in a new city after all.

So, I reported to my interview just as if nothing happened. I talked to the manager for a few minutes and then stood and watched some of the other stylists work for a while. I quickly realized that the three years I had spent in the Forever Family had severely retarded my abilities in this field. Hairstyling had moved forward in leaps and bounds and I was skilled only as if I had just graduated from class.

When the actual interview was started, I simply explained to the manager that I could see that was very behind on my skills. So I excused myself from the interview.

I did not deal with that rape experience until nearly six months later when I became romantically involved with a fellow. We started getting intimate one night and I could not relax. I could not stand to feel his hands on my body. It made me quiver inside as if I were tasting a repulsive substance. I knew what was wrong with me right away and made an appointment with a counselor the very next day.

My visit to this counselor was much the same as my first session with 'Mr. Groucho' in the hospital loony bin. I just walked in and started talking about exactly what had happened. Looking back on it now, I have to laugh at the expressions on these psychologists' faces. They did not know what to make of someone who just walked in and started talking about deep, dark issues. But, for me, I had a purpose to find and I had no time to allow things like this to get in my way.

It was while I was seeing this counselor regularly that I received word that Michael had had a terrible car accident. Apparently, he was high on LSD at the time and went into a 28-day coma. When he came out of the coma, he thought he was an insect and he'd sit for hours on the windowsill, catch flies, and eat them. A very sad ending for such a talented draftsman. And he was really talented.

Three months later, I was functioning normally again and all was right with the world. I had a great job at Gimbels Department Store, I was meeting new friends, disco was all the rage, and I was so good at it. I often tell people that I was born in Reading, Pennsylvania, but I grew up in Philly.

Within six months, I was promoted to the buying office from the sales' floor at Gimbels. My duties were glorified secretary for the actual buyer, but the pay was executive level. It was more money than I'd ever made in my life. I really enjoyed the people I worked with. Life was perfect. I even assisted the police in a drug bust in my neighborhood. I still carry the fraternity card in my wallet that was used to identify me in case I was in the house at the time of the bust. That was a really exciting experience too.

I really lived all the life I missed out on growing up with my 'jail-warden' parents. At one point, I was dating six different men. One night I'd be at the opera and the next night I'd be at a rock concert. One night I'd be ballroom dancing and the next night I'd be at a Karaoke bar.

I started guitar lessons. I bought a beautiful acoustic guitar. Within a month, I was playing at the 'open mic' evening at a quaint European pub in the renovated area near the docks. My first performance was 'Hang Down Your Head, Tom Dooley'. Later, I joined in with a few other players and just jammed to some tunes that seemed to sound good, but I have no idea what they were or if they were actual published tunes at all.

But all the glory had to come to an end sometime, and it did when Gimbels was bought out by a British tobacco company. The new management insisted that everyone above sales' clerk had to have a college degree. I tried to go back to school then; I really did. But every time I'd get near campus, I'd get so sick to my stomach and woozy in my head. I just could not do it.

Then I met Craig. He was just back from California and looking for a new adventure. He had his masters in psychology and his parents wanted him to get his Ph.D. But he was taking some time off school and planning to import some items from South America. We hit it off the minute we said hello.

He was a beautiful, tall, dark, Italian fellow. And whatever you have heard about Italian lovers... believe it! Looking back now, I think it's their arrogant confidence that gives them an edge. Anyway, whatever it was, let me tell you I was not complaining the morning after... whew... or any morning after for that matter!

We had a whirlwind romance accompanied by making lots of money and having a great time doing it all. Craig had relatives in South America who sent artifacts, beautiful hand-loomed area rugs, pottery, jewelry, and some pullover-type tops. I quit my job at Gimbels and took off with Craig.

We'd have to drive to Florida to pick the stuff up when it came in and get it into the warehouse. Then we'd have to assess what we had, go to the library, and look up the information on different pieces so we could sell them to museums and art galleries. We'd take pictures of the items and create a catalog in a three-ring photo-binder to show the buyers.

I should be embarrassed to admit how much money I made in that year, and blew it all. I had no idea about investment then – none whatsoever. I'd never been told about investing by anyone in my life. And saving? Well, why bother at that age, is what I thought. Besides, I had no idea where I was going to be living for any length of time. Craig and I traveled from New York to Florida on a monthly basis. I was afraid that if I opened a savings account in one city, we'd move on and I'd forget where it was.

Then, South America put a new tariff on exporting, so Craig's relatives sent a huge shipment and wired us that it was the last one. We sold our last pieces in San Francisco, then took several months off, and just played in the California sun.

I got an apartment in San Rafael that had a picture window in the living room that framed Mt Tamalpais perfectly. I was on the main floor. It was motel style, so windows only to the front. It had hard wood floors, a kitchen right off the main living area with a breakfast nook counter. One bedroom and bath. Laundry was just two doors down from my door and I was second to the end.

Our whirlwind romance soon wound down when we had to get on with regular day-to-day living. It did not bother me so much. I knew all along that the money and glamor would have to come to an end, and so I prepared myself for that. Craig, on the other hand, couldn't settle into a daily, mundane routine. After a number of very serious arguments, one of which nearly turned physical when he grabbed me by the arm; he went to Hawaii to finish his Doctorate degree.

When Craig grabbed my arm in a very aggressive manner we were both very surprised. Having a masters in Psychology, he immediately caught himself and just walked away. He left the next day and I never heard from him again. There really is such a thing as bringing out the worst in each other. Please do keep that in mind and examine your own relationships accordingly. Make necessary changes sooner rather than later.

Meanwhile, I had started a job with a young women's clothing chain as a sales' clerk. It was called 'Pick-A-Dilly', I was with them only three months when I was covering the evening shift with one of the other saleswomen, Janet. Well, Janet snapped and thought I was someone else and started beating me up in the store.

This was a mind-blower for a few reasons. One, it seemed that wherever I went, I had to be attacked, raped, or beat up. Was I wearing a sign on my back that read 'kick me', or something? Two, the manager of the store did not sympathize with me at all. In fact, when I phoned her after the ordeal was over and explained what had happened, all she wanted to know was whether I was going to cash out or not! Lastly, I got fired over it! Looking back now, I really wish I would have sued them.

Wait, it gets worse! They fired Janet as well, so she came to my apartment with a handgun. She shoved this thing in my nose and stuck it in my mouth and all the time she was saying that if she didn't finish me off, she knew plenty of people who could. And I knew that she hung around with a pretty rough crowd.

I finally broke free from her and ran out of the apartment. I hid behind some bushes in the parking lot and waited till she left. Then I ran in, got my purse, and took off for Carmel, a little town south of San Francisco where Craig had introduced me to some very hospitable people only a few months before.

I drove nonstop for hours, and when I got to my destination, I was thoroughly exhausted. They were very obliging to give me use of their spare room. I didn't even burden them with what I'd just been through. I just went to my room and slept for almost eighteen hours.

For the next three days, I did nothing but sit on the beach and look out over the ocean. I recapped my life up to that point. I saw myself as having had a full portion of both the high life and the low life. I felt as if I'd done it all, and so what? There was no one depending on me. I certainly could not go back home to Pennsylvania. I was ostracized from my own family. Michael had eventually come down off the windowsill and was working in a donut shop by that time, but he was not yet back to normal.

I could not file for divorce until Michael regained his senses enough to be able to sign the papers and know what he was signing. So, I was still legally married to him. However, after Craig, it was not going to be possible to go back to the small-town man and play Suzie Homemaker. I decided that I'd probably lived straight through my purpose, and because I was going so fast, I just missed it.

At that point, I also recognized a pattern of extreme highs and lows in my life. I also saw a pattern of lack of respect and that people seemed to think I was fair game for punishment for some reason. What was that? Why was that so? Was I just imagining it? I finally had to ask myself what I was doing to attract such people into my life.

And I prayed a lot those three days. I finally decided that I had nowhere else to go, so I went back to San Francisco. I fully expected to walk into my apartment, have a bomb go off in my face, and that would be it for me. Instead, as I walked in the door, the phone rang. When I answered it, it was Charles, Janet's boyfriend. I froze when he said that he thought I should know that Janet had killed herself. When I didn't respond for a moment, Charles said, "Hello, are you still there?"

I finally whispered a weak, "Yes… how?" And he told me that she shot herself with a little handgun that morning. Then he said that he knew how close Janet and I'd become and he thought I should know.

So, I questioned him and it came out that he did not even know that Janet had been fired. He didn't know that she'd come to my apartment with that same handgun she'd killed herself with. It sounded like this woman lived two completely different lives. Charles said she talked about me very affectionately and he thought she and I were best friends.

I hung up the phone and I remember that everything went black. The next thing I remember is that I got up and was going to eat breakfast. As I walked out into the kitchen, I felt confused and I couldn't remember what I had to do that day. I walked back into the bedroom and saw a small, white appointment book lying beside the bed on the floor. I opened it up and saw two weeks of notes written in pencil, in a handwriting I did not recognize. The notes read things like wash hair, get groceries, do laundry. I had lost almost two weeks, and I didn't even remember buying that appointment book nor the mechanical pencil clipped onto the page to mark the current week.

My neighbor came by just then and rapped on the window. I went to the door and she asked me where I'd been. She said she hadn't seen me for two weeks. She asked me if I'd been sick and sleeping the whole time. I showed her the book and told her the story about Janet. She just said, "Wow! Far out," and asked me if I wanted to smoke a joint. I declined politely.

Ever since that time, I cannot function without an appointment book. I believe that I definitely lost a section of brain cells over that one. I also firmly believe that I experienced divine intervention. I believe that I blacked out after the conversation with Charles because it was so contrary to what I expected and thought I knew.

This led to yet another obvious pattern. I seemed to always find myself caught between two completely different perspectives or realities. I decided to write everything down from then on. And so began my journaling that continues to this day.

A few days later, I landed a job with a figure salon and was sent to Los Angeles for training. The experience with this company is a story in itself. Suffice it to say that I was a total misfit, having never had a weight problem in my life. But it was during my two-week training session in L.A. that I met my second husband, Robert.

He invited himself to sit at our table as I was sitting with two of my friends in the lounge, listening to a live band. My skin crawled as soon as he sat down. I did not like him. It felt as if he had the attitude that we'd be blessed to have him in our company. I was actually rude to him, hoping he'd go away. But my two friends were sucked in by his good looks and seemingly pleasant personality.

I left and went back to my room, leaving my two married friends to enjoy this self-indulgent impostor. Just before I turned out my light to get some sleep, my friends were knocking on my door. They came in, all excited, and said that this Robert character was very interested in me. They went on and on about how wonderful he was, that they'd danced with him, and he seemed to be very well known by the staff of the hotel. They said I'd be downright foolish if I didn't give him a chance. After all, they pointed out, I was very unattached and not getting any younger.

Once again, it seemed that everyone around me was seeing the world one way and I was seeing it totally differently. Then I remembered how my mom would sarcastically and repeatedly tell me that surely it wasn't me who was wrong; it must be everyone else in the world. This always shed a light onto a subject that did seem to reveal the total absurdity of my point of view. How in the world could I, all alone with no one else who agreed with my perspective, be right? So, time after time, I would shut down my intuition and follow the crowd. And this was one of those times.

We went back to the lounge the following night and dear Robert was on his bar stool just waiting for us. We sat down and he came right over and offered to buy us all drinks. He sat himself down without even asking if he was welcome and immediately took over the conversation. As soon as the band started playing, he asked me to dance, and so I did.

Writing about this, even now; after more than seventeen years have passed, is very hard for me. I am so sorry I did this to myself. Of all the foolish things I ever did, this was indeed the biggest, dumbest, stupidest thing ever! I let myself be talked into opening up to this guy. I pushed all the warning feelings aside and looked at this guy through the eyes of my friends.

He was very good looking. He looked like a young Jack Nicholson. He was five foot ten inches and had that robust build. A broad strong chest and shoulders with a smile that just melted you from the bottom up. He wore graduated tinted aviator glasses that just accentuated his smile from under a Magnim PI mustache.

He took me to dinner every night after that for the remainder of my stay in Los Angeles. He sent flowers to the training room and impressed every other female in the place, including me by that time.

He took a vacation very soon after I returned to San Francisco and came to visit me. Since he owned his own business, he was able to set his own vacation schedule. We spent three more romantic weeks together and he asked me if I could get a transfer to L.A. The company I was working for had their head office in L.A. and it seemed a reasonable possibility. He helped me draft a letter of request for transfer before he left to return home. I had decided that if the company did not grant me a transfer, I would take that as a signal to cool things down a bit with this guy. Unfortunately, this idea did not set itself firmly enough in my mind.

Three days after Robert left, I received a call from the hospital in San Luis Obispo, a small town just south of San Francisco. They said that Robert had had a terrible accident with his hang glider and had broken both his legs. He had gone through major surgery and would be in a wheelchair for at least six months before he could walk again.

My first inclination was to just leave it as it was. I certainly did not feel qualified to play nursemaid. On the other hand, to dump a guy in such a condition was beyond cruel. That same day, I received word that my request for transfer was denied for the time being. However, I was told that I would be first in line as soon as a position was available. I looked at these series of events as road signs indicating that I should take care of Robert during his convalescence, and by the time he was on his feet again, there would be a position available for me in Los Angeles.

I thought, perhaps, I was learning what true love really meant. I knew that romantic love was not the real thing, and maybe it was time I started living reality instead of expecting my heart and feelings to always match what was really going on.

So, I moved in with this guy in Whittier California when he was released from the hospital and took complete care of him while he was in a wheelchair. He was not one to be stopped by his condition, either. No, he allowed me to drive him around to visit everyone he knew to show his scars and tell his story. This process included lifting a wheelchair that weighed nearly as much as I did onto a bike rack affixed onto the back of my '65 Mustang.

He did not pay me for my services. I earned room and board and the 'privilege' of sleeping with him for my efforts. Stupidly, I accepted those terms as fair, and stayed in touch with the figure salon company in the meantime.

A position never did open up for me with that company and, when Robert was able to return to work, I applied for a sales' position with Jordache Jeans.

The Jordache Company hired me right away, and as soon as I was established with them, I moved out of Robert's apartment and rented a room closer to downtown Los Angeles. I felt so confused. I really did not love this guy, no matter how hard I tried. Yet, there I was again, all alone in a strange city and Robert would not leave me alone.

He phoned every night. He called me at work during the day, insisting that we set a definite schedule so he'd know when he could see me. He'd have his friends and relatives call me. He'd send me flowers all the time, and on the surface, it made for a great romantic movie. So, why did it feel so wrong inside?

I made an appointment with a counselor and we talked for more than the allotted hour during the first visit. After several sessions, I was driving home one night when it hit me like a ton of bricks. The problem I was having was due to the fact that I did not know how to let someone love me!

This made so much sense. Here I had someone who was willing to go to great lengths to have me in his life, and I didn't know how to accept that. I had been told that the world was divided into two basic categories of people: the givers and the takers. I had to learn that it was okay for me to do some taking for a change. (It's amazing how right something can sound when framed within the corresponding con game!) The next time Robert and I were together, I expressed this to him and he was delighted to hear that I was finally coming to my senses.

Meanwhile, Robert's business was not doing very well. He said that his partner really messed things up while he was laid up. Robert had been in touch with a cousin of his in Canada who offered him a job in the oil industry. Apparently, being in the oil industry in Alberta, Canada, was a license to print money in those days. Robert suggested that if we were to move to Canada together, it would level the playing field in our relationship. It would no longer be his place or his city versus mine; it would be both of us exploring new territory together.

At the same time, Jordache was talking about investigating the Canadian market. I told them that I had an opportunity to move to Alberta and asked them if I could be their Canadian connection. When they agreed, I saw it as a positive signal from the universe, and we immediately listed an ad for my replacement in the paper. I trained my replacement the following month, then Robert and I were off to Canada.

We took a trip to Europe before we packed up for Canada. We decided that we'd probably have to work very hard for the next few years before we'd be in a financial position to travel again.

If we could stop the story here, with Robert and me driving off into the sun... hmmm... can't be a sunset because we were driving northeast. Well, whatever. If we could stop the story here, it could make for the perfect Cinderella story.

Unfortunately, I was still short-circuiting my intuition. I was still talking myself into things against what my true feelings were. Of course, we know that now because we are looking back. Remember, at the time, I thought I was learning what true love was. I thought I was living a love other than the romantic one.

During our drive to Canada, we stopped at many of the tourist sights. I decided to write a book about my life as I looked out over the Grand Canyon. I thought that my experiences from birth up to that point were noteworthy enough to deserve a book.

But, the truth was, I had no idea what hell was yet!

Chapter Four
An American Female in Alberta

At this point, I let go and allowed myself to love Robert. I reframed my life and made a conscious decision to focus on the positive.

We arrived in Calgary, Alberta, driving my Mustang and towing Robert's Volkswagen Beetle with our immediate needs packed inside of it. We had plans to stay with Robert's cousin, Cameron (who was arranging to get Robert into the oil industry), and his wife, Olivia, until we found out where Robert would be stationed.

He was assigned to the station in Red Deer, a small town about 150 miles north of Calgary. I must say here, too, that moving to Alberta, Canada from nearly three years in California was a tremendous culture shock for both of us.

We were settled in an apartment together in Red Deer for less than a month when I got word that Jordache was using a marketing company in Toronto to do all their necessary research. This meant that I had no job and was not able to stay in Canada. Instead of seeing that as a sign to get the heck out of there, we went through the necessary procedures to obtain landed immigrant status. This included marrying Robert. But first, I had to obtain a legal divorce from my first husband.

The appropriate time had lapsed to allow me to obtain a divorce by mail. There was no joint property between Michael and I anymore. We had been separated for just over seven years, so it was just a matter of paperwork. I received my legal divorce papers on a Wednesday and married Robert that following Saturday in the living room of our apartment in Red Deer. That was October 13, 1979.

The wedding was canceled once. Robert and I fought about everything. It amazed me how he insisted on seemingly competing with everything I did. It was as if he had to have the spotlight all the time. And, he had hit me!

But, he reacted as if he caught himself right away. He apologized immediately and promised that it would never happen again.

Well, it did happen again. And again, and again. We were not married very long when he would come home from an assignment with all sorts of weird ideas. He'd accuse me of running around on him and sleeping with other men.

His assignments would take him away to the oil fields for, sometimes, three weeks straight. These workers often worked straight through a 36-hour shift with no sleep. Then he'd have three weeks off and lots of money to spend. And spend it he did. Every dime. Then he'd hand me the checkbook for an empty bank account and tell me that I was in charge of the money.

I finally decided that I had to get money of my own, but I still had to wait nearly a year before I could legally work in Canada. So, I just went downtown and spoke to some of the business people to get a feel for the city. I learned that it was an election year for the town's mayor and that this mayor had tried several times to develop a downtown beautification project yet it had failed to materialize.

With a bit more research, I decided that what the mayor needed was a liaison to sell the project to the business people for him. I offered to be his door-to-door representative of sorts. I went to see the mayor, told him about my idea, and offered to perform this task free-of-charge, since I couldn't legally work anyway. He agreed to work with me on the idea and I asked for his commitment to the project in writing. He immediately obliged.

Then I approached the landscaping companies in the area with the letter in hand and said that I wanted a commission on the value of the project, if and when they were awarded the job. By the time the project was complete and the landscaping done and paid for, I was going to be legally able to work. And I knew I had no time to waste in escaping my abusive husband.

When I originally told Robert about my plan to work for the mayor, he laughed at me. He said I was such a dreamer and that I really thought far too highly of myself. When I came back to him and announced that I had actually accomplished everything

75

I planned, he was furious and his abuse got worse, even though I hadn't told him I had a plan to leave him.

He used to hold my nose and mouth so that I couldn't breathe, and whisper in my ear that I could not even breathe without his permission. He would slap me around the room every morning before I'd go to work so that I'd have to get ready all over again. He'd break my curling iron on a weekly basis. And his favorite thing was to move things around or throw things away so I couldn't find them, and then taunt me saying that I was obviously losing it.

No, actually that was his second favorite thing to do. His very best favorite thing was to force me to have sex with him because it was his marital right. He especially enjoyed sex with me after a good beating when I was crying and pleading for him to stop.

Robert was a Vietnam vet. He was highly trained in hand-to-hand combat and he had retained every bit of it. He could throw me around a room and there was never a bruise on me. He could cause me to pass out from lack of oxygen, leaving me to believe I was dying, and yet I'd always wake up again. No one can imagine what hell that was! No one can know the degradation and the feelings of fear and desperation I felt.

The only things that kept me sane were my self-help books and the fact that I had a plan. It was during this horrific ordeal that I found my strength in self-help. The first book I read was *I'm Okay, You're Okay* by Dr. Thomas Harris, and I followed that with *Children the Challenge* by Dr. Rudolf Dreikurs. Between those books and my notes from my counseling sessions, I had a pretty good idea that my own childhood experiences had something to do with the current mess I was in. To keep myself going, I also read *The Sky's The Limit* by Dr. Wayne Dyer and *Winning Through Intimidation* by Robert Ringer.

I was also able to enlist the help of a neighbor and Cameron's wife, Olivia. But, the freedom I thought would be mine as soon as I got away did not materialize. Instead, things got even worse.

Before I left Red Deer, I managed to get a job in Calgary as a sales' representative for an IBM Selectric Typewriter ribbon manufacturer. They were actually one of the first knock-off ribbons and much more affordable.

Robert would follow me around Calgary as I went about my business of visiting potential users of the product and let the oil out of my car or the air out of my tires. So, I'd come out from an appointment and have to spend the rest of the day getting my car running again. At one point, he actually broke into my employer's office and stole all the client files. Then he called the owner and told him that he'd return all the files if the company would fire me.

I'd called the police repeatedly and they'd just say that, unless the man hurt me, they couldn't do anything. I could tell that the police didn't have one ounce of sympathy for my situation either. In fact, it often appeared as if they were on Robert's side, rooting for him to win the girl back.

It was amazing how crafty Robert could be to get my unlisted phone number over and over again. Somehow, he knew every move I made and was able to show up at the same restaurant or the same bar where I was.

I lived *Fatal Attraction* long before it became a movie. I also lived the confusion and internal conflict that abused wives go through. I can understand, first-hand, why they keep going back. Absolutely everything is against a woman trying to free herself from an abusive situation. Society frowns upon a woman who cannot manage her household. The law is on the side of the abuser because the abuser is the one being abandoned in the eyes of everyone looking on. People, in general, sympathize with the one being left behind and literally condone whatever it takes for this poor, suffering victim to hold onto their family structure. It is absolutely the greatest mind game anyone can get into because your own mind is against you. Plus, it is so exhausting. The pursuer has a great deal of help and encouragement by everyone. The real victim gets little to no understanding and so, the temptation to just give up and use the energy that's left to just survive the abuse from inside the relationship is very great.

All that the situation offers, by itself, was enough to crush even the strongest of abuse escapees. But, I had the added stress of being in a foreign country in the Canadian mid-west.

It was 1980 and at that time, women's equality was still quite primitive. At that time, they still had brochures in the police stations entitled 'Lady, Beware' to inform the public how best to avoid an attack. It blatantly suggested that women had to wear unsuggestive clothing and walk with her head down and her eyes to the ground. The brochure identified an attack on a woman as a sexually inspired act – and placed the burden of blame for the attack on the woman herself!

In 1974, when I was in Philadelphia, literature was being distributed which identified rape as an act of violence. I know this for sure because I was going through counseling for my own rape experience at that time. Six years had not updated Alberta Canada. When I tried to tell the Calgary police that my husband was having a nervous breakdown, they would just smile their superior, all-knowing smile and then they would all but pat me on the head, tell me to be a good little girl, and go back to my husband where I belonged. After all, he couldn't chase me around if I was on his living-room sofa, now could he?

Finally, the peer group that I was establishing a rapport with acknowledged that I really did have a problem. I was dating one of the fellows, Richard. He had family in Jasper and suggested that we take a ski trip for a week or two, and perhaps if Robert couldn't find me, he'd get bored and go away.

And just so you know, Richard lived across the street from one of the local SWAT team members. Between this peer group of Richards; and his neighbor, you'd think we could have gotten ahead of Robert's insanity. But no! It was not to be!

When we got back, Robert had managed to break into my apartment and take everything. So, all I had to my name at that point was what I had packed in one suitcase for a ski trip. Then, while I was discovering my apartment was robbed, he got ahold of my car and took that too. It was found in a very remote part of the area and he'd taken a sledgehammer to every inch of it.

All the windows and lights were broken. He'd slashed the seats (that were leather by the way) and had somehow broken the steering column and gearshift. The police said they were surprised that he hadn't burned it. To which I replied that we would have found it sooner that way, and that's the only reason he didn't burn it.

Richard felt so bad that things were only getting worse, he suggested I stay at his place for a few days. The police finally had a break and enter charge they could use, and maybe this would solve the problem.

Well, that just started a series of arrests and then he'd get out on bail and do something else. Once he tried to run me off the road. He'd repeatedly call and say that he would never give up until one of us was dead. I did eventually lose my job over it, and there was seemingly no end to this hell. This went on from the time I moved to Calgary, which was August of 1980, to February of 1981. And I had to deal with something that he initiated every single day of those seven months, except for the ten days I was in Jasper.

If it had not been for one of the clerks at the police station being better informed of the true dangers of situations like these, I am sure the police wouldn't have ever taken me seriously enough to even have him arrested for the break and enter. She admitted to me later that she used to hear the officers laughing about my situation around the coffee pot between shifts.

We finally had enough evidence to go to trial and with that, Robert took off back to California. He never appeared for this hearing. I learned only later that he'd gone back to California. Before he left; however, he had to leave one final mark.

He took cans of paint, splashed them all over the front of Richard's house, and threw the 8 empty cans all over the front yard. And, once again, no one saw him do it. He never got caught in the act. He was like a phantom. Yes indeed, his Vietnam training served him well.

At this point I snapped. Up to now everyone kept telling me to just ignore him and he'd get bored. But they did not know this man the way I did. He was determined and I knew that he would never be bored if he was able to continue to torment me. Remember, at this point I did not know he was leaving for California.

Richard had a 357-magnum gun. He and his SWAT team neighbor used to take me to the shooting range occasionally and I was pretty good with it as soon as I got used to the recoil.

I knew where that gun was and where the key to the safe was. And you guessed it, I got that gun, fully loaded it and took off after Robert. I knew he had to go back to Red Deer to pick up his VW that was in the shop for repairs. He'd installed a hitch on his pick-up truck to tow it around since he had no one to help him move it. He'd alienated all his friends, work mates, and even his relatives saying that they were all on my side.

I was driving a friends little pick-up at the time and I was determined to find him and finish this. I drove and drove and went to every place I knew he'd go and each time I'd ask if anyone had seen him; at the garage where the VW was repaired; at his work office; at his apartment; at his favorite restaurant, and they would all say that I'd just missed him.

To this day I am so thankful that I never found him that day because I would have shot him. I absolutely would have shot him and I would have shot to kill.

The drive back to Calgary from Red Deer is just over an hour and a half at speed limit. As I drove I felt the anger melt away into pure hopelessness. Suddenly the fact that I had a loaded gun stuck in the waistband of my jeans gave me a very interesting solution.

There was a lot of open field between Red Deer and Calgary. The pick-up truck would have no problem driving into one of those open fields. I'd be sure to not mess up the truck. I'd aim away from it. But do you want to know what stopped me at that moment? The one thought that changed my mind so that I dismissed suicide? I didn't have anything to leave a note with! I had no paper or pencil with me.

When I got home Richard greeted me at the door, as he was watching out the window looking for me to come home. When I walked in he was holding the empty box the gun belonged in and he was white as a sheet. He paused for a moment and then asked if I'd found him. I hadn't looked at him yet and just said, "No, you're not harboring a murdering fugitive," and handed him the gun handle first dangling between two fingers with the barrel pointing down.

He took the gun saying, "Oh, thank God," and wrapped his arms around me in a way that felt so safe and warm that I was able to just let go. My legs buckled under me and I began to sob saying that I just could not take anymore.

Right at that moment the phone rang. It was the SWAT team neighbor saying that he'd put an APB out on Robert's vehicle and it was identified as having crossed the border into Montana while I was driving back from Red Deer. Richard and I were both listening to the call sharing the receiver between us and he looked at me and said, "It's over. He's gone."

At that I just panicked inside and collapsed onto the floor saying, "No he isn't. He just wants you to believe that. He will double back, I guarantee you he will. He vowed to go until one of us was dead and he will not give up. He does not know how to give up." Richard sat down beside me and scooped me up into his arms and said that because he did not show up for the court appearance his picture and information was released Province wide. The SWAT neighbor had seen to that. Richard said that the borders will be watching for him because they've been told that he is armed and dangerous. To which I looked at Richard for the first time since I got back and I said, "He was armed? I was the one armed, not him!" And then Richard took my face in his hands and said that only himself, myself, and the SWAT neighbor knew that and we were going to keep it that way!"

To that I just curled up in Richards arms right there on the floor and let him rock me for what seemed like days. He just kept saying it was over as much for himself as for me.

Even then I reflected on how awful it would have been if I had found him and shot him; and then had to spend years in jail for it. I would not have been free of him at that point. Rather my life would have been even more disrupted by him. Truly, violence is never the answer, NEVER!

Two months later, I was holding down a very good job as a representative with a personnel agency. In fact, this was my first independent contract position. I was still living with Richard and things seemed really good between us. Richard dropped hints of marriage and I'd squirm a bit because my divorce to Robert still had to come through. Plus, Richard had a young son from a previous marriage. The boy was only four at the time, and I found myself feeling like I was living a soap opera. The visitations were certainly reasonable and he had a very good rapport with his ex-wife, maybe even too good. It just didn't feel right. After all, I had just come through a pretty trying ordeal. And I had no therapy for it. We did not discuss it anymore. We just got on with our lives as if it never happened.

Then, as if nearly killing someone and a new job wasn't enough, I found myself pregnant with Richard's baby. I was so shocked, you cannot imagine! I must have missed a pill or two during the final crisis with Robert, or, I don't know what happened. Truly, I really don't know how that happened, but it did.

When I told Richard, I immediately said that I did not think this was a good time for me to be starting a family. He looked very relieved and said that he would never suggest an abortion unless the woman felt she could handle it. Then, he said that he was meaning to tell me that his company wanted to transfer him to Saudi Arabia for a couple of years. It meant a great deal of money and an advancement in his career that he could not refuse. He said that he thought the timing was good because it would allow me to settle myself a bit after the ordeal with Robert. He said he envisioned me taking care of the house while he was gone. And he said that he would charge me only the cost of the utilities to live there and he'd be back for every major holiday, and sometimes in between holidays, until we decided what we wanted to do about the relationship. He felt very strongly that a baby would dictate everything and not allow us to make our own clear-headed choices.

I agreed and Richard made arrangements for the abortion, somehow. I ended up just going to the local hospital for a D&C operation. I remember a social worker coming to see me the day I was admitted and asking me a whole lot of questions. She never came right out and used the term abortion, but that is what she was asking me about. I remember feeling very sure of myself at the time. I really did not want to have a baby at that point in my life.

What I didn't expect were the feelings I subsequently went through. The first time I had a D&C when the fetus absorbed all the drugs I took in an attempt to die, I never felt anything afterward. It was almost as if there never really was a fetus the first time. But this time, my breasts enlarged and milk came in and leaked out. I wanted to cry all the time. I felt so sad and guilty. I had nightmares. I could not stand to have Richard's little boy around. I was cranky and irritable. It was awful!

Richard was very supportive and the worst side effects were over before he had to leave for Saudi Arabia. But the afternoon that I returned to the house after his plane took off, I sat in the armchair and cried and cried. I knew I could never have a future with Richard. I was not going to be dumb enough to follow another man to another foreign country, no matter how sane he appeared to be. And I knew that was what this Saudi Arabia thing was leading up to. I knew Richard planned to ask me to marry him that coming Christmas, after I'd proved myself worthy by taking care of his house. Then the next step would be moving me over to Saudi Arabia. No thanks!

The reason I was in Canada was because I followed some man and talked myself into being in love. No, all I wanted to do was get my act together, move on and get back to Philadelphia as soon as possible. I just needed to earn enough money to move back and line up a job there. I figured it would take me a year; maybe two.

I always had such great plans for myself. I always seemed to think clearly and sanely to a point, then something would come along and derail me again. Or should I say, some MAN would come along and I'd allow myself to be derailed.

It took almost thirty days for Paul to turn me right around again. There he was, all six-foot, two-inches of him. He was sleek and young, with a very stable background. It started out as friends for the first time in my life. I knew Paul from the gliding association that Richard was president of at the time. We had socialized and partied together quite a bit before Richard left. In fact, Paul was at Richard's farewell party put on by the club at Richard's house.

All the unattached fellows were teasing Richard that night about who would take care of me while he was gone. The members of the club all made it very clear to me that I would not be abandoned by them. They all took vows to maintain the party spirit during Richard's absence and ensured him that I'd be included.

Paul was amongst that crowd and was probably the least threatening because he was younger than the rest of us by four years. I didn't even give it a second thought when he first called me and asked me out to dinner. I really thought that he was dutifully babysitting me for Richard. One thing led to another, and the next thing I knew, I was moving into an apartment downtown with him.

Richard had not come back for his first visit yet when I told him I was moving in with Paul and that I was sorry, but I didn't see a future for us. Richard was quite put out about the whole thing, and understandably so, I suppose.

On the other hand I'm thinking that; of course he would have no understanding for me. Rather, he called his ex-wife and she came rushing over the day of the move to be sure that I didn't take anything that didn't belong to me. It was ridiculous, really. But I was not surprised. It seemed that every relationship I had was a love/hate situation. I never managed to break up an intimate relationship and still remain friends with the guy. I marveled at how some women accomplished that.

That year, my best friend from my hairdresser school days sent me an invitation to join a friend of hers on a trip to Las Vegas for the New Year. She always said she'd repay me for all the time I spent with her when her husband worked graveyard shift at the factory; which left her virtually as a single parent. He picked me up in his private jet. I was the last to join the party. He was a card counter. He made his initial fortune on the stock market and now had plenty of money to just play on the weekends in Las Vegas. At times, he lost just enough to keep the cameras off of him. And most of the times, he made a fortune in just two days.

He needed enough players to fill the black jack table. He trained us all to watch his signals, bet, and take cards as he instructed. By playing the entire table, he usually came out on top. However, it would take us a while to all end up at the same table.

When we were not working for him, we were free to do whatever we wanted to do. He taught us the basics of counting high/low. And we always played the black jack tables where all the cards were played face-up.

It was nearing the end of the trip and I had been playing on my own for some time. I took one hundred Canadian dollars with me to play with and I was up fifteen hundred dollars.

One thing our boss always said was, "Never, never, never set a goal. Just play the cards as they fall. When the count gets too risky, *stop* and walk away. Actually get up and leave the table."

Well, I couldn't leave. I was hooked! I wanted two thousand and I was determined to get it. Then, I started losing. I was down to five hundred dollars when I was finally able to tear myself away from the table.

I went to the condo where we were staying and he was there taking a breather himself. I told him what was going on and said

I had to get out of there. I said I could feel it controlling me and I couldn't stop.

He said he was not ready to leave, so he took me to the airport and put me on standby for the next flight to Calgary. In those days, there were smoking sections in the planes. It's hard to even imagine that there were smoking sections on planes, once upon a time, with all the new regulations in place today for air travel.

The first flight to Calgary had no room for me, but my luggage went on that flight. There was three hours before another flight was leaving so back to the tables I went. I started winning again and got up to twelve hundred before I had to leave for the next flight.

As I walked towards the gate to board, I said: "Dear God, get me out of here; I'll do anything…" and as I approached the small podium at the boarding gate where the attendants stand behind to collect your boarding pass, one of the attendants said,

"We have one seat left in non-smoking."

I put out my cigarette and never smoked a cigarette again. I quit *cold-turkey*, as they call it. As I sat on the plane on my way home that night, I decided that it was time to quit smoking anyway. Paul was allergic to the smoke and I decided then that I wanted to make a life with him. He came from a good family and I did want children. That was the year that 1980 turned into 1981; and I was going to be twenty-eight that coming June. If I was going to have a family, I had to get on with it soon or miss my opportunity.

Paul and I had what I thought was my first 'real' relationship. It appeared as if it started properly – as friends with mutual respect for one another as individuals. Paul came from a generation that was more used to seeing women as equals. And with a degree from one of the top universities in Canada, I felt confident that I'd finally found someone who would nurture me and assist me through my next level of growth.

At this point, I was into reading books pertaining to sales and selling technique. I spent a great deal of time with *The Road Less Traveled* by Dr. M. Scott Peck. I was feeling very grounded and clear at this point. Paul wanted to start a family soon and I had to agree, since I was already twenty-nine when I married him.

We had a beautiful wedding on a Wednesday (December 29th of 1982) in Montreal, where all of his family was living. My Victorian dress was handmade with all natural materials as it would have been in the 1800s. It was all candle-cream lace over cream light cotton with the high neck and the long sleeves and a three-foot train that buttoned up into a bustle. We had a small reception back in Calgary for all those who did not wish to make such a trip during the holidays.

I went to work for his printing company and built it up from next to nothing to over $20,000 in sales per month. By the time I had to take time off to have our first baby, the business was in a comfortable momentum of nearly $40,000 per month and easily able to support us.

I had taken great pains to explain to Paul how taking on the responsibility of having children was extremely risky for me because of my own childhood. I thought he understood how important it was for me to know that I had an undying devotion from my partner. I had to know that it was us against the world. I had to know that my home was a sanctuary for me and not a battleground.

Just after my thirty-first birthday, our little girl was born so perfectly. I am sure no other baby was ever more beautiful than my daughter when she was born! She was a full month early, so she was very small, weighing in at only five pounds, four ounces. She was covered with a very heavy layer of wax so she looked like a porcelain doll. And she was so clean upon arrival. Again, the wax let her just slide through all the birth goop so she looked like a porcelain doll. She was so perfect! And still is to this day, by the way.

The first six months of motherhood were pure heaven for me. I made all the crib covers and matching cushions for the rocking chair. I made myself clothes to fit my new waist size. I functioned around the house the same as I had in the office. There was a routine and everything got done in prompt order. I was never happier or more fulfilled in my life as I was for that very brief time.

However, when she was three months old Paul's sister was getting married and I was terrified of traveling with my premature baby at that age. When she was born I was told to watch some videos about premature infants and their special needs. One of the videos was entitled "To Have and Not To Hold" and it talked about how holding the baby actually draws energy from them. It said that premature babies have to be left to sleep as much as possible. It strongly instructed not to wake the baby for visitors; but rather, to have the visitors adjust themselves to the baby's schedule.

Well, I made myself sick over this trip. The bags were packed and by the door. We had to leave soon or we'd miss the plane and I could not get off the toilet. My legs were weak and I could not get myself out the door with my baby.

I told Paul to just go without us. He did not have to miss his sister's wedding because of us. But he would not hear of it. He said no one wanted to see him; and that was exactly what I was afraid of. So none of us went.

Two weeks later I got a card in the mail from the woman I'd shared a room with in the hospital when our baby was born. The card was written in a very lovely poem that disclosed that her baby had died. I remember going completely numb.

I remembered her clearly because I was unable to pick that baby up and hold her after I saw the videos about premature babies. This baby, however, was not premature; and she was the third child for my roommate.

I remembered how afraid I thought that baby looked all the time. Her birth weight was over seven pounds. I also recalled how many visitors she had and everyone passed the baby around to take their turn to hold her.

I cried and cried and then I cried some more over that baby.

When Paul came home from work that day I showed him the card and said I felt it was confirmation that we still had our baby because I did not take her on that trip. He just shook his head and rolled his eyes. And that was okay with me, we still had our baby.

By June our baby was doing all the things an eight month old should be doing; and she'd caught up on her weight for her age. The crisis was over and I began to relax a bit.

Then Paul suggested that we should get back to Montreal to visit his parents; and other relatives, with the baby and then swing down to Pennsylvania to visit my family as well.

Paul's parents had come to visit us to see the baby late January and stayed for nearly two weeks. It was a really nice visit; but I had to stand guard or my mother-in-law would want to wake her up with other relatives that lived in Calgary came to visit. I was not popular due to my over-protectiveness. But to this day, I sincerely believe I did the right thing for my premie.

My parents didn't even offer to visit. In fact, I don't recall if they ever even suggested we should go visit them. And it was Paul that called them with the news when she was born. I didn't talk to my parents about it until we talked during the holidays when everyone was together at my parents place.

Anyway, I reluctantly agreed and eventually talked myself into looking forward to it. She travelled well. She was not the screaming kid on the plane. She slept through the whole thing both ways.

We stayed at my parents place to visit. They live so far from any lodging in the area that it would have taken up the better part of our trip just driving back and forth.

One day I took off on my own to visit some friends while Paul stayed behind with our baby and to spend some time with my folks on his own. What a mistake that was!

My perfect, fulfilling world started crumbling the day the city electric man came to the door and said he was going to turn our power off. I said that there must be some mistake and sincerely asked him what was going on. I suppose he saw many an innocent act at the doors of people attempting to get away with not paying their bills, and so he treated me accordingly. He was very skilled in intimidation and it took him about five minutes to reduce me to tearfully begging him not to shut the power off because I had a little baby in the house. Again, probably a typical response for him to hear, and yet, for me, this was an outrage. I was so upset and embarrassed.

That was enough in itself to throw my psyche off kilter, then the doorbell rang not half an hour later. This time, it was the gasman, and he was there to shut off the gas! Well, at that, I became furious. This poor guy did not get the enjoyment of a begging performance. This guy got his face torn off in no time flat. I knew that there had to be a formal notice before they would actually turn off the service to an occupied home. I'd learned that from the electric man. I snapped at this power tripper that he could leave the formal notice in the mailbox and that my husband would be handling it. Then I slammed the door in his face and stomped to the telephone to find that husband of mine.

Well, he was nowhere to be found and the secretary didn't know where he was or when he'd be back. By the time he sauntered in for dinner that evening, I was fit to be tied. I had had all day to rehearse this little speech, and it was not pleasant.

When he walked in, however, I did attempt to maintain a semblance of control and proper respect until I found out just what was wrong. To my horror and amazement, Paul suddenly transformed into a distant stranger. He looked down his nose at me much the same as the electric man had done, shrugged his shoulders, put his hands on his hips, and said, "But they didn't turn anything off, did they? They can't until a formal final notice is given. Did they leave the final notices?"

I produced the notices and persisted to know why the bills weren't paid. I couldn't believe it. The mental picture I had of ourselves because the bills were not paid included smelly, pot-bellied, gross men sitting and drinking beer in front of the TV. I saw kids running around without shoes and in dirty, ripped clothing. The wives slopped around with a cigarette butt hanging out one side of their mouth in ratty old slippers and housecoats, with curlers in their hair. This was not the image I wanted to uphold. I was taught that bills got paid and the responsibility was taken to attend to the necessities of life.

I started that old familiar quivering inside. My knees turned to jelly and my throat started closing up. I sat down and said, "Paul, please talk to me. What is going on? When I left to have the baby, the orders were lined up for months."

He just sighed impatiently and said that I should not worry about it. He'd take care of the utility bills the following morning. Then he went, sat in front of the TV, and put the evening newspaper up between us.

This scene was all too familiar. My ears started to sizzle and my head started spinning. I tried so hard to keep control. I went in and said as calmly as I could, "Please don't shut me out. Come and talk to me while I make supper."

With that, he folded one corner of the paper down, just enough to look at me with raised eyebrows, and said, "I am tired. I had a rough day. I want to read the paper before supper; is that too much to ask?"

My stomach started to churn and my legs were so weak. I struggled into the kitchen and just sobbed. Paul walked through the door and sternly remarked, "Deborah, there is nothing to tell. I said I will handle it tomorrow; it's no big deal. Please don't overact to this, okay? I can handle it."

Somehow, we got through supper that night, and the next day I called the company accountant. Darren, our accountant, was my friend before I even knew Paul. Therefore, I felt very confident that he would tell me if there was anything to tell. And so there was.

It turned out that, since the day I had left the company to have my baby, Paul put his feet up on the desk and figured he had it made. The truth was that the company was in receivership on paper. At any moment, any one of our suppliers could have walked in and taken everything. That included our home, our vehicle, everything.

The feelings that washed over me then were unbearable. Darren went on to tell me that all my credit cards were maxed out to the limit and there hadn't been a payment made on any one of them for months. I finally interrupted him and asked him why in the world he hadn't told me any of this before. He said he thought that I knew all this was going on and condoned it. I was just shattered!

To me, it felt like a betrayal. I sat by the phone for at least an hour after I'd spoken with Darren and reflected over the previous months' events and interactions I had had with my husband. I recalled the number of times that I'd ask how things were at work and he'd give me short, simplistic answers like a teenager responding to the questioning of a rightfully concerned parent. I remembered the conversation the evening before when he blatantly stated that there was nothing to tell. Holy smokes! Nothing to tell, he said, and all the while we are in receivership!

I tried so hard to reason with myself and stay calm. I tried to see his side of it. Maybe he was just protecting me. But I had that company in a momentum that should have carried through and continued to grow. All he had to do was maintain the process I had established. No matter how hard I tried to reason this away, the same conclusion kept coming back.

This was a power struggle plain and simple. I remembered how much Paul hated it when I worked at the company. He'd sulk and drag his ass around the office just like a bratty teenager who was going to sabotage a game just because it was not his idea to play. I simply had a system that worked, and I proved it by building the company to a point where it could support us. When I left, Paul no longer had anyone to nag him, so he didn't work, and let the company go into receivership. I had never been so angry and so hurt, all at the same time. I felt so betrayed.

I know that Paul never understood the depth of the damage that caused to our relationship. I know that, if I had not had so many other wounds, I could have withstood this and weathered this storm. But Paul knew who I was. He knew about my background and he knew how important the team bond between us was to me.

This situation broke that bond. He was playing the game without me. I was left in the dark about the realities of the situation as if I either didn't count or was not qualified to be privy to the information. He was keeping secrets from me the same way my dad kept secrets from my mom.

At that point, I realized that my daughter would end up growing up in the exact same home environment as I had, and that frightened me.

That evening when Paul came home, we had the worst fight we'd ever had. I understand now that we were going through the typical power struggle that all relationships endure. But at the time, all I saw was yet another man treating me as less than his equal in the relationship. He really pulled rank on me that night as well, regarding my lack of schooling. He poked into every sore spot I had. And he knew them all because I'd told him in trust.

This level of abuse was all new to me. This one was the abuse of the upper middle class. These men don't physically hit you because that is obviously too barbaric. These men play psychological warfare. They verbally hit you in the most sensitive areas, and then when you react in the expressive way they know you will, they sit back real calm and make your freak-out seem totally out of place. They gain even more power by being able to maintain this facade of total cool. And so they should be able to – they have all the cards, all the information, and all the control.

This situation feels as if you are a passenger in a car that is driving at extreme speeds on a road that curves and bumps. As the passenger, all you can do is get thrown around in the seat, while the driver at least has the grounding of holding onto a steering wheel, and has access to brakes. Anyone in this situation would naturally freak out. So, consider this: the person driving this (hypothetical) speeding car knows the road and is purposely driving in a manner to scare the passenger. Then the driver turns to the passenger, remains totally calm and cool and acts as if the passenger has no reason to be SO freaked out.

The impact on the passenger is magnified by existing unhealed wounds obtained from previous similar experiences. The driver increases his own power by maneuvering the car to throw the passenger directly on existing wounds. When the car finally stops, the driver, who is the only person the passenger has in their life to depend on, just walks away and offers no consoling, no understanding, and definitely no renewed communication.

I started to deal with our financial mess by going back to work nights cleaning public washrooms. I cleaned seventeen public toilets every night. I worked from five o'clock in the evening to midnight. Then I'd go home and cry for an hour or two till I could finally sleep. Then I'd get up at six the next morning and be with my baby all day. I would get a brief nap in the afternoon. This went on for four solid months.

Every time I got on my knees at one of those filthy, smelly, disgusting public toilets I'd think to myself, "So this is what true love, devotion, and having someone's baby gets for you. He gets to sit at his desk all big, important and proud. Meanwhile, the truth is our lives and our marriage is in the toilet. We were not working side by side to get where we had agreed we wanted to go together. I was the lower-class subject forced to grovel at the lowest depths to clean up the mess he made with his university degree."

When my daughter finally turned one year old, I had talked myself into putting her into daycare. This was a sacrifice that I could not forgive Paul for. Part of our marital agreement was that I would be able to stay home and raise the children. I did not want to have to work outside the home and raise kids too.

For the next two years, I worked day and night to get that company back to where it was when I'd left to have the baby. I went to the bank and presented a marketing plan, and with that, they extended our credit.

I'd be out selling all day, run home and make supper, then I'd go back to the shop and work till midnight or later getting jobs done. Paul worked just as hard and resented every minute of it, and he especially resented me.

Finally, one day I collapsed. I found myself at home in the middle of the afternoon and I didn't know why I was there. I'd think of something to get or do, but when I got to another room, I couldn't for the life of me remember what I was supposed to do. I sat down and tried to stay calm and started to call my doctor. It took four tries before I finally punched in the right number, as I kept inverting them.

I remember asking the receptionist/nurse if a person can know that they are losing their mind. She responded immediately and attentively with a firm, "Yes, what is happening... tell me slowly... take a deep breath... tell me what is happening." By that time, my entire left side was numb and my vision was closing in. I had lost my peripheral vision.

I started to cry and told her my physical symptoms. She asked who she was talking to, so I told her my name and that I was at home. She told me to stay on the line and that she'd have the assistant there call my husband at the shop and have him pick me up. She said we should go straight to the hospital and that my doctor would meet us there.

Suddenly I felt such rage inside me. I wanted to rip the house apart piece by piece with my bare hands. I lost control of my breathing and the nurse on the phone said that she could hear that I was hyperventilating. She told me to just cover my mouth with my hand and force air in and out through my fingers.

When I got to the hospital, I was so sick to my stomach. They got me onto a bed and treated me for a migraine. I fell asleep almost immediately.

This happened to me two more times within the following six months. It's what is called a complicated migraine. It's just short of a stroke and is caused by severe, prolonged stress. What it *REALLY* is, I think, is the body reacting to the mental and emotional abuse.

Paul had transformed our home, which was my sanctuary for nurturing just as much as it was his, into a battleground. The abuse was so subtle and so cleverly disguised that I would just talk myself out of trying to reason with him and just push harder and harder to dig out of the financial pit that he'd dug for us. All I could focus on was what I had some control over, and that was the work that had to be done. Meanwhile, all I got from him was resentment and neglect.

The third time I was admitted for one of these 'fits', the doctor took both of my shoulders in his hands and looked me square in the eye and said that I had to take some time off. He told me that if I didn't get away and deal with whatever was going on, that he and I would probably not get a chance to discuss it again! Then he gave me a card for a retreat owned and operated by one of the local churches.

The place was called 'Kingsfold' and was operated by church members. There were chickens and turkeys to be taken care of. They grew all their own vegetables. The main house was set up like a fraternity with at least eight bedrooms and two main bathrooms. The kitchen was huge and opened up to a main dining area with a fireplace and six tables for four. There were several cabins on the property as well. It was all very rustic and comfortable.

I cried for the first three days. I'd just go in the kitchen after meals and grab a piece of toast or something, as when I'm that upset, I cannot eat.

Finally, I was able to talk to one of the counselors. She expressed the same thing that every counselor told me. She said that I was unusual because I was so readily open and willing to talk about anything. She never felt that she had to coax me like she had to with other people. She also said that I seemed to have a very clear picture of the situation from several angles. She was amazed at how I could so easily see things from another person's point of view.

After two weeks at the retreat, I came home and Paul and I had a talk. Well, actually I talked and he held a grudge. I apologized for swinging in like Tarzan and taking over rebuilding the company. I explained how I realized that my background was very strict and that I tend to be strict with myself and everyone else. I poured my heart out, and to it, all he simply replied was, "Then we agree that it was all your fault." I couldn't believe my ears!

I said that this was not a fault-finding mission. I said that I just wanted him to understand where I was coming from and that my intentions are in the best interest of keeping the family system going. Then I asked what had caused the business to get in such a financial mess in the first place, because I knew it was fine when I left to have our baby.

Then he just got up, started walking out of the room, and said, "And here I thought this place was going to do you some good." Then he sat down in the living room, picked up the newspaper, and put it up in front of his face.

I just sat there and stared at him in amazement. I had told him all about how my parents used to do that to me. I had told him all about my first husband pulling the same silent treatment and what it did to me. He knew exactly what he was doing to me.

So, I walked into the living room very calmly and said, "So you're going to hide behind the newspaper like my parents used to do to me?" And with that, it was his turn to throw a shouting temper tantrum.

He threw the paper down and yelled that he felt as if he couldn't win no matter what he did with me. He said that he was sick and tired of me seeing everything through the eyes of my past. He said I was so negative about my parents when all they ever did was try to reach out to me. He said I squandered my inheritance and didn't respect anything or anyone other than myself.

What was so amazing about his performance was that this was the first time I had verbalized that I was feeling as if he was treating me like I'd been treated in the past. Another thing was that the company went into receivership when I was home with my baby, living happier than I'd ever lived in my life.

They'd done it again. I left Paul with them for one day and they obviously filled him in on all my shortcomings and all my failings including selling the apartment building. He'd lost all respect for me, is what was really going on. And I knew that was a battle I'd never win.

And at that moment my mind flashed back to our plane ride home from our visit to my parents. I remember how I thought I noticed a different air around Paul. He seemed to be keeping his nose in the air at me. But I remember thinking too that I was just imagining it and shook it off at the time. And at the time I was, once again, shaking off my own intuition!

I also want to add here (now that I've had healing) I do realize that my parents were not deliberately undermining me. They were simply justifying themselves. They had opened up and shared a very dark secret about our family's past and in their eyes, it did no good. I ran away in 1977 with my Italian Stallion and I did not contact them at all for years. I never even contacted them about my wedding to Paul.

They knew I had to have told my side of the story to Paul; and Robert to justify not including them in the weddings; and so naturally, they were just telling their side of the story. I doubt they had enough insight to realize the damage they were causing. Again, this is what ignorance (meaning lack of education) produces as results in the world we live in.

Having said that; it does seem that my dad never instructed Paul to 'get me in line' the way he'd instructed my first husband. Paul's statements did focus on merely respecting them and Paul never raised a hand to me like Michael did.

Paul and I had never had a serious fight prior to the company taking a nosedive financially. . We had agreed on everything from religion to childrearing techniques. We discussed things and came up with solutions with very little effort prior to this financial disaster that *HE* had, in fact, created. And he knew it was his fault and that was why it was so important to blame *me* and punish *me*.

I personally didn't care anymore whose fault it was. I just wanted out of it and back on track again. When I told him that, he just huffed off and turned on the TV. Then he said, "I suppose I'm being abusive now if I watch TV." At that point, I realized that this man didn't have the interest or the ability to fulfill my needs. All he was capable of doing was judging them.

By the same token, I suspect he felt exactly the same. He felt as if I were just judging his needs rather than supporting the techniques he wanted to test drive. Never mind the fact that the company went into receivership during his test drive. Yet, from where he stood at the time, he was right! I had a tried-and-true method that had grown the company tremendously and all he had to do was 'practice' on less vital cash flow. So in his eyes, it felt like he was working for me in the business and his own ego blinded him to the fact that his way didn't work. He had no problem living in debt.

Meantime, I was very willing to work on myself and improve myself, and I agree that perhaps some of the things that I was sensitive about were a bit extreme due to the PTSD (that I didn't know I had at the time). But, that was who I was and where I was at. It was not a contest of who was better or who was right, and I couldn't get that through his head. I guess he thought that I didn't want to play the who's right game because I was wrong.

Very soon thereafter I decided to quit working for our own company. I hated printing anyway, and sales were back in momentum once again. I told Paul that, if he decided to use a different marketing technique than the one I had implemented, he should phase the new one in more slowly the next time.

He was very pleased when I told him I was going to look for another product or service to represent and keep working for a while until we really had ourselves financially secure again. I thought we might find our way back to each other again. I wanted so much to have the communication that we had in the beginning of our relationship. I couldn't believe that Paul and I would have a home atmosphere of distant resentment like my parents had.

I went to work for a client of ours who owned and operated a small office furniture manufacturing plant. The twist there was that this fellow, Don, was an old flame of mine. Because I'd known the guy for as long as I'd been in Calgary, I could skip over the formal interview and resume submission stage and get right to work.

Although Don and I had never been intimate with each other before, there was a time when we were dating that I thought the sun, moon, and stars rose and set because of him. However, I did think that I was well over him. He had made it very clear that he never wanted children. Because I did want children, I had made the choice to marry Paul and broke off dating Don. Now, five years later, I was working for Don and was very *unhappily* married to Paul, with a family started.

Finances shaped up and Paul and I managed to plan a trip to Barbados for the Christmas holidays in 1987; so our daughter had just had her third birthday. We went to Montreal to visit Paul's parents first for Christmas, and then left our daughter with them so we could spend New Year's in Barbados. It was wonderful. We talked a great deal, but I still felt walls instead of bridges between us.

One afternoon in Barbados, Paul went scuba diving and I stayed behind to bask in the sun on the beach. I laid there all warm and enjoying the atmosphere when I got a very clear picture in my mind about my marriage.

It became obvious to me that the team dynamics had changed drastically between Paul and me. He and I were no longer working side by side toward a particular goal. Paul had definitely taken a dictatorship position in the marriage. He withheld information about the company when it was in receivership because he truly felt that I had no right to know. His behavior had become exactly like a teenager trying to gain individualism while still dependent on his parents.

It was also obvious to me that he was still holding a grudge about the way I jumped into the business and rescued it from receivership. He repeatedly contested that: if I had just left him alone, he would have turned the company around as well. His grudge was because I claimed the victory with my methods and his method never got a chance to prove itself.

On one hand, it infuriated me that he would risk our very livelihood to experiment with marketing techniques. To me, it makes far more sense to practice new things on the sidelines, not on your bread and butter source of income. And that anger was fueled by his audacity to hold a grudge against me for rebuilding the business! There was something very wrong with that picture. How many men can fault their wives for building them a business… twice?

On the other hand, I could understand his frustration. He felt that my method was tried and true and could have been reinstalled if his method didn't work. He insisted that the company was in receivership on paper only and that I simply did not understand the mechanics of running a business since I had no schooling for it. He said that all I had was 'street smarts', and that anyone could build and run a business the way I did things. He said that I was simplistic and primitive.

Well, my simplistic and primitive methods were then selling a great deal of furniture and that was what afforded us the trip that we were subsequently enjoying.

Then I flashed back to Baltimore and I remembered the feeling I'd had when it became known that I had the same Bible study as the leader of that Forever Family. I had that same 'no win' feeling now. Paul found something that he could hate me for and he needed that to establish his autonomy.

This was not about who built the business. This was Paul's need to establish himself in his own eyes as the chief just like a teenager will often rebel just because they can.

Although his parents were very careful not to interfere in our lives, they cast a very long, dark shadow over us. Every holiday had to include seeing them. They visited and called frequently. And Paul reported to them on a regular basis and provided an account of the business and our marital progression (regarding children, that is – we were the first to provide them with a grandchild).

As long as Paul built walls between himself and me, he could maintain a very active relationship with his parents and still feel independent. I provided the necessary figure for him to be independent of, and there was no way I could change that configuration. I was stuck, once again, in the 'odd man out' – or quite simply, a scapegoat position.

I am going to digress here for a minute if you can please bear with me. I look at the isolation that I felt trying to fit into the family dynamics of this upper-middle-class family. This was a family that was far better educated than mine, and quite a bit ahead of mine financially as well.

In comparison, I feel that I had just a taste, just a glimpse, into what Princess Diana went through! If anyone has ever experienced a mother-in-law who thought she was Queen Tut, just imagine actually having to deal with a mother-in-law who IS queen! My heart went out to that poor girl at the time. I had concern for her since the day she got married to Mr. Playboy himself. She was genuine and true, and he probably viewed her methods as simple and primitive too! It was a no-win situation that she was in as well. The marriage dynamic would have been very similar.

Okay, back to my story…

Later, after we were home and the holidays were over, I begged Paul to go to counseling with me. I knew that the only way I could begin to survive the marriage I was in was to heal my wounds. It had to not matter that I was isolated from my husband. I had to find a way to nurture myself and hold this family together.

Every time I brought it up, he'd just shut me down. He absolutely refused to go to counseling. He said that I was the one with the messed up childhood, not him. He also said I was the one with the trail of divorces flowing behind me like the tail of a kite. He truly saw himself as pure and perfect in contrast to me and my upbringing; and I had to admit, he was right.

Therefore, I went and blew yet another counselor away as I explained everything as I saw it. It always took three or four visits before the counselor caught up with me. Those poor people. I often wonder if I am the only client who counselors actually manipulated out of their office. None of them ever wanted to keep seeing me. The last one used to phone me and have to reschedule my appointment because she was sick. Well, by the time we'd find a time that fit both our schedules, the crisis I was in was long over and I'd end up going in and just visiting. However, I don't make enough money to pay people to visit with me! So these counseling sessions ended.

I have to add here too that I had no personal support group. Without family to assist me in weathering the normal storms every marriage encounters, I was doomed regardless. I had no one to run to unless I paid for it and then it was superficial at best. And I don't mean to minimize the value of counseling. Rather, without a support group all the counseling in the world has nothing to anchor itself to. By the same token, I am not justifying extra-marital affairs.

To magnify my loneliness from the lack of communication with my husband, Don and I were developing a very close relationship at work. He and I were having the communication level and making the kind of money together that I wanted to have and do with Paul. Don was proving that it could be done together, as a team, and that it could be very enjoyable.

Don allowed me to have a huge office space just off the manufacturing floor. It was a 12 x 14 foot room where I put beautiful drapes all along the wall behind my desk, even though the window itself was only a small 4 x 2 foot hole in that wall.

There was a mini-bar including a bar fridge. I had a wall unit against the wall to your immediate left as you entered the office with crystal glasses and bowls in it. I put a full-size couch with an end table and matching armchair against the wall in front of my desk, so the armchair was the chair someone would sit in to meet with me at my desk. There was also a beautiful area rug under a custom-made coffee table (made in our own manufacturing facility) and all candescent lighting with two floor lamps; one to one side of the couch and the other in the corner behind my desk return. There was a lamp on the end table and I had a desk light on my desk. I did not use the overhead fluorescent lighting as they gave me a headache.

Of course the desk was from our own office furniture line. Potential clients were so impressed with my office. My mini bar was fully stocked with anything you'd want to drink and the fridge held the mix. I kept caviar along with other delicacies in that fridge to entertain in my office any time of year! Don and I were living the dream. We were making money hand over fist. Sales were coming in including the first million-dollar furniture contract with the city of Calgary. It was budgeted for just over three hundred thousand per year for four years to refurnish the entire city of Calgary employees with ergonomic-friendly furniture since computers were invading the offices at light-speed. I soon found myself dreading going home. I found myself feeling the same things about going home to Paul as I used to feel going home to my parents' place. I didn't want my daughter to grow up in that environment. I started feeling desperate. I explained this to my counselor and she suggested a trial separation. She said that maybe it would give Paul a chance to see exactly what I offered in the relationship. She thought he needed a turn to feel lonely for me, and to give him some space to think as well.

Her advice made sense to me at the time. So I got a place closer to my work and our little daughter helped her mommy move out. At the time, I really didn't expect that I'd be getting a divorce. I really thought it would be temporary.

Well, once I was out and away from the nonsense, it only made my patience even less for the word games and mind games Paul played with me. His superior attitude only seemed worse from the outside looking in. I finally asked myself why I should spend so much time begging someone to know and understand me. I decided that I deserved to be treated fairly and to be given a turn in the game of family life. The world has so much crap going on that, if a person can't get validation and nurturing in their own home, where can they get it? Hence, a very common, and understandable, reason for extra-marital affairs. Since love is synonymous with sex these days, it is one way people obtain validation outside their own home.

At the same time, Don and I were getting closer and closer. We were having lunch one day and I finally admitted to him that I was having marriage problems. I even admitted that I was living in my own place. To my great surprise, Don calmly said that he wasn't surprised.

Then he went on to describe exactly what I was going through. He said he knew that Paul and I would eventually hit 'the wall', so-to-speak, because Paul was a young, highly educated, bureaucratic type who relied on books and formulas. And that I was a free-spirited, seasoned, street fighter who ran on intuition; which were totally different approaches to life. He did say, however, that if ever the two approaches could effectively combine, it would be an unbeatable team. I asked him what he thought it would take to accomplish that union. He just laughed and said if he knew that, he would not be selling furniture. He said that the conflict I was living was the human dilemma and that the same battle goes on inside every individual between the mind and the spirit.

I took that little tidbit to the counselor our very next session. She seemed unimpressed, while I thought I was having a great revelation.

Time and again I tried to communicate with Paul. I wanted to get back together and move back into my home. I would meditate before our meetings to get grounded, but it never helped. I always walked away with so much resentment that it would take days to calm down again. He knew what buttons to push to keep me at arm's length and he just kept pushing them. Clearly he did not want to get back together.

Taking a long hard look at things from Paul's point of view; the circumstances did allow him to come out smelling like a rose. Everyone would sympathize with the 'poor innocent husband whose crazy wife left him with the house, the business, and the child'. It was no wonder he was pushing me away. This is exactly what he wanted! He had all the success I'd accomplished and could lay claim to it all once I was gone and labeled as crazy.

I thought perhaps I could be my own person regardless of what my husband thought. But I soon realized that he would keep me so busy licking my wounds and chasing after his financial messes that I'd never have time to grow and nurture myself. I knew I'd be back in the hospital with another complicated migraine in no time if I moved back in with him. So, divorce was the only answer.

No one knows how hard that was for me to do. No one ever stopped to think that, for a woman to divorce her husband and grant full-time care of the three-year-old to the father, there had to be some very good reason.

Yet, I did it. I became the visiting parent every other weekend and every Wednesday night. I'd pick my daughter up from school on a Wednesday and take her back the next morning every week. Desperate moves are made by desperate people. No one asked why this seemingly capable businesswoman was falling apart on the domestic scene. Paul was all too quick to feign his suffering as the abandoned mate and to demonstrate his sacrificial attitude to go it on his own. Yet, all the while, he was orchestrating it from the inside.

Paul once told me about things I did and said during that time that I don't believe I could have been capable of. Today I truly believe that he would set my little girl up to fail. He'd tell her that I'd called to make arrangements to pick her up for a special outing. Yet I had done no such thing; therefore, naturally I would not show up. My little girl would be waiting for me and I would not show up. How cruel can a person be to put a child through such a thing?

Yet I recall being extremely conscious of making all my appointments with her and I never cancelled on her. He was lying to her to make me look bad. I once asked her about it and thankfully she did not recall such experiences.

Then that made me think that he was just telling me this story to convince me that I was really insane. Perhaps he hoped I would kill myself. Then he would really get the crowning glory of being the devout and wronged partner.

But, what I will say is this, we have often heard it said that behind every successful man stands a strong, responsible woman (probably doing all the grunt work). Well, now I dare say that behind every screaming, crazed woman stands a game-playing S.O.B. pulling all the strings. Then, of course, I have to consider my mother. She did nothing but yell and throw temper tantrums. She endured a great deal with the family she married into. And my dad was so abused that he just ran from conflict.

Dad used to tell that he was 5 years old when he was strapped onto a tractor that was set to run in low gear. He'd have to steer it around the field to plow it. The adults would leave him to do the job and come back when they thought the job should be done. No bathroom break! No lunch break! Just get the job done.

He also told the story of how he was in his early teens and was in charge of the horses. He did something wrong and they took off in a gallop across the field, dragging him along on his back. When the adults finally caught up with the situation, my dad was laid under the grape arbor in the shade for the rest of the workday. Only after the work was done could such issues be dealt with. They did get a doctor in and his back was not broken, but he had so much dirt and stones embedded in his flesh that it had to be cleaned out to prevent infection.

The treatment consisted of them putting some sort of tape on his back and then ripping it off to pull out all the dirt and stones! Imagine the pain that would have caused on an already raw back from being dragged for hundreds of yards in an open field. He said he did pass out from the pain. When he came to, his dad beat him for being so stupid and for the fact that he would not be able to participate in the work for a month, as the doctor ordered bed rest for at least a week and no work for a full month.

One of my dad's nine brothers was beaten so badly by the man that my dad called his father, that he developed a learning disability. He was diagnosed as 'retarded' in those days. He never matured past the age he was when he was so badly beaten; and that was about fourteen. Anyway, I digress.

At this point in my life my immediate plan was to get on my feet, financially, and then go back to court and gain day-to-day (full time) custody of my daughter without seeking any child support. I knew that, if I had my daughter and had to get financial support from Paul, he would just make my life even more unbearable. The point of the divorce was to establish the autonomy I needed to regain respect as an individual. As long as I was 'the wife', I was 'the appendage' to be tossed about at Sir Paul's will.

All plans look so good on paper. This one was a great deal more difficult to live than I ever expected. I had nightmares and so did my little girl. I fought one physical affliction after another. And I wrestled with guilt over indulging in an affair with Don.

When Don first showed interest, I immediately backed off and said that I didn't think it was a good idea to mix business with pleasure. I needed to maintain my career first and foremost. I explained that I had no one else to depend on besides myself. But he assured me that, if we attempted to put a future together and it failed to happen, I would never have to worry about being able to work with him. I took him at his word and he never went back on it either... you'll see what I mean a little further on.

I ended up moving into Don's new mansion in one of the finest neighborhoods in Calgary. Sales were through the roof and his furniture company was growing substantially.

We took a vacation together to Laguna Beach California. One afternoon we went to the Ferrari dealership and he sat in the car of his dreams. The very same one that Magnum PI drove in the TV series. Then the salesman told him they were discontinuing the production of that model that year. If he wanted that model, he had to order it before the year was out.

We had no Google in those days to check up on information of that sort. However, the salesman produced the company memo that announced that corporate decision.

Don's face went white, then gray. Then the salesman said he could order one with only one thousand dollars down as a deposit. The car had to be delivered directly to a Canadian dealership to avoid cross border issues. Needless to say, he ordered the car!

In April of 1989 we flew to Vancouver to pick up the car. I'll never forget that experience. The dealership had us picked up at the airport by limo. Driving home though the mountains that time of year in the most amazing sports car on the road (as it is even today) was a thrill of a lifetime. We drove 14 hours straight through with only one quick stop in Golden BC. The leather seats cradled your body and the vibration of the engine was like a full body massage. When we got out of the car after nearly 14 hours straight driving, it felt like we'd just driven around the block. And as we pulled into his driveway the first snowflakes started to fall. We'd made it home before the weather turned; which was vital because those cars are not built for snow and ice driving. And in Canada, the seasons can change within an hour.

I thought Don and I were clear on my intentions to get day-to-day custody of my daughter. However, when that time came, he became very irate. He said he did not want children in his life, ever. To that I asked him why he hooked up with me since he knew I had a child. He said that he thought my successful career would outweigh my need for mothering. He fully expected me to marry him and leave my daughter behind with her father. I could not believe my ears when he said that.

After days and weeks of fighting and arguing, we agreed that I would get a house of my own and we would maintain a steady, monogamous relationship.

However, this change in living arrangements caused me to hesitate in going back to court. I wanted to be sure I could actually maintain myself financially before I took on the life of another human being. I really think that, subconsciously, I didn't trust Don to keep his word about my career.

As soon as I was moved and settled, the head games began between Don and me. I moved into the house in August 1990. We dated and maintained a fairly comfortable routine until Christmas. Then suddenly, there seemed to be all sorts of misunderstandings between us.

At that point, I braced myself because I saw the ever-familiar signs of a disintegrating relationship. Yet I was so sure that Don and I were destined for each other that I maintained a corner, in my mind, of confidence. I just looked at the situation as part of the process and believed with all my heart that the 'phase' Don and I were going through was going to serve to only make our bond stronger.

This chapter of my life was evidence that I was finally beginning to get closer to matching my actions with my instinct.

Although I could see things from several points of view, I was able to act from only one point of view. When I resumed going to see counselors, I just overwhelmed them with so much information and so many angles that they just wanted me to go away so they could breathe. I was going so fast that I had no time to really weigh things out, or let time resolve some things. I was just so panicked inside.

Another problem, too, was that I had gone so far so fast that to get back to working from intuition was going to be a very long journey. I felt as if I were standing on top of a mountain and looking across many, many miles at the other mountain which was where I really wanted to be. The only way to the mountain where I really wanted to be was through the valley below. This valley was thick with dark forest. It had many turns and hills that could easily cause one to lose their way. It was frightening and dangerous, and the only way to get through it was to use intuition to its maximum strength.

I thought this journey was going to produce a new, and finally a very real, relationship in which I'd have a friend, confidant, and business partner.

Chapter Five
Harsh Realities

Don had told me that he was making plans to go see his mother in Florida for the holidays. I naturally assumed I was included since I had always been included in his plans for the previous four years.

On December twenty-second, the day I thought we were flying out of Calgary for Florida, I went to his office to say I needed to get home to finish packing. He then informed me, and very coldly (I might add), that I was not accompanying him. He also expressed great surprise that I didn't realize that. He then continued in a very detached and business-like manner and said that he and I had to talk, after the holidays, about my commission structure. He felt that it needed to be cut back a bit in light of the severe downturn in the market. With that, he said, "See ya later, and Merry Christmas," and walked out with his suitcase. I was left sitting in his office completely stunned.

As I said, it was the twenty-second of December. All my friends had plans and they all expected me to be off to Florida. It was too late to get tickets to go back to Pennsylvania to visit my relatives and friends there, and besides, if my commissions were going to be cut back, I didn't feel confident to spend the money on airfare. I had no tree or any decorations up at all because I thought I was going away. I had no groceries in the house for the same reason. I sat there in his office for what seemed like an eternity with my head just spinning.

That was the most torturous Christmas I'd ever spent. I had been reading *The Intimate Enemy; Lethal Lovers and Poisonous People;* and *Soul Murder.* And at that point, I felt like I was living proof of every one of them. Loneliness actually roared and echoed off the four walls of my home. I laid on the floor in my living room and cried and cried and then cried some more. I couldn't believe that I had just gone from the frying pan into the fire with this relationship.

I finally saw the pattern. Not only was I moving from one man to another so fast that I had no time to heal in between, I was also arming every one of them with everything they needed to destroy me. I would enter each relationship with practically a written dossier of all the things that really hurt me, along with lists of all the things I really needed from them. What I was not realizing was that there was an unspoken clause in each agreement with these men that read, "As long as the woman did exactly as was expected and fulfilled every preconceived notion of the man, the needs the woman had would be filled. However, when the woman offended the man in any way, these exact needs would be revoked and all the things that were shared in confidence would be turned and used against the woman."

You must understand that most participants in relationships do not sit and devise methods to literally undermine the other. These things fall into place naturally and subconsciously. But, with Don, it was very conscious.

He used to amaze me with his cold, calculating perspective on business. He used to demonstrate to me how he could manipulate staff into doing what he wanted. And he explained to me in detail how he mentally tortured one of his previous staff whom he thought was trying to strike a deal behind his back. This man spent years studying motivational techniques so that he could use them both ways. He could either manipulate someone into a positive direction, or he could destroy them without them even realizing what happened to them. And, he took great pride in the mastery of this ability.

I remember saying to him once that it made no sense to me to spend so much energy manipulating people when all you should have to do is ask them and then explain why and how what they are doing fits into the big picture. If they don't get it, they'll quit and then you simply hire someone who will appreciate the simple, straight-forward approach. And I remember his reply. He said, "If you want to play for the big bucks, you have to learn to play by the big bucks rules because they've been there long before you got there. So, you play by their rules or you don't play at all."

So I knew I was up against something I was totally unprepared to deal with at this point in my life. This guy's mind games made Paul look like a cartoon. My first thought was to try to reconcile with him. But he was too smart for that. So, I just backed off.

When we finally got together again to talk I did make sure that I mentioned the promise he had made me and I told him I knew that I could trust his word. He always prided himself in keeping his word.

He assured me that I could trust that I would always have an opportunity to work for his company, and we agreed that if either one of us decided to start dating someone else, we would admit it to the other. That conversation was just after the holidays.

We dated less and less. Our relationship at the office was strained and remained strictly professional. My commissions were cut. I started combing the newspaper for another job, but there was nothing that paid as much as what I was making with the furniture job, even with my commissions cut.

This change also completely removed the possibility that I could take my daughter on full time. This was the most devastating aspect of the whole situation. When I cried about this, I cried so hard that it felt like I was about to throw up my intestines. I would expect that the only pain worse than what I was experiencing, at that time, would be to lose a child in death. When I say I understand what that must feel like, you can trust me on that for sure.

I remember sitting back one weekend and taking an account of the progress in my life to that point. I realized that my life was still a series of extreme highs and lows. I lived a repeated boom and bust cycle. And this bust in relationship with Don was the most severe and the most threatening to my well-being.

The cycle was: I would go out into the world and do something magnificent and make all kinds of money, for example, the importing from South America in the '70s with Craig. Then I'd allow some man to help me squander all the money away and treat me badly.

Then I'd find myself emotionally and financially bankrupt. So, I'd suffer through a breakup of the relationship and then I'd go out and make more good money again. Then I'd hook up with another man like I did with my second husband until he nearly killed me.

The cycle continued through my marriage to Paul and was repeating again with this relationship with Don. In fact, Don had me over a barrel better than anyone ever had before. He held all the cards in this game and he knew it.

This insight made me very angry with myself. I immediately reread *Pulling Your Own Strings* by Dr. Wayne Dyer and made a solemn oath to myself to ensure that this was going to be the end of the boom and bust cycle, come what may.

May I suggest here that one should be very careful what one promises to one's self when one is totally dependent upon a master game player!

The very next day Don told me that he had decided to proceed with my marketing program as I had originally outlined it. That meant that it was time for me to hire an assistant to enable me to cover more territory in the same amount of time. I was amazed and foolishly thought that he was doing this with the best interest of the company and myself in mind. I even began to think to myself that perhaps I was being too harsh in my expectations of him. After all, why would Don bother to squash me? I certainly didn't pose a threat to him. It made far more sense to build on what we had already established to continue the growth of the company than to rip it down and start over.

In fact, Don and I had discussed that very thing. Don said that the reason Paul's company had gone into receivership on paper was because Paul had obviously switched marketing programs too abruptly. And I remember telling Don that was exactly what I'd thought. I showed Don the marketing plan I'd presented to the bank to obtain additional credit to bail the printing company out of receivership. So why would Don turn around now and shoot himself in the foot by doing the exact same thing as Paul did? He was too shrewd for that. So I relaxed a bit and started to interview potential assistants.

The applicant who won Don's approval was the one I liked the least. She reminded me of the type of girls in high school that were always challenging everyone else to a brawl after school. I just did not like her. But Don had final say, so sweet Ruby got the job.

From the moment she started I could feel the tension between us. She had no intention of being my assistant. She had her own agenda, and that was going to be evident really soon.

It took all of two weeks before I figured out that she and Don were seeing each other after work. The pattern he had used on me was being repeated. But I knew she was married and living with her husband. So I gave him a call. Since Don had not fulfilled his end of the bargain by telling me that he'd decided to date someone else, I thought I'd check things out from the other end.

Big mistake! And this was the second time I pulled this stupidity on myself. Never, never, never catch the naughty boy in the act. That was my mistake with Paul. I found out about the receivership and responded and exposed it accordingly. Therefore, Paul could contend, from then and ever after, that if I'd left things alone, everything would have worked out okay. But it was my reaction that made the receivership look so severe, and because I jumped in and took over, we'll never know.

Well, yours truly was jumping in once again, swinging in on the vine of truth to expose the evils within. Sure enough, Ruby's husband had had his suspicions, but the bummer for me was that Ruby and her husband were talking about divorce anyway. So to him, it was just part of the process.

And truly, truly, this really happened. This man gave his blessing to his wife to move on; and I quote, "while she still had her looks" unquote! How do these women get men to support them no matter what?

This woman had been a dependent all her life. She'd gone from living with her mommy and daddy to living with her husband. He took responsibility to ensure her best interests were met and now that she wanted to divorce and move on, her husband was in full support of that too!

In fact, he was most grateful because she was leaving their two children; ages 16 and 18 with him to, and I quote, "not disrupt their lives in the process". I'm standing there, listening to this over the phone is pure disbelief. What was it with people in this area? How much more bizarre could things get?

The next thing I knew, Ruby was moving into an apartment within blocks of Don's house and a meeting was called for the following day.

This meeting consisted of Ruby crying the blues because she had been treated so badly by me. She said that she learned that this condescending attitude of mine was chronic and that others in the company had experienced the same thing. She felt that she could no longer work for the company under these circumstances. To that, Don piped up and said that he felt a review was necessary to decipher whether or not this marketing program was, in fact, meeting projections.

This was totally ridiculous. The program had not been implemented long enough to produce enough results to distinguish either way. The program had obviously produced enough to afford us the ability to hire another person, but phase two had been operating less than two months. We needed at least 6 to 9 months to assess the second phase of the program, and Don knew that. This was a railroad job and I knew it. So I decided to just sit back and watch what transpired next.

Don announced that Ruby would be his personal assistant instead of working for me, since I obviously didn't know how to handle people. He then proceeded to reduce my territory to a fraction of its original size. Then he challenged me to build my territory back up in the manner that I was so gifted in doing. Then he announced to everyone at the meeting that he always promised me that I'd have an opportunity to work at his company and he was true to his word. He also said that he was looking forward to moving on to a more lucrative marketing program with Ruby by his side as he had given her charge over the territory he'd just taken from me.

So, all she had to do was nurture my clients, grow the territory from within through referrals and increased sales from existing clients while I slugged it out as the new rep all over again to build a territory where there was no business yet.

Four years of backbreaking, door-to-door, in the trenches, grind your face and get your eyes scratched out by competition effort was just handed over to a bimbo. Naturally, Don took the accounts that had evolved into ongoing, repeat business and left me with the existing business that was proving very difficult to develop. . Ruby walked into the advanced position that I had worked four years to create, and I got left to do it all over again.

Absolutely everyone there knew what was going on. Everyone was sure that I'd leave and then they'd have ALL my effort to themselves. The humiliation was enough by itself without Ruby bouncing and singing around the place afterward. She just reveled in rubbing it in and flaunting her relationship with Don in my face.

I went home that night after that meeting and thought to myself; "Well, I really got myself into it this time. I've managed to boom and bust myself from the frying pan into the fire. And this time, there is nowhere to run to. If I leave this company now, I can make only a lateral move, at best, considering the territory I now had. I can't afford this house now and I can't even think of getting my daughter full-time. So now, what do I do?"

The next morning I woke up at four a.m. and realized that if I left this company it would take me three to four years to be at the commission level I had achieved before my territory was reduced. Not to mention, I'd just be at some other asshole's mercy. I realized that, as a woman alone, with no family name or established position in the community, I was totally S.O.L. All I had going for me was the contacts I'd made in the furniture business and my own 'street smarts'. And, somehow I had to make them work for me.

By this time I was thirty-seven years old. I was just approaching the burnout stage that salespeople reach after too much time in the field. Introducing a line or a company into the marketplace is far more difficult than carrying a product that already has a track record or at least a momentum of some repeat business.

Between the printing company I grew for my ex-husband and this furniture company, I had put in nine years of start-up pace, direct sales. I knew that I didn't have the stamina to go and learn a new line and start all over again.

My only hope was to ride out the momentum I had created with the furniture company and use the income to start my own business. I hated the very thought of it. I didn't want to run my own business. I knew I would get consumed by it because my expertise was confined to such a narrow aspect of business. I'd have to spend a great deal of time researching and learning all the other things like full business plans (not just the marketing and sales aspects) and accounting. I was not interested in these things. I just wanted to do my job. I just wanted to do what I was the best at doing; namely direct sales. In that capacity, I was of most value to the company and I was the happiest.

I couldn't figure out why I couldn't just work for someone honest and sincere who would just pay me for my skills. It made no sense to me that a company would not appreciate their salespeople. Without sales, a company does not exist. There can be hundreds of accountants and secretaries just lined up from here to forever, but without a sale, there is nothing for them to do.

There was another pattern coming into view now. I realized that in this game, the man demands that the woman build or make something that he promises to share with her become reality. After she has performed her service and the thing exists, the man gets mean and ugly and scares the woman away so that he doesn't have to share it after all. And, at the same time, he can say that he would have shared it IF the woman would have stayed. I had to admit, it was very effective.

That very day I made appointments to meet with the biggest companies I'd brought in. I visited with every one of them and told them honestly what was going on.

And each and every one of them contacted Don and told him that; if he removed me from their account, they'd go to tender! Let me tell you truthfully, 'go to tender' are words NO company wants to hear, ever. But especially not when they are trying to grow their company, impress the new girlfriend and screw over the ex-girlfriend at the same time.

So, I got my main commission producing companies back and that definitely eased the financial crisis back into something feasible for me.

The next thing Don tried was to introduce incentive for the sales team; a team that consisted of Ruby & myself.

Now, prior to this meeting I'd gone to Don and asked him if I could talk to him about something; but he refused several times and insisted I could talk to him after the sales meeting.

He opened that meeting saying that he really needed to see the sales for this month to go up and in order to motivate us, he had a plan.

He said that for thirty thousand dollars in sales we'd win tickets to the hockey game. He had season's tickets, so he was offering to give them to the winner.

For forty thousand dollars in sales for the month, he said he'd provide a car phone. He'd purchase it and pay for the installation. Keep in mind, this was 1991. Car phones then were hard wired into your car and hooked up to the car battery. So installation was significant, at least in Canada in those days.

For fifty thousand dollars in sales, he said he'd provide the car phone and pick up all the business call charges for one year.

So I asked him what sixty thousand dollars in sales would win. To that he said he's pay for the all the calls on the phone within reason.

What he didn't know was that I had a seventy-two thousand dollar order on my desk for a client I'd been working on for some time and had not told him. This was what I wanted to tell him before the meeting when he would not talk to me.

So then I asked him why he stopped the total sales at fifty thousand dollars; and he said since the month was half over, he wanted to be fair and for the quota to be attainable.

I said, "Oh, so seventy thousand dollars would be unattainable in your estimations?" and he said, "Pretty much."

Then Ruby piped up and produced an order for fifty thousand dollars that the two of them had picked up the day before. Don acted surprised, but we all knew what was going on.

I'm sure you know what I did next! I said, "Wait a minute!" and went to my office to retrieve the paperwork returning promptly announcing that I did believe that my seventy-two thousand dollar order did trump the 'previously submitted entry' for the contest.

You'd think an owner of a business would be ecstatic to have just received over two hundred thousand dollars in orders in a month that was blank up to that point. But no! For some reason he was not happy. He up and stormed out of the boardroom and Ruby followed close behind.

Meantime, I have to admit; it was one of very few victorious moments for me... I went to my office and enjoyed my favorite drink. Don had convinced himself that he was the wind beneath the wings of my sales success. The truth was, however, he was from Newfoundland and Ruby was from Lethbridge; a windy city to the south of Calgary. She knew nothing about sales. All she knew how to do was play manipulative boy-catching games.

And while Don had been successful in sales to the point where we joined forces, he was no match for me.

His technique hinged on the who's who process. He had buddies in places where he could make deals. I, on the other hand, had mastered the techniques necessary to establish rapport and develop clientele; and I dare say that was a dying process then already. Yet, he had himself convinced that if he was in the mix, there was no stopping them.

The fact that I'd landed a seventy-two thousand dollar sale, all on my own, without having him involved at all in the close process; was way too much for him to withstand. So, needless to say, from that day forward, he and Ruby did everything they could to undermine me.

I remember once when I had government officials coming in to consider our furniture for the Provincial government offices, I received a written phone message to call home; meaning home to Pennsylvania.

My dad had been diagnosed with cancer recently and I'd made that known to the receptionist in case I did get a call.
The meeting was scheduled for ten o'clock. It was nine thirty when I got the message. Naturally I reacted emotionally and called immediately. My mom answered the phone quite surprised that I was calling. When I asked her if anyone had called and left a message for me, she said, "No, why would we have done that?" I was then that I heard the laughter outside my office door. As I hung up the phone I got the intercom message from the receptionist that my guests had arrived. I had no time to regroup. I was flustered and my presentation was not my best. I'll never know if that's why we didn't get the contract. But I do know that losing that contract was worth the torment to Don. He did not care because he thought he'd never need anyone but himself to continue his success in business.

Chapter Six
From Recovery to Discovery

So, I stayed at that furniture company for five more years! No more running. No more boom and bust cycle. This time I was going to work *through* the things, within myself, that were putting me in the same situation over and over again. And I was not going to leave everything that I'd built this time.

If you are surprised to read that decision, imagine the shock Mr. Manipulator himself felt. He actually admitted to me around the middle of the third year after the big marketing program switch, that he couldn't believe I stayed.

The company expanded and we moved to another building in 1993. This time I had a typical salesman's office just off of the reception area. Ruby had the office next to Don's; as she still remained his personal assistant.

Don and Ruby got married in 1994. It continued to be a nightmare to work there. They did everything in their power to ostracize me from the natural socialization that occurs in an office, and they were in the powerful position to do so.

Don robbed me of tens of thousands of dollars in commissions. For example, he would wait until payday, then he'd call me into his office and say the job that we'd agreed on at eight or nine percent commission had to be reduced to two or three percent because the delivery men had damaged some pieces in shipping (as if delivery mistakes were the salesperson's responsibility!)

I went to a lawyer and, over time, we developed a file nearly three inches thick. The lawyer was very convinced that we had an airtight case and he was just itching to go to court. But, I just kept remembering the lesson I'd learned previously from my divorce from Vietnam Vet Robert – 'Don't stir the hornet's nest'. My visits to the lawyer's office served as counseling for me, and

I was learning a great deal about how people like Don operate. I wanted to be sure that I'd never be caught in this type of situation again. I never told the lawyer that I had no intention of taking it to court. I paid for the time he spent counseling me and I felt that was fair.

In August of 1992 I did incorporate my own company and contracted myself back to Don's company because I'd just landed a million-dollar contract with one of the larger local oil companies. This time Don was involved. In fact, it took four years to attract this company away from Steel Case furniture.

They were opening a new building and wanted to refurnish the entire company. While this sounds wonderful, the problem is that a contract of that size can make or break you. Don could not ask for any up-front money because Steel Case would never put a demand on them of that nature. Meantime, the bottom had fallen out from under us as the economy took a nosedive.

The slower economy meant that we had no other work to do in between the big order for cash flow! Don had to finance the entire project and the installations would take up to eighteen months. The city of Calgary contract was long over as well by that time. So, by contracting myself back to the company I was back to commission only with no company benefits or expense account.

I rounded out my library in those five years with John Bradshaw's books *Homecoming* and *Creating Love.* I spent a great deal of time on inner-child work during what I call my 'five-year sentence'.

I will mention *Lip Service* by Kate Fillion at this point. It is an excellent account of the true nature of women. The hell that bimbo put me through during my five-year sentence inspired a great deal of notes and observations. I was thankful to see *Lip Service* on the bookstore shelves. It saved me the time of writing it myself.

Also, I took the *Course in Miracles.* The rest of my suggested reading at the end of my story was acquired during this time, and without it, I would have surely died.

I had to accept that I would never be in a position to have my daughter full-time. That was enough to justify feelings of total uselessness and suicide was a great temptation for a long time.

I had to watch as Paul got remarried to a woman who got herself pregnant to entrap him. And worst of all, I had to allow that woman to be with my daughter on a daily basis. Although, as it turned out, she provided an excellent contrast! As a result, my daughter really appreciates her straight-talking, no-games, 'real' mom, thanks to that game player.

The unique position that my daughter has had through all this is most interesting. She has had the opportunity to see the contrast, first-hand, of the difference between game playing and living your 'authentic self' (as most psychologists call it).

As she gets older, I am finding our relationship becoming richer rather than distant, as I had been so forewarned about. I can only hope, as every parent, that the foundation is there. And as the years go by, I become more and more aware that I have to check my words and keep the communication open and honest.

My father died in June of 1992. I had a real struggle with that. In fact, I crashed for several months and I was extremely distraught. I wasn't able to go home for his funeral because, to me, that would be playing games that I do not know how to play. My father and I had no relationship. I felt that it was just as foolish to attend his funeral as it would be to attend any other stranger's funeral. I understand that funerals are for the sake of the dearly beloved left behind, but I had no relationship with my mother; siblings, or anyone else in the family either; except for one cousin. My mom is far more comfortable with me at a great distance. I was sure my presence would only add to her stress.

I eventually came to realize that all my drive to succeed in business came from wanting to prove to my father that I could do it on my own. When he died before my great success was realized, there seemed no reason to go on. I will tell you this segment of the story in detail because I found it so healing, at the time.

I was driving my car when I recalled the song by Whitney Houston entitled "The Greatest Love of All". In fact, all the words went through my head...

And then I understood! My own father was so blinded by his old ways, his old ideas, and his own abuse issues that he would have never appreciated my accomplishments while still looking through the eyes of his own upbringing and lack of education. So, the next time I see him, we will be able to communicate through the clarity of truth. At the time, that understanding gave me a renewed inspiration to carry on and a feeling of comfort.

My health suffered tremendously over those five years. And I still wonder if I didn't push it too far by staying with the furniture company as long as I did. But when I did finally leave, I had the pleasure of selling Don a dry territory for five-thousand dollars. Although it was not a great deal of money, it did represent a great deal of principle.

I had spent the first year of my five-year sentence with Don and Ruby in charge trying to go back to school and found that I just could not handle the pace. Sales is too demanding to leave any energy for anything else in the evening. In fact, sales often demands evening hours for paperwork and planning.

So, in 1992, I incorporated my own company – Alternatives Unlimited Inc. It started out as a promotion for self-help and personal development. I felt that I had gained so much ground and had come so far in my own development that I was a perfect example of what a person can do by applying the techniques offered through that industry. And I continue to pass on information and give away books to people on a regular basis.

I also dabbled in tourism. In 1992 Calgary was very immature in tourism. The Calgary Stampede was the big draw. So I tried to establish "Western Dance Tours" and created bus parties that drove from one western bar to another (otherwise known as a pub crawl). It was a tremendous amount of work. It demanded work during the day to obtain party participants and then work at night to run the tours. It was next to impossible as I did not have the infrastructure to accomplish it, so I abandoned the idea.

Eventually I began to contract myself out on a temporary basis as a sales assistant. I even contracted myself to the furniture company between 1993 and 1996. That helped to plug the holes in the agreement that my commissions kept leaking through.

I developed a program of telemarketing (however I called it *teleScouting*®) and direct sales support that would either boost an existing business that was lagging for some reason, or it was extremely effective in starting new companies and/or introducing new products to the market. This provided sporadic contract work as well.

By contracting my skills for a specific amount of time, I escaped the seemingly common process of building a territory and then watching the management tear it apart and distribute the bits to their girlfriends or to members of their own 'good old boys club'.

I managed to get a contract with the Canadian Cancer Society for a major fundraising event in 1993. This established a momentum for me in fundraising and eventually led me to a contract with the Alberta Liberal Party.

It was the establishment of the contract with the Alberta Liberal Party in May of 1996 that set my company on a steady incline. This put me in a position to start hiring support staff and developing an infrastructure for continued growth.

This gave me the ability to leave the furniture company; and it was none too soon. It was so nice to wake up in the morning and not have to force myself to get on with the day.

I also organized the occasional convention, which added variety to my daily routine and broadened my contact base. These are listed as projects rather than contracts in my business plan.

Oh, and I have to tell you this as well: just after the New Year of 1993, I was talking to my ex-husband about our daughter when he began to push me for child support. His young son was about two at the time and my daughter was nine. The red lights went on in my head. Why would he suddenly be insisting on collecting child support from me?

I went to my corporate lawyer and asked him what the chances were that he could demand support payments from me. The lawyer said that he would have to return to court and have our agreement changed. The lawyer suggested that, in light of the past performance of my ex-husband's business decisions, perhaps a receivership was in full swing this time. My lawyer knew of a way that he could find out for me, and so he did. And guess what!

Paul had taken out a second mortgage on the house and apparently, the business was suffering. Naturally, the bank is going to inform Paul that someone was inquiring about the financial status of the house and business. Needless to say, he was furious because, once again, I found out the truth.

Although he would never admit it, I know Paul's daddy came to the rescue this time. Sir Paul had to learn that textbook recipes for business are missing one key ingredient – *experience*. I suppose it is okay, by macho standards, to let daddy bail you out of financial trouble. It just doesn't look good if the wife does it.

I will close this chapter with acknowledgment to the publication *Women Who Run with the Wolves* by Dr. Clarissa Pinkola Estés. I didn't read this book until one year after I had written the first draft of this story. I found myself and my story best described in her chapter about the red shoes.

I found that, throughout my journey, every time I picked up a publication or attended a motivational seminar, it simply confirmed what I was already doing. Or it explained in better detail and in more eloquent vocabulary what I already knew. Therefore, I was provided with the much-needed reference check to assure myself that I was on the right track and that things were just taking longer than I thought they would.

I spoke with the owner of an organization that offered a yearly membership and, in turn, brought in a top-noted motivational speaker once a month. I belonged to this group for over two years. The owner said that very few, if any, of the members ever really applied what they heard in the seminars. When I told him that I found it to be confirmation for my processes, he just smiled and said, "Oh really? Well, that's a unique approach," and placated me right out of his office. The following year I didn't renew my membership and he, apparently, moved into personal coaching and sold the original organization.

At this point in my life, I decided that I was all right and it was the world around me that was wrong. I was surrounding myself with the wrong people and, consequently, creating a world of conflict around myself. I was not taking the time to really assess the decisions I was making before I was committing myself to something.

I found myself with a constant tugging inside me. I felt that I was always needing to get somewhere else. No matter what I was doing, I felt like I should be doing something else.

Staying with the furniture company was almost the most difficult thing I ever did, second only to leaving my daughter with her dad and that woman on a full time basis. But I knew I had to change the way I was doing things if I wanted different results.

And by the way, Don and Ruby did go on to be very successful thanks to Don's friend in a huge national accounting firm that ended up contracting his company to refurnish the whole company. Don built two buildings for his company with the arch windows that seemed to be his obsession.

However, the company had a reputation of extremely high turnover. After that big contract was done, Don ended up having to sell off one of his buildings. And eventually he sold out to a larger US company so he could retire.

His bimbo from Lethbridge never brought him any sales like I did. And his own technique was based purely in who he knew. It was all superficial and unsustainable.

Last I heard Don and Ruby were living in California. He always hated the winter and when the NDP took power in Alberta in 2015, I am sure that; if he wasn't already living elsewhere, he would have been by then!

Chapter Seven
New Patterns

In the summer of 1993 I went on the best vacation I ever had up to that point. It was a backpack trip with two schoolteachers and one of the schoolteacher's mate to Belize. And that trip is still at the top of my list of best things I ever did.

Don traveled all the time. I ended up spending way too much money chasing after him and his vacations… oh, the things we do for love. We went to Hawaii once. Bora Bora, Haiti, and that group of islands another time. The Virgin Islands, and he'd taken me to see Newfoundland and some of his relatives at one point. That was a real impressive experience.

However, this schoolteacher I was with for the Belize trip was a real penny pinche. This guy could find a deal where there was no deal. When I traveled with him it was fun, educational, and economical. Too bad he was so shallow.

He was brilliant with money; but even better as a handyman. He could fix anything. He owned several apartment buildings around Calgary and kept them in repair himself. Our relationship lasted only a little over a year. It was such a bizarre peer group that he belonged to that I can't even, to this day, begin to explain the dynamics. Suffice it to say that we were a very poor match due to his peer group. Had it not been for the influences they put upon him, I believe he and I could have had a wonderful life together.

In October of 1993, I established a very serious, intimate relationship with a very fine local fellow. We met at the Canadian Cancer Society during one of my searching expeditions for a contract. We lived together until August of 1998, which was when his mother passed away.

At that time, he moved back home to live with his father. We then took time separately from each other for some personal development. We found a lot of differences between us when we were living together. The main difference was in the area of organization. This man had absolutely no rhyme or reason as to where he put things around the house. If he used a hammer in the bathroom to adjust the window screen, that's where you'd find the hammer the next time you needed it. It took him only two years to totally destroy my routine and organization around my home. By the time he left to live with his dad again, I was on the brink of disaster both mentally and emotionally. I realized that my personal and professional strength was in my ability to be extraordinarily organized.

My life's pattern of boom and bust also had a subplot to it (and I may have mentioned this before?) that included a very definite and recurring symptom regarding relationships versus career. When my career was going good, my personal love life was nil. And, if I had a wonderful lover and the future looked good in that area, my career suffered.

This situation had, once again, evolved into that pattern. In spite of the crazy-making aspects of the disarray of my home, my business was growing and my career was moving forward. So, the natural progression, according to my life's pattern, was that now it was time for the man and I to break up and for the man to relieve me of everything I had built up for myself professionally and personally during our time together.

But this time it was different. A new pattern was in place. This man did not need to seek revenge. In fact, he was able to acknowledge that we each simply had a different approach to life, and living, and that our relationship deserved the effort of remaining consistent with each other as friends for a while. So, for the first time in my life, my career and my personal life were equal. Both were in a healthy holding pattern and gaining strength from within.

For the first time in my life, I had a male friend, who was once a lover, who did not strip me of my dignity, or my finances, when the physical intimacy ceased to exist. He was the first male friend I had ever truly had! He was, indeed, an incredible and wonderful man.

I never experienced the dating phase of my development. I married the first boy I dated from high school. Since then, I moved from one relationship to the other so fast, there was no time for dating. Although, I had to wonder what good it would do me to finally appreciate the value of dating at forty-seven years of age. I decided that my new appreciation for dating would benefit my daughter the most.

And yes, my daughter, I am so thankful for her every day. I am so glad that I didn't miss out on having children altogether. Although I never saw myself as needing to perform the function of parenting to fulfill myself; since I had done it, I realized the tremendous inner personal growth parenting offers. It really takes you to a new level of perspective about yourself if you are open to working *with* the children as opposed to working *on* them.

The most incredible revelation I had through the entire journey of writing my story out was when I realized that I had been subconsciously searching for the love bond that I experienced with Norman when I was fifteen years old.

In every counseling session I ever had, I would identify my first intimate relationship as being my first husband, Michael. Yet I had been subconsciously looking for my rescuer to return. On one hand, I can see the damage that did to me, to have a sexual relationship so young. And yet, it was a beautiful experience. I have to remain focused on what little positive aspect there is in a situation like that.

And, (brace yourself!) I called him! After twenty-eight years, I called and spoke to Norman. I never knew what my dad had said to him for sure. I never knew whether he didn't come back to me when I was finally of age because he had seen my engagement announcement in the paper. I wanted to know. One thing I did know was that he hadn't gotten married until at least three or four years after I was married the first time.

I had to call three people to get his phone number because it was unlisted. I found that interesting. It was a weird experience. When he picked up the phone and said, "Hello," I was swooshed back in time and I became that fifteen-year-old girl again.

I asked if it was Norman and he said, "Yes."

Then I said, "You probably don't remember me, this is Deborah."

And he said, "Deborah? Leon's Deborah?" By now my heart was pounding so fast I could barely breathe.

And I said, "No, the Deborah who used to be the girl next door – Deborah Susan."

There was a brief moment of silence and I heard him almost gasp. Then he said, "Oh, I don't want to talk." My voice dropped to a very sympathetic tone (you must understand that I telemarket for a living and I know how to communicate and read people over the phone). So my voice was projecting sympathy and understanding as I said, "Oh, you don't?"

He interrupted me and I heard the twenty-four-year-old young man that I know loved me at that time say, "No, I'm sorry" from the perspective of a grown, responsible father's position, as Norman was then the father of more than one girl.

I responded with, "Well, I'm sorry too. I was writing my autobiography and I wanted to talk to you at least one more time to…"

He cut me off again and said, "Oh, I think you have the wrong number," and hung up.

I sat there for the longest time just listening to my heart pound. Then I opened up to the feelings I was having. I just wanted him to know that we were just two country kids who got carried away. I knew for sure, at that moment, that I had been his first. Perhaps my mom was right, maybe he was just using me for practice, I don't know. But, it was my parents who made it dirty.

I really had to resist the temptation to call him back. But, since he went to the trouble of keeping his number unlisted, I thought I'd better not. So, I called his sister who had given me his number and told her that he had not been glad to hear from me and that I thought it best if he was not questioned about my searching for him. She agreed and we hung up.

Later I felt a warm glow inside where an unrequited love used to be. I hoped he felt the same. I really hoped that he wasn't carrying a shameful guilt about what happened to us in the past.

I have made incredible progress, considering where I started! And I trust that you won't mind if I blow my own horn. I've been told that if we don't blow our own horn for ourselves occasionally, no one will know we are coming.

Today I hold a very deep and sincere respect and admiration for my mother. She survived a great deal and kept faithful to her vows. Vows she made before she really knew what she was in for with my father and his family. That type of faithfulness is long gone from our society as a whole.

My mother, alone, protected me from my father's long-established traditional thinking that could have resulted in scars and wounds far worse than what I actually experienced. She led the challenge and faced the battle to create change. She worked with what she had, and she got the job done! I only pray now that she can reap the reward of her toil and sacrifice in joy and fulfillment and live and enjoy the rest of her days here on earth in peace, in comfort, in self-discovery, and in love. She and I won't be going out for coffee anytime soon. But I can appreciate her from a safe distance for now.

As I look back, I see the organization of people I was placed into through the sequence of events that, I believe, were part of a continuing path to my purpose. When I was under contract with the Alberta Liberal Party as Director of Development, I saw in the leader of the Liberal Party as a man who was humble and sincerely concerned for his constituents. And then I saw the Premier of Alberta as a man who once had a heart. He once walked closely with conscience and intuition but he allowed himself to be bought. He compromised his true beliefs, his true self, for the sake of power. Why? Why does power so often change us?

I've been told there are three basic laws that must be observed to maintain proper balance in your life's journey: poverty, chastity, and humility.

Poverty means that you cannot be bought. It means that you will choose your principles over power, money, or fame. It does not mean you have to live in financial depravity.

Chastity means 'morally pure' – honesty and loyalty in business and in personal life.

Humility is pretty obvious. Humility is the perfect balance of self-esteem. You know that you are worthy of a particular title or leadership and that you can handle the responsibilities while, at the same time; if you truly knew of someone else who could do a better job, you would gladly step aside for that person to take over. Then again, perhaps you prefer the simple definitions of poverty, chastity, and humility in the dictionary. And if that is the case, that's okay with me.

To me humility also includes an aspect of self-evaluation on a regular basis. For example, one burning question that seems to haunt everyone who feels compelled to take action on their compassion for the less fortunate as in regard to the third-world countries is: how do you choose from among so much need? So in our evaluation of ourselves we see ourselves as overwhelmed with the vast need. We look at entire countries under severe dictatorships causing individuals to live in totally inhuman conditions. But what can we do about it?

At the same time, we ask why children are born with birth defects. And, more often than not, the suffering is usually inflicted upon the most unlikely candidates. By that, I mean that the question would read, 'Why do bad things happen to good people?'

In another great book entitled, *When Bad Things Happen to Good People* by Rabbi Harold S. Kushner, it is explained that God does not interfere with the natural order of things that have been put in place by our own free will. The lineage of your family carries with it a series of genes inherited from generation to generation. Very often the gene or chromosome that causes a particular dysfunction was inherited generations ago. This, therefore, relieves the current bearer of the condition direct blame. However, the effort to deal with the problem is now totally upon someone who is not to blame. How fair is that?

The answer to that question may surprise you. Quite simply, it took that many generations to develop the balance of strength and insight to deal with it. Stop and think about the people who do handle the challenges of birth defects, for example. Are they not the strongest people you've ever met? Do we, who are blessed with all of our faculties, not say to ourselves that we know we could not possibly handle that type of challenge with as much finesse as they do?

Lineage applies to the concern about starving countries as well, but we call it history or politics. Meanwhile, we must not allow ourselves to be paralyzed by the fact that we cannot do it all. We must step out and do the job that has been assigned us by fate, circumstance, or by our own inner drive.

I could write an entire book about those types of insights, and perhaps someday I will.

The point is that we are never given more than we can handle. You may think that the suicide statistics bear some weight to argue otherwise. To that I must say that having faced such temptation on many occasions myself, I feel qualified to tell you there is always an opportunity to live and see things through. One just has to be willing to accept the long, hard road sometimes rather than indulging in a quick-fix answer.

Writing this book, in itself, for me was healing and revitalizing. Allowing it to be made public is another matter that is both exciting and frightening. To have one's whole life laid out on paper for all to see is a vulnerability that I'm not quite sure I'm ready for. And so I say that, if this is meant to be made public for the purpose of helping others, then the path for that to happen will open and be made smooth and easy. I suppose that if you have just finished reading this, then we all know what the outcome was.

I hope my story has helped you to see that, even though life can be tough, and sometimes even unbearable at times, you can reach down and find that inner strength you need, and you can get through it. Hey, if I can do it, so can you!

May I suggest that if anything in this story triggered familiarity, either in your own life or in someone else's life who you know, go out and buy one of the books I've listed on my page of suggested readings, and give it as a gift to yourself, or to them. Read it and digest it and make the changes that you know you must.

To be continued...

Writer's note: this work was then put away with the intention of picking it up again at some point in the future when I'd realized my success both personally and consequently financially.

I envisioned tremendous success that would render all the past suffering worthwhile and give me enough money to be financially independent and in a position to help others on a volunteer basis.

I did approach a couple of publishers, including the producers of the Chicken Soup series. I still have the letter Chicken Soup sent me to tell me that I was on their short list. However, I never heard back from them. So I put it away along with the first draft of these first seven chapters.

It was June of 2015 when I pulled the three ring binder that housed these first seven chapters out of the box it was packed away in to give it to my EMDR therapist so she could understand the past traumas I'd experienced that finally led to the recent diagnosis of PTSD.

I did approach this therapy with the same reserved hope that I'd finally find some relief from the uncontrollable self-destructive behaviors that kept derailing my life.

And yet by this time I'd realized that sometimes my life derailed and I had nothing to do with it. It was as if I was targeted by some bad Karma that just kept finding me and no matter what I did, 'it' was going to ensure my ongoing failure.

Here's what happened next...

Chapter Eight
And the Beat Goes on 20 Years Later

To start this segment, let me tell you more about my Ken. I'll call him Ken because people said we looked like Barbie and Ken when we were together. He was gorgeous. Nathan Fillion gorgeous. Or Richard Gere gorgeous in "American Gigilo". In fact, he looked very much like Nathan Fillion when he played Richard Castle. Ken was the man I met at the Canadian Cancer Society.

Ken was a model in his younger years; and he was still doing commercials locally when we met. We were extras together in a movie initially entitled *Portraits of Innocence* with Michael Ironside as the star. Michael Ironside always reminded me of a younger rendition of Jack Nicholson.

I was also an extra in a training video he was hired to play a role in for a well-known Gas Station chain.

He could juggle with the best of them. He could do close up magic that would blow your mind. He was quick-witted and always on the ball. I dare say I loved him more than I ever loved any other man.

It was with Ken that I learned how to treat men properly. Where I grew up the women all wore the pants in the family. They were short tempered and ruled the roost with a sharp tongue, a shallow perspective, and an even narrower opinion.

So consequently, I treated men much the same. I realize how devastating that was for my daughter's father. I really did not know who I was with at the time. My ability to discern others was so clouded with my own demons that I just went into a sort of autopilot in my relationships and therefore destroyed every one of them accordingly, except the one with Don. He wanted me to leave my daughter and I wouldn't do that. So that failure is on him.

It was during my time with Ken that I wrote (what I call) a thesis entitled *Men Are People Too*. It started out asking where the shelters were for abused men. Where I come from, that was the case. The men were beaten down and treated very cruelly by the wives. I often wondered what brought them home every night after work. And in my research I discovered that it was just pure habit.

The same way a person returns to the bottle; or to the drugs they know are ruining their lives, these men just kept coming back for more. And yes, the same way an abused woman returns to her home, so does an abused man.

My thesis concluded that the shelters for these men are every sports bar, golf course, and locker room. They just tough it out and find solace amongst themselves where they can be themselves with no judgment, no criticism, and no unrealistic demands.

And the day I knew I'd finally turned a corner in my treatment of men was the evening Ken and I had friends over for movie night. Ken had wired my living room for surround sound. Keep in mind that this was 1993. This technology was very new and not necessarily easily available in Calgary Alberta.

The ceiling in my townhouse living room was 22 feet high. I loved that place. Nestled in a quiet complex just off of one of the main streets very near the center of town; yet once inside you'd never think you were within the city limits.

The homes were built 4 together on the inside of the road and at the curve of the cul-de-sac there were 12 connected. All multi-level and beautifully landscaped so that everyone had a private deck off the living room; or dining room (depending upon the layout).

The bedrooms were on the upper level, of course, so you were at the treetops with the birds in the morning. And regardless of the season, they would always sing in the morning.

I'll never forget one of Ken's first overnight stays with me when he woke up saying, "Frickin' birds!" Well, maybe his language was a bit more colorful. He was raised the youngest with four siblings in a huge house in one of the original 'oil money' neighborhoods. His bedroom was always in the basement. And the house was built solid with great insulation. So he never heard birds in the morning.

And I am laughing so hard writing this… I said, "But they are loving and wanting to make more birds."

To which he replied, "Can't they go fornicate somewhere else?"

I laughed then too until tears came and my sides hurt. I said, "It's not considered fornication for them!"

He had two Shih Tzu dogs, a male and a female. Up until this encounter I was so anti little dogs. To me they were all just little yappers. I preferred the larger breeds. Labradors, German Shepherds, and the like. However, these two just stole your heart and kept it cozy within their soft fur and wagging tails; as they were always so eager to bring you the toy for the next throw.

We ended up breeding the female and kept one of the puppies for our own. His sister had adopted the two dogs while Ken stayed with her through his divorce. So we had visiting time with them, but they were considered his sister's dogs by the time I met them.

We presented our new puppy to the kids Christmas of 1994. I had the video of it transferred to DVD a couple of years ago. It was an amazing time in all of our lives. That little dog brought so much joy and happiness to us I cannot even begin to describe.

Anyway, I digress; back to the movie night… This was the first entertaining Ken and I were doing as a couple. You see, he also had a 2 (almost 3) year old son. I was the visiting parent for my daughter, who was 9 at the time. Therefore, Ken arranged his visitations with his son to match mine with my daughter. This allowed us to play house every other weekend with the kids; and yet we had every other weekend to ourselves as a couple; as did our estranged spouses. Life was perfect for us at the time.

Okay, back to my original train of thought: so we're having movie night and Ken offered to make the popcorn. You cannot imagine the horror that went through me when he came down the stairs with my oldest, stained, and broken on one corner, plastic bowl with all the popcorn in it… But I caught myself!

Rather than grabbing the bowl and running back to the kitchen to distribute the popcorn in proper presentation (for company) bowls. I said "Oh, let's give our guests their own popcorn bowl" and got up to retrieve one of my crystal bowls always kept on display in the wall unit that also held the huge TV.

Those bowls never saw the light of day; or night, for that matter. They were for show. But this time, one of them was put to great use. I poured half the popcorn into the crystal bowl for our guests and Ken and I snuggled up on the second couch in my living room to enjoy the movie with our usual popcorn bowl.

I was so proud of myself. I felt as if I'd definitely turned a corner. I'd finally reached nirvana and was living consciously and respectfully of my partner and treating him like the sensitive human being he rightfully was. This time the relationship was going to stick; and my career with my own little home-based micro business was seemingly going good as well. At least I was able to take a draw every month to cover necessities of life.

Those first four years with Ken were amazing. I actually tasted what it feels like to be in a functional relationship and have balance in my life.

While Ken and I were spending time apart we started to explore the world of marriage counseling by video tape programs. It was Barbara De Angelis in those days. She was at the top of the charts for her couples-healing power. Her approach was 'Making Love Work'. Meaning, making it succeed.

However, her competition rephrased it into 'making love... *work*'. Meaning, making it hard effort.

We were doing well with the program we'd purchased and then we heard that Barbara herself was coming to Calgary! We were thrilled. So we got tickets and attended with all the enthusiasm any couple renewing their deep love for each other would have.

She picked us out of the crowd and asked for our 'testimony' regarding the program and we both gave it the rave review it deserved. She asked us to stay behind after the symposium was over. And so of course, we did.

And it turned out that she was looking for people who had success with the program to do an infomercial with her. She invited us to Hollywood, where she lived, to do the shoot. Ken and I both knew it was because of our Barbie and Ken look that we were selected because there were at least a hundred couples there to choose from.

In our interview for the spot she also learned that we were familiar with being on camera; which is actually a very serious thing. To have people who are not actors and who have not ever

136

been on camera, there is a bit of a learning curve in taking direction accordingly. With us, they knew they could just get right down to the business of shooting our segment.

The home where we did the shoot was magnificent. It was not Barbara's house. I'm not sure who it belonged to; but whoever it was, they lived in the typical lap of luxury we would expect anyone in the film industry to live.

Ken and I strolled the beautiful garden around the pool and out to the gazebo arm in arm with the fragrance of the amazing flowers all around us. And this was the first time we discussed marriage since we'd become a serious, dedicated couple.

Initially I told all my potential partners that I did not want to get married again until my daughter was of age to really understand that she would remain part of the family nucleus regardless.

You see, her dad got remarried very quickly after we divorced as mentioned in chapter six. This put my daughter outside of that family nucleus formed by the stepmother, Paul, and the new baby. I felt that if I were to remarry also that my daughter would be outside of two complete families leaving her caught in the twilight zone somewhere in the middle. I could not do that to her.

Initially Ken completely agreed. We'd often comment to each other about how perfect our life was. Yet here we were discussing marriage as if my concerns had never been mentioned before. The discussion did remain very friendly and I thought it was again legitimately established that we did not need to get married.

One of the producers gave Ken two tickets to a private restaurant for magicians. As usual, Ken had entertained the film crew with his up-close magic and had impressed them so much that these tickets were given to us for an experience few 'outsiders' like us could ever afford.

We were taken by limo (as we were driven around the whole time we were there mostly so the filming would stay on time) up a winding road to the top of one of the few mountains in the area to a place that looked like a castle.

We entered through two sets of very heavy doors into a very small dark wood-paneled room where a very striking couple stood behind a very small podium with the guest book open. We reported our name and presented our tickets. The woman greeted us and checked off our name in the book and told us to go to the far wall facing the stone carved owl perched in a small alcove in the wall; and we were to say 'open says-a-me'.

Of course, I am sure they pressed a button at that moment, and the paneled wall slid to one side to expose a hallway dimly lit by movie theatre floor lights. The panel closed behind us and we climbed a narrow stairway to the right to another podium with another handsome couple and a guest book in a small paneled room with another owl in an alcove on the far wall.

Here we were to sign the book upon entering and we were told that before we leave we would be given an opportunity to write our comments about our experience.

Let me tell you; this was amazing. We proceeded to pass through another sliding panel that opened to a dining room with two fantastic *Phantom of the Opera* type chandeliers. We had to walk down about eight steps where a waiter; dressed in a formal evening-tails tuxedo with a white linen towel over his left arm, awaited to seat us.

With a slight bow he motioned with his right hand to follow him. Most of the tables were big enough for four; however, most of the tables were seated with only two sitting across a corner from each other, rather than directly across from each other. Keep in mind that this was mid-week. It was a Wednesday night as opposed to a Friday or Saturday; which we were told are always booked months in advance.

This was the first time in my life that I ate quail in a sweet and sour sauce. And it was amazing. And while we dined a harp played in the background. After dinner we were invited to retire to the library… which was through another paneled sliding door at the far end of the dining room.

Here we found several card tables with magicians performing the up-close magic that Ken always did. However, these illusions were far more complex. Of course, Ken loved every minute of it. The room was small and had filled bookcases, ceiling to floor, on all four walls.

On the far corner it appeared as if the bookcase had moved forward slightly; and upon closer inspection it certainly had! Behind this wall was what appeared to be a storage area. More bookcases lined the walls, however, these were not as full. In the center of the room were large square tables with plain plywood tops and crude two by four legs. Another plywood shelf was underneath and about half way to the floor with large sketchbooks and loose papers on it.

On top of one of these tables was a copy of Houdini's notes! Ken and I started paging through these to our amazement when suddenly one of the magicians came into the room and quietly told us that this was a restricted area and we could not be in here. As there were several other couples browsing in amazement, it took a while to get us all out of there; but wow, what a find!

The place is called the Magic Castle; and thinking back on it, I have to suspect that the discovery of the back room is probably part of the experience. Yet, it made for an amazing evening for both of us and we certainly filled in our comments with great and well-deserved accolades.

Ken and I also took the kids to Disneyland. I think it was 1996 or 97. My memory blurs the sequence of events around most of my life; and even the most recent is still blurry. To find my personal day-timers for these years would require a great deal of digging through boxes that have been packed away for some time and I just don't have the energy for that right now.

So suffice it to say I believe my daughter was 12 and Ken's son was 5 when we took a ten-day trip to Disneyland in California. I still have a full picture album dedicated to that trip. Ken and I moved in sync with each other to the point where we rarely stood in line for very long. At home we'd often walk into movies at the last minute before the lights went down and find the best seats in the house just waiting for us. And this trip was no different.

We saw everything and we did everything that was available on the Disneyland grounds. We had perfect weather the whole time. We shared a room with two queen size beds. The boys slept in one bed and the girls in the other. We even spent some time by the pool of our motel where the shuttle bus came twice in the morning and twice in the afternoon and once again later in the evening. I can still feel the afterglow of that trip even today as I write this. Yes indeed, I tasted what a functional relationship would be like. But alas, it was only a taste...

Ken's mother died in 1998. His father was demonstrating that he was unable to be left alone because he'd lose track of time. He'd forget to eat and spent a lot of time crying. So it was unanimously decided amongst the entire remaining family that, since Ken was not married and had his son only part time, he'd be the best one to move in and live with his father.

That was the beginning of the end for us; although, at the time it seemed like a good idea even to us.

It is well known that the Alberta election in 1997 was won by the PCs yet again. Grant Mitchell ended up watching his party go from 32 seats to 18 and he was promptly replaced by Nancy MacBeth. Yes, we remained under the PC torturous rule until 2015 when the NDP won and PCs were finally put in their place. However, that's another book all together!

Grant Mitchell was replaced by Nancy MacBeth. I was let go, along with a number of others who were 'branded' as one of Grant Mitchell's supporters; as Nancy had her own fundraiser and office staff in mind. This was all perfectly normal and expected under the circumstances and everyone involved cooperated with the new direction one way or another.

However, at the same time, the pressure on those of us in the office was tremendous after the election. The loss hung in the air like a thick fog and everyone was polishing up their resumes and feverishly scouring the want ads.

I was completely burnt out; and I knew it. I was also now very unemployed. My contract payout was enough to sustain me for a couple of months and then I had to be collecting a paycheck again. Yet I was in no shape to even interview at that time.

The Calgary Stampede was coming soon and they had started advertising for the small extra paid staff necessary to run the food stands and other permanent facilities that made up the entire 'greatest outdoor show on earth'.

I thought there would be no better place to convalesce that working the Calgary Stampede. I love the Stampede to this day; and I passed that love onto my daughter, who is now passing it on to her son; who was born July 10, 2016.

But you can be sure that my daughter and I were at the Thursday night 'sneak-a-peek' as always; which was July 9th that year! Yep, she walked the grounds before she when into labor and 2016 was the only Stampede she ever missed.

It was July 4 to 13, 1997 that I manned the food stand in the infield of the rodeo grounds. This was where the true cowboys came to eat as well as the royalty of the Stampede! And by royalty I mean the people who could afford infield tickets to the rodeo along with their esteemed guests.

I had the time of my life. I was 44 years old and still able to turn heads. I was loud and loose calling out the orders so even the guests way back at the end of the line could hear me. I put on quite a show for the people who had infield tickets. Twice I was asked to take a managers role rather than just manning a cash register; but as much as I would have loved to, I was not able to.

Believe it or not, I could not count the cups in the morning before we opened because my brain was so fried. I'd lose track of where I was by 15… and there were hundreds of them! At least at the cash register it told me the amount of change and it was never more than I could count out. It was embarrassing, but that was all I had to give at the time.

And by the way, I still have the t-shirt we wore as Stampede-workers that year in my closet. It was officially 20 years old this past July 2017! I have fond memories of that experience and wish I could work that same spot every year. As it is, my daughter and I try to attend the grounds as many times as possible during the 10-day event.

This past year (2017) they finally introduced a pass that the public can buy for a reduced daily entry fee. Of course you pay for the pass to the equivalent of four dollars a day and then you can come and go through the gates whenever your schedule allows.

That was especially handy for my daughter this past year while the baby was so young. Next year he'll be two and far more interactive; and of course we can't wait. And while my son-in-law shakes his head in disbelief, we are both really looking forward to Stampede 2018…

So back to the 1997 Stampede when I was more closely in touch with a friend of mine whose husband was president of the Chuck Wagon Association. They owned and operated a small industrial cleaning company and were experiencing difficulty growing their sales. They told me that they had brought on several sales people over the years to find no increase in sales. In fact, their sales were dwindling.

This actually continued the effort I'd begun with Ken. Ken changed jobs several times while we were together. The commercials and other small acting roles were just side cash for him. He always held down a 'day-job'.

Ken started in sales in 1994 or '95 for a large international moving and storage company who had been main contributors to the Canadian Cancer Society. I would assist him by making the initial cold calls to schedule appointments for him to establish the people looking to relocate as clients for his company. I also assisted him when he sold photocopiers for more than one distributor.

Working for my friend and her husband would be the first project I'd carry that was a contract and I had to justify my hourly rate for the service. You have to understand that, even today Calgary Alberta is not a city where opportunities abound to introduce a new approach to anything; much less to what the majority of the working population would consider mere grunt work that anyone can do. And they feel that the only reason they don't do this particular grunt work (of searching for new business by phone) is because they don't have the time.

Therefore in 1998, in their minds; there was no talent necessary. In their minds any monkey who had the time could do this job of cold calling and scheduling appointments. So, having to pay someone to do it was acceptable; however, the pay structure was not going to be very high. Minimum wage to just a touch over minimum wage seemed fair to them.

To further complicate the situation, working with married couples that own and operate companies is not like working with companies that have human resource departments where you can go if you don't get along with management. Rather, it's more like being the unwelcomed relative who's down on their luck and you are sleeping on their couch until you get your life together.

Did I realize all that going into it…? No way! No, I waltzed in there for our scheduled meeting thinking they'd appreciate my talent, my skills and my abilities; and that they would be happy to pay me for my efforts.

We went back and forth for what seemed like days until we finally reached an agreement of effort and remuneration. And just to give you a real good idea of what working with people like this was like; and keep in mind that these were 'friends of mine'… At one point in our meeting this guy actually said I should not talk back to him!

I kid you not! He voiced an objection regarding the pay schedule I'd presented; to which I answered clearly and with evidence to justify the pay structure; and he said I was not to talk back to him. Fortunately, I laughed out loud and said, "Seriously? Who do you think you're talking to? How well will I work for you if I cannot answer objections?" To which he realized what he'd done and we all just laughed it off. But trust me when I tell you that he was dead serious when he first said I should not talk back.

Keep in mind that in 1998 I was not yet working on a computer. I was working off of paper company lists acquired by visiting the local library and copying pages of the Alberta Corporate Registry where all companies were listed by their business category. They were also listed by Province.

The company listings in the book included the owner(s) name; management names; annual income; number of employees; and more. It was public record and open to anyone who wanted to copy the pages.

The type was so small that I had to enlarge it to two hundred percent just to make it legible. I'd copy the pages onto letter-size paper and then tape that to an eleven by seventeen-inch page, draw lines to isolate each company within about a half inch section for hand written notes of the call.

These pages transformed into worksheets would then be three hole-punched and placed in three ring binders. Fortunately the companies were listed in alphabetical order so that if; on the odd occasion, someone actually called back when a message was left, the company could be found to update the notes.

The callback schedule was also on paper to ensure that the companies received a sufficient amount of information to make a sound business decision to interview the company I was representing. Looking back at that now I marvel at the amount of effort that was necessary just to keep track of the calls. And one had to be able to write extremely small, yet legibly, to use the manual call sheets.

It was decided that I would schedule the appointments and the two of them would do the actual sales calls. This was the best thing they could have done; because, it did not take them long to realize that what their previous sales people had been telling them was true.

They kept firing the sales representatives they'd hired thinking that they were lazy and not doing the job. They told me that all the information the reps were bringing back was just excuses for their inability to increase sales. However, I knew differently and therefore encouraged them to experience the sales calls for themselves and hear first-hand what the prospective new clients were saying. I told them that way they could increase the business and hire a new rep once the sales were increasing.

I worked for these people until year 2000 when I finally placed a fellow with them to take over the phoning for them. We all learned a great deal during that two years we worked together.

The fellow I trained to do the calling for them stayed with them another two years and I am sorry to say I am no longer in touch with them.

During that project I really studied the process and perfected it. I developed a math formula that demonstrated the ratio of calls to appointments. I learned how many calls it really required to obtain that appointment.

I perfected the greeting and the voice mail messages that gently moved the client along the sales process by providing new information with each call. That way every call was productive, even when leaving a voice mail message.

Then I tracked the ratio of appointments to those resulting in an actual sale. In 1999 I wrote the manual that contained all the information to make the cold calling effort the most productive it could be while still remaining less of a nuisance. Truly, everyone hates cold calling; both the caller and the recipient. However, I'd made it the best it could be. Truly, it was a one-to-one marketing program complete with word-of-mouth advertising that produced new clients for years to come if they were properly maintained with follow-up contact.

By 2003 I developed an Excel Spreadsheet that calculated the number of calls necessary to achieve a desired amount of increased sales; and it never failed! It never failed if the caller remained disciplined and did the calls as instructed, that is.

However, more often than not; anyone I trained would eventually spend more time trying to beat the system and therefore failed to reach the previously proven results; which were the results I achieved every time. They would fulfill their own prophesy of failure by refusing to do the job as instructed.

And I have to admit I struggled to get past the monotony of the effort. You do eventually 'hit the wall' so to speak. You do reach a point where you think you cannot possibly repeat that introductory line yet again and still sound as if it is your first call, and not your one thousand and first call.

So, just as the people hiring the cold caller felt that the calling was an unskilled, grunt position; the callers I trained all started out great, however, only one managed to take it past three months. And that was the first person I trained to take over the calling for that commercial janitorial company.

In fact, he moved to another sales position after leaving the janitorial company and remained on the top of the sales-leader board there for years using the technique I taught him.

However between year 1997, when I had a team of callers for Ken's first photocopier distributor and 2014 (when I resigned myself to being a one-man show again) I trained seven more people, and only two of those continued on with the effort.

Between 1997 and year 2000 I thought I had accomplished a good balance in my life. I was taking on contract work for the cold calling. I was working through the challenges of a long-term relationship. My daughter was doing well in school, and in her life.

In 1996 I had researched and produced a gift line that I initially called 'Angel-Folios'. It consisted of the leather-like folios most often used for wedding photos boxed with the appropriate mats. Then there was a series of poems I'd written that a person could purchase to put on one side of the folio. The buyer would then select a photo, that they themselves had taken and which was appropriate for the occasion, whether it be wedding, birthday, valentines, (even funerals) and the like; and the photo would be included on the other side of the folio to form a handcrafted, and so personalized, gift that they brought tears to most recipients.

I poured about fifty thousand dollars into this gift line between 1996 and 2000. I did everything right. I'd been in sales and marketing all my life. I had the business plan, the cash flow chart, I'd even test marketed sales in a prominent department store; and these things sold out at every craft show.

I approached the manufacturer of the folios to partner with me; or just buy me out... I approached all the greeting card manufacturers only to see greeting cards appear on the shelves six months later that mirrored my concept.

Then, in May of 2000 things began to change again. If I'd known how bad the coming personal and professional storm was going to be, I may not have allowed myself to even attempt to navigate it.

This time the pain and challenges were far beyond what I could have ever anticipated. The three year reprieve from adversity had not strengthened me nearly enough to face what was about to come.

Turn the page, as I did then, and see what years 2000 to 2014 had in store for me. Truly the worst was yet to come... and of course I had no idea at the time. No one ever sees the challenges before they hit.

Chapter Nine
The One/Two/Three Punch

The 1999 New Year's celebration was everything a 1999 New Year celebration should be. Ken and I were with our best friends. It was the year we had the children for New Year so we had our celebration in the basement of his father's house; the house he grew up in.

Ken was still living with his father at the time and we were working things out; or so I thought.

I have to mention here that after we had that second conversation about marriage, Ken proposed to me twice in public thinking I could not possibly turn him down in public. All of a sudden what we had was not enough for Ken. He wasn't as attentive anymore either.

When we first got together and we'd plan going to the zoo with the kids, for example; he and I moved as one. We both knew what had to be done to accomplish the task at hand. Without much discussion, he'd go one way and I'd go the other and we'd end up at the car with everything we needed. There was never any resentment about how much each of us did around the house. There was never any discussion about who should do what; we just got it all done together.

But by 1999, he'd come over with is son and stand at the door saying, "hurry up, hurry up," rather than pitching in and helping like he used to.

Of course, he was not living with me anymore, so I could see why he would therefore not be as involved as he was before. But standing at the door saying, "Hurry up," that was so out of character. Who was this guy now?

It had become very clear to me the second time he proposed that he was very seriously unsettled with our arrangement. We had another discussion about it and I suggested perhaps we could have a commitment ceremony. We'd send out announcements that we felt we wanted to make our relationship as committed as any other marriage; and we'd have a reception. And so we did.

We had the reception at a sports bar where there were not only pool tables, but also virtual games and pinball machines. There was a dance floor and I ended up on it by myself several times hoping to have at least one dance with my 'husband'... but that never did happen.

He was having the time of his life with his buddies playing the games and doing what men do in a sports bar. We were very tired and late that night, so sleep was the number one activity on the agenda that night.

The next morning, Ken got up early to go on a golf tour with his dad and other male friends who did this every year. We kissed goodbye at the door and I'll never forget the hollow loneliness that pulled my heart down to the pit of my stomach as I watched him drive away.

I took a walk by the river with our little Shih Tzu, something that always made me feel so good. But this time it was just so painful. Ken had changed so much since he'd gone to live with his Dad and for some reason, at that moment, it became so clear.

Ken was a man's man and I recognized that very early in our relationship. He maintained a routine of playing tennis and baseball with his buddies throughout our relationship. I never objected; and I never complained that he spent too much time in such activities; because he never did. It was always so balanced.

I also knew that a relationship has to evolve. In fact, it will evolve and if you don't keep up with that you will lose it... however, that was not the problem.

The problem was that Ken and I were no longer in sync like we were the first four years we were together. He didn't want to dance with me anymore. Yet, when we were first dating we danced together like pros.

We had both gained weight, but not enough that our friends even noticed. I thought back to the months before we planned the commitment ceremony. A couple we'd recently befriended indicated that they were interested in switching partners... you know, sometimes it's called swinging...

Now you have to know that the guy in this other couple was drop dead gorgeous. He was Armenian or something like that.

He had jet-black hair, the deepest brown eyes you've ever seen and lashes around them that most women can only wish for no matter how much mascara is used.

He was shorter than Ken. Ken was exactly 6 feet tall. This guy was maybe 5 foot 8 inches and he was built like a body-builder; but not overdone. It was just enough to be super-hot. And I don't know about you, but I like body hair that is complimentary; and trust me, his was! His wife however was quite plain.

So on the way home on the night they suggested this I asked Ken what he thought about the offer; and his reply was: "Well, I can see you and him, but look what I get stuck with…"

I could not hide my distaste when I expressed that I was shocked that he'd even consider it. To that he tried to back-peddle and say he was just commenting on the imbalance; and not that he'd be interested. We discussed it further and it did seem to me that if the woman would have been more appealing, he would have been quite prepared to participate.

We laughed it off at the time, but that was the turning point. I also recalled that during our couples counseling I learned that Ken had been introduced to pornography by his brothers when he was only fourteen. At the time I did not realize how damaging that can be. However since then I have learned a great deal about the effects of porn on young minds. It breaks my heart every time I think about how that robbed Ken of the fulfilling love life he truly deserved; and perhaps is still doing so today.

I was never into porn. Ken had tried to introduce it into our sex life; but it disgusted me. I did not find it inspiring at all. And I tried, I really did, for his sake. But I just could not get into the perversions involved.

My girlfriends took me out to one of these strip clubs for my stagette before I married Paul and I hated it. It embarrassed me. And trust me when I say I was not a total prude in bed. I had some pretty racy lingerie, with the moves to match; and enjoyed role-playing… I just did not enjoy watching others do it.

I do pinpoint that as yet another disappointment for Ken. I get it that, after four years things were becoming a bit routine and he was trying to spice things up and I was resisting. Actually, it was more than resisting. I'd tried to step into that world and I just could not do it; and he recognized that I could not do it.

On July 1st 2000 Ken called me to tell me he was going to start seeing other women. Apparently he was scouting the online dating sites; and they were scouting him. He found a woman named Deborah who was raising her granddaughter who was 7 at the time, I believe. Ken's son was 9 by then; so the distance in ages was much less.

Ken and this new Deborah were married less than a year later. They moved within blocks of me and had two dogs. Ken came to visit me soon after he was married so I could see the ring on his finger. It was all a game to him, I guess…

He proved, just as all the men in my life proved, just how easy I could be replaced. He wanted to be married. It didn't matter who it was, just so the position was filled. Even now I can feel dull remnants of the pain of realizing that he was just like all the rest. He was no different after all.

Seven years and all we'd enjoyed together was not enough. I heard that he once said, to a mutual friend of ours, that he was just with the wrong Deborah all that time. What? Seriously?

Looking back now I can see that deep down I expected that he would date a few women and would realize what we had the way I did when I strayed… Oh yes, I'd strayed.

When we first separated and Ken moved in with his father I took up with a fellow I met through work. This fellow and I had exchanged flirtations on a regular basis for years and it became real for me when Ken was gone.

I was very up front with it. I did not try to hide it. I told Ken that I felt we needed to move on to other people. And at the time I meant it and I really thought that was it for us. At the time I really believed that Ken and I were finished.

See, that's what PTSD does for a person. It prevents a person from being able to really think a thing through. After I'd come so far along with making sure that I treated him right and I was being so careful to respect him as a person; I turned around and abruptly walked away for some guy I hardly knew? Really? Clearly I was not 'thinking'.

However, for the first time in my life I regretted 'moving on'. All this fellow did was magnify how hollow our relationship was compared to Ken and me. All I could do was compare him to Ken and there was just *NO* contest. The more I was with this other guy, the more I missed Ken.

There is a song out right now entitled *Reminding Me* by Shawn Hook where a man and woman both say that 'He (she) keeps reminding me how good it was when we were crazy… in love. He (She) keeps reminding me that you're still gone and I'm still lonely'.

The reason I moved on was because I was convinced, by that time, that I was just a rebound for Ken. He was still very emotionally attached to his ex-wife during the initial phase of our relationship. . She was all he talked about.

We had friends over one evening who knew Ken and his ex for a number of years. The entire evening was spent talking about her. The red flags went up; but I ignored them. I really wanted him and I was willing to ride it out until he got over it.

And after I'd strayed Ken worked so hard to get me back. And he was so open about it to everyone he worked with at the time. He was selling photocopiers for a large distributor who had a dozen sales representatives and an equal number of support staff. He had quite the audience for his pursuit and determination to get me back; and so he did. He won me back; however, I was already halfway there before he even started.

Yet I never told him these things at the time. Most of it was so far beyond my reach cognitively that I would not be able to put it into words. PTSD is all about reacting to triggers… you bounce around like a pinball; occasionally you hear a bell or two go off, and you know that the bells mean something; but you have no clue what that is… so you just keep reacting… fight or flight; and for me it was always flight.

So, I only realize *NOW* that, at the time, I subliminally thought he'd experience the same thing with dating other women; and we'd reunite again with both of us firmly on the same page. But that is not how it happened.

There was no happy ending where we run across a field into each other's arms so clearly aware of ourselves and each other with a love so deep, so solid, that nothing could ever block it again.

At the time the pain was so severe for me that it was like a bear plunging its claws into my throat as deep as possible and tearing down to the top of my pelvic bone. Not cutting, but tearing, shredding, pulling my guts out and I could see them spill out onto the floor.

Every breath I took just sent sharper pain across my chest so I could not breathe properly, but I'd breathe real shallow to try to prevent another bolt of lightning from shooting and searing across my heart.

However; at the time, I just put my head down and dedicated myself to my work and to my daughter. I thought that if Ken and I could not make marriage work, then I could not make any relationship work in this life. I was finished. I was truly finished. At the time it was simply like being completely done eating your favorite meal over and over and over again until you could not possibly eat another bite of it. I did *NOT* feel pain at the time... the PTSD protected me from that; rather, I just fled to the next thing to keep me occupied.

At the time, when our little Shih Tzu would sit at the top of the stairs watching the door waiting for Ken to come home, my heart would break for her. I'd say, "No Ken, baby... Ken's not coming back..." and she'd hang her head and drop her tail and come to me and I'd hold her, and rock her, and I am certain I saw tears in her eyes more than once... But I did not cry; not at the time.

I'd been chasing relationships since I was fifteen; and each and every man in my life abandoned me; or betrayed me; plus robbed me; and that's starting with my own father!

Until Ken, I took the full blame for the deterioration of the relationship because I recognized that I was emotionally absent, I had a sharp tongue, and very little patience.

But with Ken I'd corrected all of that. But thanks to porn, it was not enough for him. The man that walked out of my home the day I discovered he was remarried was not the man I'd met and fallen in love with; fell madly in love with (I might add) in 1993. This time it was not my fault that the relationship did not stand the test of time.

Ken could not bridge the gap that porn created between us any more than I could. I understood that.

At the time; and every time I faced such harsh loss, PTSD allowed me to see it logically and enabled me to take steps to flee to the next thing that would keep me occupied and emotionally absent.

PTSD both robbed me and rescued me. It caused me to make poor choices and blocked me from proper communication; but it also enabled me to survive the consequences.

I often wonder how happy Ken is now in his sixties. I wonder if the orgies and the porn are enough at age 60. What we had for those four short years was rare indeed. I am grateful that I was able to taste, and live, what a true love would feel like. At least now I know I'm not missing anything in this life regarding love relationships; because for me, that came around only once in this life. So I don't have to go looking for it again. I can be content with the memories for now while I look forward to the next life when I will have true love again.

And sometimes I see people who appear as if they have their true love here and now; and have had for some time. When that happens I am so happy for them because I really do know how they feel.

I can also completely sympathize with anyone who loses their loved one to death. How devastating that is. I know that pain of loss that is so final. There is no waiting for it to get better like having a bad cold that keeps you from enjoying life for a while, but eventually goes away and you can get on with life as you knew it before you caught the cold.

There are no words that can truly describe the pain of that bear claw starting at your throat and shredding all the way to your pelvic bone. It leaves very deep scars. And just as any scar tissue does, these scars feel nothing. Scars replace live tissue with dead, dry, coarse cells that feel nothing at all. All the nerves have been ripped away, to never grow back.

I wonder if my early introduction to intimate relations between a man and a woman is what set the perception for me. What I mean is that I never feel sexual arousal unless I am in a relationship with someone I am attracted to; and who I know is attracted to me.

I never understood my girlfriends saying they 'needed to get laid'. They talked about it as if it was like getting your teeth cleaned at the dentist. They 'needed to'? To me that behavior is not something that is independently initiated. Without the reciprocal exchange of mutual attraction, the drive to have sex does not initiate with me at all…

And if that's hard to believe, get this: I was thinking back to my junior high school days once and I recalled the guys teasing us girls and saying that we girls all had big hairy lips. I argued with these guys saying that was ridiculous because it was men who got beards, not women. And even then it made no sense to me because beard hair did not grow on the lips; but around the mouth. I just wrote it off to them being stupid…

I was fifty years old before I finally got it and finally understood what they were referring to. I kid you not! Anyway, back to my story.

So, after Ken found a suitable replacement for me (punch number one), I put my head down and focused on my work and my daughter. And the first thing that happened after Ken left was that I'd exhausted all my options to get my gift line off the ground to no avail!!

Punch number two… I had to put the gift line down with a debt of fifty thousand dollars of research and development with no prospect of bringing in a dime to cover it. So all I could do was turn to the only revenue stream I had going for myself; the cold calling.

Between year 2000 and 2006 I maintained a steady stream of contract work providing the cold calling efforts to grow businesses.

I would answer ads for a sales person and then introduce my program offering to make the sales people the company already had more productive. Most of the time I would gain a new contract just before the money from the last contract ran out. At least it worked enough to keep me warm and well fed. However, the gaps between projects were beginning to prove costly and I could not get ahead of the debt incurred during the down time. At the same time, I was just getting older!

And losing Ken and the gift line was just the first and second of the 'one/two/three punch' that was going to send me into a tailspin and then directly into an emotional crash.

However, before I tell you about the third punch; I want you to understand more about the work I was doing regarding the cold calling efforts.

First of all it was all business-to-business. The only exception to that was when I worked for Ken while he was with the moving companies. I described the effort to my perspective new clients as being similar to launching a rocket. The amount of fuel that is blown out to lift that rocket the first three inches off the ground is tremendous. However, the amount of fuel necessary would diminish as the rocket gained momentum; and, once the rocket was out of the gravitational pull, it would be easy to maneuver and maintain ongoing follow up to acquire new clients.

Likewise, the project had to be front-loaded with an extremely high level of effort. The number of contacts accomplished to effectively arouse interest in whatever my client was offering had to provide a sufficient number of new sales to, not only pay for the project; but realize a profit as well.

I would take an initial payment up front, usually fifty percent of the entire project cost. A set amount of time would be established to realize the desired results. The balance of the project cost was then paid out as a monthly retainer; and finally, a percentage of the profit would follow the conclusion of the project. The final payment was actually my profit. Up until that point, I was merely breaking even.

Sounds and looks great on paper. However, each and every time the client would crash the program before the necessary time to realize the results would elapse. That way they could pick up the calls at the follow up stage and not pay anything more!

And they'd be really harsh about it too. They wanted to really crush me so I'd have no fight to take them to court. And this went on for at least two years.

I kept upgrading my contract and improving my presentation to ensure that I was managing expectation; but they'd always crash it. It was exhausting. And it was excruciating to have to go on and try to obtain another contract; but it was all I knew how to do. I was trapped and suffering punishment for my own success; because the program always produced new business… always!

I did finally discover that one of the photocopier managers that I was able to use as a reference was coaching these business owners and managers how to screw me over! Rather than take the goose that laid the golden eggs and run with it so everyone could make lots of money; they were content with just that initial success and then reveled in crushing me for it. They'd have the goose that laid the golden eggs for dinner and think they were shrewd businessmen for it.

I ended up taking the last of that group to court and got three-quarters of my money and that ended the cycle. And that was in 2003. I rewrote the manual (the first manual was written in 1999) on the calling effort that I'd studied since 1995 and from there contracts were better and the clients held up their end of the deal.

In 2006 when I obtained a contract with a local marketing company; who had gained its position in the market in the late 80s to the early 90s when the thriving oil companies had to prepare a mandatory annual report to the Alberta Government. To supplement this main income stream they also developed logos and branding for printed marketing materials such as brochures and letterhead; and of course websites.

It was yet another husband and wife run business. That was the only level of business that was willing to consider my offer; because businesses on the next level up already had a marketing department and therefore already had a marketing plan of their own.

The wife ran the show and her husband just needled her to get more business by emotionally manipulated her; so she in turn manipulated all the workers. Their staff of 25 turned over on a regular basis. She was pure hell to work for; but she really believed in the cold calling marketing method, so this was the first project that just kept renewing and growing!

In February of 2006 my daughter's dad died of cancer. He was only forty-eight at the time. His son was only fourteen at the time. It was truly heartbreaking and; even though she wrote an incredible eulogy and delivered it at his funeral like a pro, my daughter did not adjust to his death at all.

All she did was cry. She'd lay on the floor because; she said, she could not get any lower, and if she could, she would have. She lost weight until she was just skin over bones. She went to university every day, as it was her junior year. However she was not learning anything. She just could not concentrate.

She did not see me as a confidant in this case because of the divorce. Finally I did call the school. I said that I was well aware that, by the time a student is in University, the parents no longer meet the teacher, or call the school. However, when I explained to them what was going on they said they'd intervene. And they did! I am sure they saved my daughter's life.

My daughter was a straight A student all through high school. Her average was 3.8 right up to and until this semester. However, the school did step in and rearranged her exams and provided a support group for her. I truly do not believe she would have survived it otherwise.

By 2012 I was able to hire staff of my own and this marketing company client became my corner stone account around which I could take on additional short-term projects and run a staff of callers.

We all worked from home; and by that time, being on the computer was so convenient for us all. We worked off of simple Excel spreadsheets; and communication between us was either by phone or email. It was going great. I was finally into six figures and my overhead was just the hours I had to pay my staff; and so I paid them very well!

As the year 2012 started I also hired a fellow who was a retired insurance salesman. I'd known him and his wife for several years. They had initially retired to Mexico, but had to return to Calgary to assist their daughter who had a two year old with cancer; who did eventually survive it by the way.

He really needed to work again; and we will call him Dominick. I hired him and I hired the first of my calling staff at the same time; and we'll call her Lizah (pronounced: Lies-ah). These names are very fitting for this duo.

Dominick actually knew Lizah, as she was their neighbor. He had gotten to know her and her husband rather well. And because I knew him and trusted him, I felt confident to hire Lizah and train both of them to do the cold calling according to my process.

Please remember here again, I'd studied this process to the point where I had an Excel spreadsheet that calculated exactly how many calls had to be done to achieve the desired results. And it had never failed up to this point. I tracked every project and I had proof that the program worked.

As soon as Lizah was trained I had her take over the calling I was still doing for my cornerstone account to; therefore, free up more time for myself to seek and gain more projects.

Dominick was to be my GM and maintain existing clients for me so the cash flow remained steady and healthy.

I would start every project. When it achieved a certain level of success, I'd transition it to one of my staff to continue to grow it. The plan had benchmarks that corresponded to a particular length of time.

The clients were fully aware of how the program worked, as I would leave them with a copy of the manual. In fact, I often trained someone to stay with the client as an employee (as a one-to-one marketing person, as I called it); and I would collect a small placement fee to cover the training of a new staff member. Everybody won. It was a wonderful program and it was making great process.

That transition occurred around March of 2012. By December of the same year, Dominick and Lizah had managed to 'steal' my cornerstone account for themselves! Even as I type these words my legs start shaking and my knees go to jelly. My heart is pounding and I have to breathe in a shallow manner to prevent those shredding, tearing pains… even though it is somewhat in the background for me now, it is still there. This was the third punch that nearly took my life.

Two other short-term projects had just concluded. The girls I had phoning for those projects were looking to move onto the one I was just grooming to transition into having the both of them do the calling rather than myself. In fact, I'd already introduced them both to the project and everyone was getting along; and the project was moving along very well.

This, by the way, was a local media company who produced TV commercials and/or video for a website. They were second in their industry; and soon to be number one, as rumor had it that the current number one in the industry was dismantling. The owner had passed away.

Regarding my own situation however, with my main cornerstone project just gone out from under me; along with my GM and senior caller; and with no placement fee, I had maybe sixty days till the money ran out.

The time of year was against me as sell, plus I had no real prospects to bring on any new projects within the sixty days that I had to survive (financially). You see, whenever I started a project it took at least three full months to get the momentum established. Therefore, that removed me from seeking other business for the duration of the start-up of any new project.

It also took three months to convince an interested company to take the risk and make an investment in the program. I wasn't the only game in town.

(Note: after I finished writing the segment about the third punch I had to go and take a very hot bubble bath. I'd broken out into a sweat and I just felt like I really needed a bath. So I did that; and now I'm back...)

Due to the circumstances, I had to keep the only project operating at the time as my own so I could continue to eat and pay rent. All the others were married and their income earned working with me was extra income for them. They were all very understanding; even sympathetic, for my situation.

And even though they were all very understanding, even to the point of being offended by what Dominick and Lizah had done; it was extremely devastating to me.

You may recall how my guidance counselors encouraged me to go into the college-prep division of my high school? Well, I was completely devastated then, as well, when my parents took that dream away. You may recall that I'd feebly attempted suicide at that time.

When my brother was born, we were still living in the trailer. Dad had taken the wall out between my sister's room and my own to make one bedroom for us both. So, when my brother was born, he was put in the bedroom, in his crib, with my sister and I had to sleep on a rollaway bed in the living room.

Because my mom wanted to stay up and watch TV until midnight; I had to go sleep in their bed until she'd come to get me and I'd roll my bed to the living room and finish the night there.

The reason I am bringing this up now is because I was twelve or thirteen at the time that I took a whole bottle of Aspirin hoping I'd not wake up the next morning. And when I did, I was so surprised and I commented, "Oh, I'm awake?"

And my dad said, "Well, of course you're awake, what did you expect?" And I said, "I took the pills hoping I wouldn't wake up."

And he said, "What pills?" So I told him and he went and got the empty bottle from the medicine cabinet in the bathroom and brought it out.

He said I was stupid for thinking such a thing and that this medicine was expensive and how he'd have to buy another bottle. He said if I ever tried something like that again that I'd better do it right or he'd do it for me.

Looking back on it now, to me it was a 'whole bottle'. However, it was probably only a few left in the bottom of the bottle. I remember they filled the palm of my hand; but it was certainly not a full bottle.

My ears were ringing and I felt light-headed at the time, but that soon wore off and I had no other reaction to it.

And throughout my life, after that attempt (and the one when I was pregnant *not by my husband*), I would think about how to best commit suicide to really get it right.

Well, after Dominick and Lizah pulled their client-stealing stunt the drive to finally do it right was so overwhelming. I could not cry hard enough or long enough to relieve the pain. I couldn't get drunk, because I'd drink myself sober and just go straight to the hangover.

The drive to just plunge a knife into my heart was equally as strong as my conscience was telling me it would be the unforgivable sin to take my own life. It was not my life to take. My life had been given to me by God, and God had been there for me before, so he could be there for me again through this…

So, I went back to the deal with God. The deal was that I would sit down and write out my plan and my note regarding how I wanted things taken care of after I was gone.

Then I would put the plan in the envelope and wait one more day. If, after one more day, I still felt the same; I could go ahead and take my own life. And of course, the effort relieved the nagging in my head so I could finally sleep; and so by the next day the drive would be gone and I'd tear up the plan and the letter that was meant for my survivors.

And that's how I survived 2012. After waiting that one more day, I shook it off (long before Taylor Swift did so) and carried on.

Chapter Ten
Can It Get Any Worse?

Working at home presented a double-edged sword. On one hand it was great to save the time and expense travelling to and from an office every day; along with not having to buy clothes to keep up with the fashion statements, and packing lunch. But best of all, it spared me the office politics. I could put my head down and just do the job. And that's when I was at my best. When I was left alone to just do the job, to be absorbed in it, to feel the momentum.

When I sat down to hunt for new clients I could hear the thunder of horse's hooves as they charged past the starting line at the Calgary Stampede Chuck Wagon Races. I could feel the exhilaration of rounding the first curve in a stock car race. And yes, I'd driven a stock car once at a training facility just so I could know that feeling.

On the other hand, the out-of-sight-out-of-mind aspect of working at home became the challenge of this particular project. Managing client expectation was always a pain where I sit; however, up until this project I had been able to do it very effectively by maintaining a marketing plan and referring back to it as the project moved along. When the client would see that the benchmarks were being met, they were always satisfied that their investment was evolving as forecast.

However, this time I was working for yet another person who would rather compete with me. You could tell that she was always disappointed when I answered her questions as she'd always reply with 'that's interesting'.

I'd met her and worked with her for a short time at the marketing company that had just been stolen from me. She was a project manager for a while there and ended up leaving because the owner was such a bag to work for.

Apparently one day the owner of the marketing company yelled at this woman (who was now my boss) in front of everyone and actually called her some very shocking things. She (my current boss) handed in her resignation the next day; but still stayed to work the final two weeks. I thought she and I had an understanding between us. I really thought she and I were on the same page and understood direct sales for what it is.

Eventually she hired a wanna-be consultant who she found on LinkedIn. This would-be hero (who I always called 'boy wonder') came in and stomped all over my work. He dug into the database, like they always do, and just destroyed the momentum. Needless to say, I was let go so they could afford boy wonder. Fortunately, I did see this one coming and had put out several resumes to a number of published opportunities. That is, I managed to answer a number of want ads for sales people in between writing another suicide plan as well.

I could tell that boy-wonder was all talk and more impressed with himself than anything else. I found out later that he never did bring in any new business worth mentioning. All he did was destroy the existing momentum I'd established and cost them a great deal of time and money.

By now it was the early spring of 2014 and I interviewed with two opportunities that I didn't even want. However, I'd always take an interview opportunity just for the practice. And currently the third option was very interesting.

It was with a fairly well established software developer who offered a full inventory/accounting program complete with the hardware (actual computers) to go with it. The minimum anyone could work with them for was twenty-five thousand; and that was bare bones. Thirty thousand was far more realistic.

My interview went very well. I really connected with the President. I went home after my first interview and prepared a presentation for my second interview. I researched their competition and prepared a one-to-one marketing plan to grow their business.

On my second interview this fellow was totally impressed. I demonstrated my Excel spreadsheet and revealed how many calls I knew I had to make to find that first sale. I forecast six to eight months to find it.

The research on the competition was very impressive as well. He was most intrigued as I demonstrated to him how they fit into the current market and what market share he could hope to capture within the first, second, and third years of my one-to-one marketing program.

I was asked to return for a third interview; and as I was leaving, the receptionist said I was the only candidate that had prepared a presentation. With that bit of information I was confident that; if I was not offered the job, it was definitely not meant to be. And, I would not want to work with a company that was not willing to give the job to the candidate who demonstrated that they'd do their homework.

Not to mention the fact that I had tangible evidence that I knew what I was doing. So many sales people come into a company and spend most of their time selling and reselling the management on how great they are in spite of their lack of results; like boy-wonder did. My attitude was that I was going to come into the company and put my head down and do the job and bring in the results, period. I maintained the marketing plan and updated it with the results to demonstrate to my client that the job was being done; and done right.

The third interview involved meeting the other managers of the other departments and answering 'skill testing questions'; as I like to call it. Everyone thinks they are so clever and they rarely realize that the candidate is sizing them up just as much as they are sizing up the candidate.

The second in command was a young (mid-thirties) ex-minor-league baseball player. And yes, he'd been the pitcher. Prior to working for this software company, he had been a manager of one of the businesses this software company had acquired early in their history. I was going to have to work very closely with this fellow.

For the past ten years this fellow (we'll call him #2, because he was so full of it) had grown the company organically by obtaining referrals from the existing clientele; and, through some of the people he'd known in the industry. While this is a very legitimate process; and a delicate one, it is very different than cold direct sales into companies who don't know you from Adam; and especially when you are talking about introducing these companies to a thirty thousand dollar investment.

The president of the company, who I'd report to directly, was a sixty year old (so my age) ex-stock-car racer who had not been out on any sales calls for twenty years. And while he had been on the front lines at that time; and did the direct cold sales, twenty years had changed the market drastically. Plus, I was female; and we have to do things differently, especially in sales, because women cannot get away with what men can get away with when approaching business owners. We'll call this guy #1; because he, himself, was all he really cared about.

I also met the two software developers who were surprisingly my age as well. This really surprised me. Being somewhat technically challenged myself, I did fully expect the developer to be in their mid-thirties like #2. However, after I thought it through, it made sense that #1 and the developers launched the business together twenty years ago; and therefore, all the additional support staff would be younger. However, the founders of the company were my age or slightly older.

The final interview of my third visit was back with #1. I told him then that my main concern was the fact that I was technically challenged. I told him that I can work the initial educational aspects of the sale. However, when it got to the technicalities of demonstrating how the system would work for them, I'd need #2 to be willing to carry that segment to the close until I learned it; which could take some time.

To that #1 said that they were fully aware of my technical-ignorance and said that was exactly what they wanted. He told me that they'd hired someone a year or so ago who proved uncooperative in that he felt he knew how to program better than #2. So, rather than getting on the phone and getting the job of selling under way, this new salesperson wanted to reprogram and upgrade their software to better suit the current demands.

Well, that was music to my ears. If they didn't expect me to become a programmer I was ready for the challenge.

The remuneration package was wonderful too. Because the initial sale was the biggest cash investment; and because the ongoing support was where they made ongoing profit, they offered me a base of forty-two thousand per year paid monthly; and twenty percent of the net initial sale!

After one year I'd be eligible for their health benefit package which would apply only if I became an employee; which I did not want to do. So it was at this point that I introduce the option of just contracting me; and I'd forego the benefit package. I had my own benefits through my own company.

I'd already prepared a proposal for contracting me and left it with #1. He told me that they would all get together and discuss the candidates and I was to come back the following week, on the same day of the week, and at the same time for their answer. He said that if I was not awarded the position, I'd be told why. To which I thought to myself that I would not care why at that point.

I decided right then and there that if he said I was not awarded the position, I'd just up and walk out. I would not have wasted one more second of my time with them.

The position was awarded to me and they agreed to contract me. However, they demanded that I work from their offices rather than from home. By this time I had been working from home since I left the position with the Alberta Liberal Party in March 1997. It was now May 2014… do the math!

And to further complicate the matter, they were in the worst possible location for me to access from where I lived at the time. However, I had to agree. I needed to get to work as the bank account was in desperate need of input. Besides, the office they were giving me was a huge corner office an executive cherry-faux-wood desk and credenza; and boy did I have plans for it.

We went back and forth for nearly three weeks before the contract was finally acceptable to them. I must admit that by that time I was not paying much attention to their moving a comma here and changing a semi-colon there… rather, I was already deeply entrenched on developing my list to begin calling.

The training was conducted solely by #1. He was a real Brian Tracey fan. And while I appreciate Brian Tracey very much; he was just one aspect of sales. In fact, all of the paperback sales training was designed to address a specific set of circumstances.

It wasn't until I had studied so many of them that I found the perfect combination was: Xerox; Brian Tracey; Tom Hopkins; and Dale Carnegie to provide the complete and full spectrum of skills; processes and procedures; and insight to be really effective in direct (stone cold, business-to-business) sales.

Throughout the six full weeks of training #1 focused upon product knowledge. He said he was not going to teach me how to sell, but rather WHAT to sell. He recognized our likenesses and our differences and he was comfortable with both.

I found their program to be very easy to understand from a user's point of view; which was the one I had to have to sell it to users. However, demonstrating it did take some time for me to become proficient and smooth.

There was another plus with this company. It was *NOT* a mom and pop shop! This was a small company of actual professionals who came together and built a four million dollar company. Of course I researched this company, as I did all my prospective projects to see if they could afford me.

Finally! I had finally found the company that was going to take me to retirement. It was so perfect for me. There was no whispering at the water cooler. Everyone came to work and kept their nose to the grindstone from the time they arrived until the time that they left. I felt that all my previous experience culminated into providing me with the honed expertise to do this job.

All my previous projects had also left me with a broad range of contacts. Because I changed industries every time I changed projects, there was no conflict. Therefore, I had a database of people who at least knew me and who I could draw upon initially to obtain at least one sale to make up for the fact that the monthly draw I was being paid was two hundred dollars short of my overhead costs at the time.

#1 told me that I should not expect to close a sale for at least eighteen months from the time I finished the initial training. Well, that was not soon enough for me! I had to close a sale within six to eight months to survive the stolen client and being fired from the media company within two years of each other. Had my sales forecast not clearly shown the possibility to close a sale within six to eight months, I would not have pursued the opportunity. However, I certainly did not tell them that little fact. I thought it best to let them be pleasantly surprised when my program produced an initial sale within eight months maximum.

In the meantime, my daughter was planning a wedding. The date was August 16th of that year. And on top of that, my landlord decided she was going to sell the townhouse I'd been renting as my business location since 1991.

There was certainly no money to buy the place and it broke my heart. I tried to get my daughter and her future husband to assist me in keeping it; but they saw no value in my place. To them it was old and outdated and in need of so much renovation that they though it was better if I moved into my daughters townhouse; that was about one fourth of the size, and even further from where I worked.

So, after losing my cornerstone account in December 2012; getting let go before the media project properly matured in March 2014; I started the new job with the computer systems company in May 2014 that demanded a great deal of product knowledge training. In August my only daughter, my only family, was getting married.

A bright spot was, in October (six months from my start date of May 4) of that same year when I had the signature of my first Computer Systems sale; and then I had to move out of the place I called home for 22 years and loved dearly; and painfully had to downsize severely; which was not my idea; and I was not ready for it either

Yet, by mid-December (eight months from my start date with the Computer Systems Company) I picked up the check for the down payment of that first sale and was one more step closer to a 14,301.25 commission! My first sale was over seventy-two thousand dollars for the entire system that they needed.

Oh yeah! Victory dance in the end zone... However, keep in mind that I was really running on empty during all of this. I struggled to get through the day each and every day. The commute every morning was grueling. By lunchtime every day I had to put my head down on the desk and just catch a quick nap. Even though I was getting to bed early every night, and I was laying low on weekends, I just could not seem to catch up. I felt exhausted all the time.

In addition, there was a catch to the commission payment (there always is). The commissions were not paid until the company paid out the initial cash investment; which actually made perfect sense.

Payment terms were not an option with the Computer Systems Company. Rather, the new client had to either find a leasing company; or get a loan from their bank; or find some way to pay for the entire system within thirty days of the installation; providing everything was working properly.

Understand too that this was a catch only for the first sale for me just because I was so desperate for cash myself by this time. The credit line balance just kept getting higher with a wedding dress and some of the other necessary accessories for the wedding on top of drawing two hundred every month to cover the shortfall of my paychecks.

And I was warned that these deals often go sideways. It's a lot of money and buyer's remorse was a huge possibility when working with big ticket items like this.

On the other hand; my first sale was to a very well established mom and pop company, who I met stone cold, over the phone in August 2014, by the way. It was actually the very first online presentation that I did completely on my own because #2 was not available for the appointment the only day the prospect had time to spend forty minutes getting to know the program enough to make an initial informed decision to spend the hours it was going to take to plan the installation.

It was the end of October when the prospect signed the plans and committed to the sale. The fifty percent deposit for the system was due on or before December fifteenth. The full installation date was scheduled for March first. If all went well, and the client paid on time thirty days after installation; I'd have my commission check by mid-April or the beginning of May at the latest.

I'll never forget the day I walked out of the prospects office with their deposit check in hand. It truly felt like redemption. And even though there was plenty of time for things to fall apart, I just knew it wouldn't fall apart.

This well-established mom and pop company had been looking at computer systems for over a year. This fellow understood computer programming enough to recognize the best program for his company. He told me several times that this program was, by far, the best one he'd seen and was so glad that he'd waited until he found us rather than settling for something that was just close enough.

I allowed myself to finally exhale. I felt grounded and secure in the job and looked forward to growing with them. I still had lots to learn; but I was fully immersed in this, and I was confident with it. I also had three more companies I was nurturing along the exact same way I'd worked with this company. I expected I'd have another close within the first quarter of the coming new year.

Then I took the last two weeks of December off that year and I just slept, and slept, and slept some more. However, it didn't seem to help. Maybe I slept too much?

No matter what I did I was struggling with such low energy that I'd still have to take a twenty-minute power nap at lunch just to get through the day. The pressure was off, but I was not invigorated by it this time. I dragged through January and since my sale closed it seemed that #1 and #2 were not pleased with it.

It was such a bizarre reaction. They congratulated me, but it was almost as if they were embarrassed that I'd accomplished this. They were meeting often to work out the details of setting up the new client and all that seemed normal; yet I sensed something was wrong. But I was just too exhausted to try to figure it out. I wrote off the feelings to exhaustion and just ignored them. It was all I could do to get myself to work and back home every day.

I thought back to the first in-house sales meeting I'd arranged for myself and #2. He seemed nervous and I was confused by that. He also let me know how inconvenient this was for him because he was always *SO* busy.

When he finally did join us I had already completed the demonstration as far as I was able to.

My prospect was a perfect candidate for the minimum program. His business was just about to cross the three million dollar mark this year. He brought his accountant with him who had been with him for the past two years of growth.

I recognized this accountant from my years as a participant in the Chamber of Commerce social events for networking between 1998 and 2000. She approached me at one of these events wanting to do my books for my business. She worked out of her home like the rest of us; and I actually did try to work with her. However, after I dropped off my books and files (which consisted of a huge Tupperware-like portable file box; all very well organized) she just gave me excuse after excuse and the work just did not get done. I finally had to go to her home and demand that she return my documents. I was nearly late with my year-end that year.

Fortunately she did not recognize me. When #2 came in we were at the stage of the presentation where the accounting segment needed to be demonstrated. #2 started and this accountant immediately interrupted and asked a series of questions one after another like rapid-fire from a machine gun.

#2 looked like a deer in the headlights… so I stepped in and started writing her questions down one at a time and made sure we had her questions correct.

Then I said to #2 that he could address the questions one at a time and read the first one from my notes. While he still looked like deer in the headlights, he managed to answer the first three questions. However, on the fourth one he stumbled a bit and she interrupted again and said that the program looked like it was weak in this area. She said it was an inventory program and that her process handled the inventory just fine and remained focused on the accounting; which she said was the most important aspect of growing a business.

Again, #2 just sat there looking stunned and stupid. I could not believe that he did not have an answer for her. He'd been with this company seventeen years and he could not answer this objection? Panic started in the pit of my stomach; however, no one would have seen it. So I said that perhaps we could ask our accountant to come in and cover this aspect. I turned to my prospective client and said we all work as a team here and everyone has their area of expertise as I walked over to the phone to call in our head accountant who trains the clients on the accounting component upon installation.

However, she didn't pick up. So I said I'd go to her office and then #2 finally found his voice enough to say that she was out training this morning; along with our other accounting expert. To which our little snip accountant said, "Oh, so what happens if one of your clients has an accounting problem this morning? Who would assist them if your entire accounting team is off-site? It sounds to me as if you are not in a position to be taking on any more new clients."

She then turned to my prospect and said, "We should just go, this is clearly a waste of time." And he was all too happy to jump up and get out of there.

To this day I wish I had called her out right then and there for who I knew she really was. But what good would that do at this point? I could not answer her objection as my training stopped at the superficial at that point; and yet, neither could #2 answer her objection. I would have just looked like a bitter rookie and would seal off any future possibilities with this prospect if I'd responded aggressively. At least by letting it go I could get back to him in a year or so when I knew more and could demonstrate that we'd grown enough to take him on…

On the other hand, to this day I wish I would have called out #2… he clearly demonstrated that he was *NOT* a sales person. He was the same as any housewife selling Avon or Tupperware. He was fine with the warm market efforts; but no way could he stand up to open market sales, even after seventeen years with the same product.

He had been the counter person in an auto parts distributor and thought he was a salesperson, when he was actually just customer service, and order taker.

He came out of the boardroom after they'd left as white as a sheet and said, "What a piece of work that chick is, hey?"

Right then I should have said, "Seventeen years and you could not answer her questions?" But I didn't. I just turned and headed for my office to lick my wounds.

Then on February 16, 2015 #1 called me into his office. #2 was in BC visiting a client that was expanding their business and would need additional computers and software. I grabbed my clipboard fully prepared to take notes. As I walked in it felt like the air was thick and I wasn't able to breathe except for those short shallow breaths I'd come to know all too well.

I sat down in my usual spot on the opposite side of his desk and he said, "Today will be our last day together. There is nothing you can say to change the decision; it is final. However, I do want to explain to you why this decision was made…" and from there, I could not hear what he was saying because my ears were sizzling, my head was light, and now I really couldn't breathe.

All I could do was say, "What? What?" And then the flood of tears burst forth and I could not control it. He was taken quite by surprise and said he realized that this was probably a shock to me and offered me a glass of water. He left the room promptly and returned just as fast with a glass of water.

My skin burned as if on fire. The clothes on my skin felt like sandpaper on rug burns. I could not think. I did not see this coming at all. Not this time. Not right after my victory and I had three more companies, who were very interested; and who just needed to find time to get all their decision-makers together for my demo of the software so they could make a decision.

I'd perfected doing the demo right over the internet so I didn't have to travel to their offices in the middle of the day and in all kinds of traffic. #1 felt it was necessary for me to just drop in on these prospective clients and persist in asking them questions before I offered the demo. And because I was not doing this, he was saying that it was reason to let me go.

It made sense to me that after I'd managed to get a sale closed; with the help of #2 of course, that #1 would simply realize that women just do things a bit differently. Twenty years ago when he dropped in on people and asked questions, those business owners saw a colleague and perhaps a mentor. If I dropped in on them and started asking questions they'd see their mother checking up on them and demanding justification for what they were doing and why they were doing it.

And after he made such a big deal out of not wanting to teach me how to sell, but just *WHAT* to sell, he was now sitting there going on and on about how I was not selling *the way* he wanted me to.

The shock was too much for me. I was too exhausted to deal with this. I was finally broken. I'd never reacted this way in a professional setting, ever in my life, no matter how awful things got.

I could not respond except to cry uncontrollably. Somehow I went back to my office and called my daughter from my desk and told her I was fired. They wanted my key and they wanted me to leave right away; but I could not drive. So #1 called a taxi and said they'd reimburse me for the cost. He just could not get me out of that company fast enough.

I was all by myself with no one to run to; no one to ask for help; no one to talk to.

You can imagine how loud and forceful suicide came to me at this point! All the suicide plans I'd ever made all came rushing back to me like a tsunami. Write it all down again? Really? And why bother? Should I wait one more day? For what? Where in the world do I go from here?

The truth was, I was just too exhausted to act on anything. When I got home, I collapsed and just slept. I do not recall what happened between the day I was fired to the day that I went back to get all my personal things from the office. I do know it was about a week later.

Remember when I said I had plans for that beautiful office? It was a ten-foot by twelve-foot room with windows to the outside as well as to the inside. I'd brought in artificial plants, a beautiful painting entitled "The Window" graced the wall to my immediate right, over the return portion of my desk. I had two computer screens and I really loved that.

There were two guest chairs facing my desk and I was going to get a couch for just inside the door with my first commission check. In the meantime, I'd brought in my chaise lounge chair from my deck and that's where I took my power naps starting in January.

My décor was in stark contrast to the rest of the offices. There was *NOTHING* on the walls. No pictures, no motivational posters, nothing. One of the customer service personnel had a few plants and pictures of her family in her cubicle. There was one plant on the stairs going to the second floor. The reception area had an artificial tree; three guest chairs, a small area rug. The wall behind the reception guest chairs, where a picture could have gone, was a window into #1's office. Oh, yes, there were two pictures on the wall behind the reception desk (beside the window to #1 office). I cannot tell you what they were now. And there was one picture on the wall in the boardroom.

Please understand, I have no idea how a person without PTSD would have reacted to this repeated punishment and disrespect by companies where I'd been successful in obtaining new business for them. All I know is how I reacted. And I was afraid to challenge the firing for fear it would delay my commission payment. Remember, they still owed me over fourteen thousand dollars!

And after the shock wore off, I was so angry this time. This time I could have spit fire. This time I was not going to allow all the past injustices to replay and add to the pain of this most recent blow. This time I was so angry that words like 'fury' and 'infuriated' are just not descriptive enough.

I immediately went to my binder where I kept all of my contracts. And where was the one from the Computer Systems Company? It was not in its proper place in the binder. I stood there looking at the empty spot for the longest time not believing my eyes and my heart pounding in my chest like I'd just run a marathon.

I checked the front cover pocket, perhaps I'd just not filed it. But it was not there either. I checked everywhere through all my files that I thought I'd packed so carefully when I moved.

I still wasn't used to my new place. I felt very unorganized and for me that is very bad. And at this point my anger was quickly turning into shear panic. I tried so hard to think... what had I done with it? Of all times to be careless, of course it had to be now with a 14,000 dollar commission hanging in mid-air.

I recalled that I'd looked at my contract in my desk at work and decided not to take it home until I moved so I could be sure not to lose it. Yet I also seemed to recall taking it home anyway and putting it into its proper place in my company business plan binder. Even though I no longer had to prepare a report for my bank manager for my business credit line, I still maintained the business plan in case I ever had to approach the bank again.

My head started to spin. Did they fire me so they didn't have to pay me my commission? And I had asked #1 the day before if he was happy with the progress. I asked him directly if there was anything else he wanted from me and he replied, "No, everything is fine," which was not what I wanted to hear.

I wanted to hear that he was totally impressed that I'd secured a sale a full year before he projected that I would. At the time I went back to my office wondering what the *H* a person had to do to get a compliment around there. I really thought I'd out-lived the male vs. female issues in the work place by this age. However, I remained confident that my sale gave me some grounding; and yet here I was fired yet again... a victim of my own success... my anger became fury and the fury became the most intense anger I'd ever felt. And again, had I had more testosterone in my system, I may have been building a bomb by now...

But instead, my mind was whisked back to the personnel company I worked for in the early eighties. I was back in the washroom stall listening to my workmates conspire about what they were going to get me to apologize for this time. They practiced their manipulation techniques by taking turns being offended by something I'd done or said. Then through staged gossip they'd make sure I'd learn of the offense and then the current offended party would bask in toying with me to see how far they could push me and how often they could get me to apologize.

I relived that humiliation as their laughter rang in my head. My mom's voice saying I'd never amount to anything was blending in with the laughter of the kids on the school bus throwing apples at me so they'd splat against the metal window frame throwing pieces into my hair as I ducked to avoid being hit. Anger raging with pain swirling with fear and vulnerability flooded every cell of my being, it seemed.

All I had to do was to get in my car leaving it parked in the garage and start the engine. I didn't need to go to any effort to fix a hose to the exhaust… I just had to roll down the windows. It was a small garage. And that would do it. That would finally end this seemingly unending succession of failure and punishment.

I didn't have to plan anything. There was no need for a note. My daughter knew I was fired yet again and had seen all I'd been going through all these years since my corner stone client had been stolen from me. She'd understand for sure.

She certainly didn't need me anymore. She was married now and had an entire life of her own to keep her fulfilled. I was just baggage. I certainly was no strength for her. My work was really done with her and now I could finally check out and be done with all this.

Exhaustion would win out this time again; and I fell asleep and slept for hours into the early morning.

I woke up numb and made breakfast. I ate and slumped down in the chair in front of my laptop and even to my own amazement, I started looking at want ads… want ads for salespeople.

Next thing I knew I'd updated my resume and was sending it to six possibilities. It was just mindless routine this time. I felt nothing as I researched each company's website. None of them aroused my enthusiasm to grow their company… why should I grow their company? What's in it for me other than getting fired again before I can actually obtain the reward they'd promised?

And yet I had bills to pay and food to buy. Who was I kidding that I'd actually go through with suicide? I could not leave my daughter with that to live with. How would she cope as people would look at her so sympathetically?

And truth be told, even in my darkest hours I'd always have this weird tiny pinhole of light that seemed to represent hope. Why did I always think things had to change for the better? Why did I see each firing as if it must be the last one and that the next opportunity would therefore be the one to pay off like it promises to? Why was I doing the same thing over and over again and expecting different results? Then I remembered:

"The darkest hour is just before dawn…" All of the self-help books and sales training publication I ever read and incorporated into my process always identified failure as just a learning opportunity. Edison (apparently) had thousands of failed attempts to develop the light bulb and identified each failure as a demonstration on how NOT to invent a light bulb. Walt Disney (apparently) went bankrupt several times before successfully launching Disneyland. And that's the determination I had and that's what I was doing! I was not going to be beaten. This was the first time that I stopped and tried to understand why I just kept going on and finding new jobs that would ultimately rip me off. So, that's what drove me. I was convinced each time that it was so bad that it could not get any worse. However, that begged the question: what did I need to change to stop this pattern of boom and bust. What was I doing to perpetuate this cycle? All I was doing was getting older. I was going to be sixty-two in June of 2015.

So, then I have to wonder: with the computer company, should I have not focused upon finding the first sale and spent more time schmoozing # 1? Should I have followed his projection and held off getting that first sale for the first year and a half? And yet I have no idea how that would look. How does one do that? I simply did not know how to do my job except the way I did it; because the way I did it produced sales every time, and that's what I was hired to do. And yet I hear that doing the same thing over and over again while expecting different results is the first sign of insanity...

The truth of the matter was that I was *NOT* expecting 'different' results from my performance. I was expecting to make sales. I was always hired to make sales so, why was I fired every time even though I was doing the job I was hired to do?

I was managing expectation with my reports and yet they'd always find some other reason to fire me.

Could it possibly be that, due to my success they somehow felt that I was bettering them? I always said that I proved every project the same way. I never felt that the success from one company proved the process would work for any other company. They watched the effort. I provided full disclosure into my process; and when the program proved itself for them, was it proving them wrong somehow?

Were there bets going on behind my back with other management; or other peers of theirs, where they were saying it couldn't be done so that; when it did happen, they saw themselves losing somehow?

I remembered the office furniture company I worked for in the eighties. One day Don said to me, "You know how people ask if you want to be right or rich?" and I said I did; and he continued, "Well, I know I can be both!" So, were these guys proving they could be both right and rich by eliminating me from the success and taking it all for themselves?

I also remembered how Paul hated me because I rebuilt the company twice 'my way'... as he put it. It wasn't his company if I built it. Yet to me it was *'US'* building it. Why did he see it as either himself or me?

And how in the world could I possibly be responsible for every manager seeing it that way? Was it the mid-western culture? Would the response have been different if I had been on the east or west coasts?

I was convinced, at this point, that if I had a man to negotiate with (and to buddy-buddy with) the client; and all I did was the grunt work, everything would have been just fine. Clearly the mid-western culture did not permit the woman (alone, with no male counterpart) to be this successful with any sales program.

Not even with her own husband; as Paul had clearly demonstrated.

AND; that was why I'd hired Dominick... and it did work for a while, until he decided to take my corner-stone company for his own... That was his rendition of firing me. One way or another everyone seemed to be determined to separate me from my success so they could claim it for their own.

And this time the computer company was going to accomplish it because I could not find the contract! This time I assisted them in screwing me to the wall because I fell asleep at the wheel. Clearly I had not yet learned how to defend myself properly. Well okay then, let's do better next time.

I did go on several interviews that proved unsuitable for my program; but again, I needed the interview practice.

The one fellow was looking for a jogging partner as well as a salesman to take over a very well established territory.

Now that was worth drooling over. Something I thought I'd never have the opportunity to do; and that was to take over a territory behind a salesman retiring. That would have been heaven on earth for me. Just have to sell to the warm market and not beat my head against the brick wall of the open market.

I'll digress here just a moment to explain. You see, the 'warm market' are the people that already know you; or the product/service you are representing. Tupperware and Mary Kay thrived on turning timid housewives into sales giants by simply giving them a product they could introduce to everyone they knew; and in turn, to everyone their friends and acquaintances knew. This is often referred to as the 'farming' aspect of sales. All the elements are provided and the individual follows a pre-set routine and process and the sales simply just grow from there. And because everyone knows everyone, the results materialize rather quickly. Tupperware and Mary Kay are also 'business-to-consumer' where the numbers of buyers are naturally very high.

The open market is quite a different story. In the open market you, along with your product, are unknown to the people you are approaching about it. Herein lays the true skill of manipulation and education. The skills of manipulation are employed mostly by the con artists who are selling something that does not really benefit the buyer as much as the sale benefits the salesman.

Therefore, a great deal of emotional manipulation is required to move the 'victim' to actually make a purchase.

I, on the other hand, always carried products or services that actually benefitted the buyer; and it was always 'business-to-business'. I saw my job as education and timing. First I wanted to educate the buyer on how the product or service would benefit them; and did so with concrete facts and evidence. And secondly, I would learn when the buyer would be able to buy, and I'd be sure to be there when the time came.

Of course as time went by awaiting the buying cycle to come full circle, a rapport was built so the buyer could have the confidence and trust to actually do business with you.

Buying cycles in business are determined by annual budgeting, change in technology, their own company growth; while consumer buying is often determined just by their wanting to have it.

Rather than manipulate, I paid the dues of time to earn trust based on the work I was willing to do for the buyer to finally fulfill all of his needs necessary to make a sound business decision to make the purchase; and to make the purchase from me. This required time; but more importantly, large numbers of potential buyers. That meant a lot of legwork to obtain the sufficient numbers to produce the required sales to justify my earnings. This is often referred to as 'hunting' as opposed to 'farming'. And one has to be able to withstand a great deal of rejection; and to possess an insurmountable amount of determination to be consistently successful.

I always said that the difference between the amateurs and the professionals was consistency. Anyone who plays golf can go and have a great game, one day. However, having that great game consistently and bettering it with time is the difference.

Also, in the first seven chapters of this book I listed a number of publications that really assisted me to survive one trauma after another.

Well, you'll notice that starting in chapter eight, which begins to cover the twenty years that followed; there are no paperbacks listed. That's because after studying the aforementioned publications and integrating them into my process; from there it was just a matter of practice making perfect. It really is no different than a doctor or dentist who completes their education and then go on to build their 'practice'.

Of course, one has to keep up with journals and new articles on the subject of direct sales, just as any other professional would keep up to date. However, the truth is that human beings are finite beings and can come up with only so many objections to any given offer. Once a sales person begins to hear the same objections over and over again; and has mastered overcoming them, then they know that they have all they need to be successful from then on selling that product or service.

So back to my story. I was definitely not able to fulfill the requirement of jogging partner for this position; and therefore thanked the interviewer for his time and wished him well. And that was the third of the six resumes I'd most recently sent out.

I'd received two rejection emails, and the last of the interviews was scheduled for the next day. And this one was the first opportunity that I'd ever been invited to interview about that was not a narrow or shallow market. Meaning, it was a product that most businesses used… office supplies!

And who does not love to get lost in the stationery store? Isles and isles of paper, pencils, pens, envelopes, sticky notes; not to mention computer accessories, and even furniture to be explored and envisioned in one's own office.

I'd actually had my first interview over the phone with the owner of the company. He (Sam) and his wife (I'll name her Priscilla) had been serving as direct competition to the big box stationery store in the city for over 14 years. In fact, they met when they worked for another stationery store that had been bought out and absorbed by this big box store in the nineteen-eighties.

During my second interview, now in person at the warehouse just north of the Airport, I met the two customer service reps; Judy and Selina, who I'll call Miss Muffet; and Barry, who was Priscilla's father. Barry handled all the accounting for the company and I suspected right away that he was very close to my own age. Later I learned that he was just one year older than me.

My interview was strictly with Sam. He was very open about the challenges they had just faced due to the dishonesty of the previous sales person. And this sales person had been with them from the very beginning of their company. He told me that she had redirected a large number of their existing clients to another smaller competitor in the area while she remained on staff and seemingly performing her sales duties for them day by day.

And that experience came on the heels of a general manager they had hired who ended up just playing internal politics and getting nothing done. Apparently they had just let that fellow go several months prior to my interview.

Clearly it was growing pains and with Sam's story I realized that no one is immune to the treachery of greed and dishonesty. Sam and his wife seemed like real good people. They were just a sweet young couple (in their early forties) wanting to run a business and realize the rewards accordingly. And they did not mind or begrudge anyone else their success either.

In response I carefully expressed my frustrations with my attempt to hire a general manager to grow my business only to experience the departure of my cornerstone account. That then led to my offer to provide my direct one-to-one marketing program to grow his business without having to hire a full sales force.

I presented my manual for the program; the outline of the marketing plan; and demonstrated the Excel spreadsheet formula for guaranteed sales success. To which he replied that he definitely wanted me to work for them; however, he did not want to contract a sales person. He wanted me all to himself rather than becoming one of several products I'd represent.

He presented me with his employment contract and I read over it right then and there. To my utter amazement this position offered benefits! I'd never had health benefits before, ever, in any position I'd ever had. Of course, I did have a program that allowed me to deduct all my health and dental costs from taxes. However, all the money had to come from what I earned. This was a real group benefit program where you paid only a share and then you're able to have the benefits cover most medical and dental expenses... wow!

However, the compensation he was offering would not nearly cover my overhead, let alone provide money for food and gas for the car. I asked if I could come back the next day to discuss the option further. While I was interested; and at this point becoming an employee with a benefit program sounded really great. Yet, I doubted that he would step up to the monthly draw I required just to cover day-to-day living.

The other drawback was that this product line was nickels and dimes compared to the twenty-five thousand dollar minimum program cost of the computer company. A box of twelve blue ink stick pens was a dollar and forty-nine cents. And my formula revealed the effort that was going to be necessary.

However, I did have a huge list of companies where I had contacts already established for other things I'd sold over the years. This would be my 'warm' market to establish a foundation of ongoing sales to cover my monthly draw and get me to commission quota a great deal sooner than Sam would ever expect. And because I changed the product or service I was representing every time I changed jobs, there would be no conflict that previous companies could legitimately claim.

On the other hand, it was yet another mom and pop shop... been here before. And the wife was the typical domestic with three children all under the age of 10. She'd been a customer service rep for the previous stationery company (that was bought out) and she had brought in all of the clients they started the company with fourteen years ago. She reminded me of #2 at the software company. Another customer service rep who thinks they are a sales person.

I had researched the company and they were grossing over four million in sales annually. So, they could afford me if they wanted to. I would not even interview with a company that was less than two million annually because they had to be in a position to fund the start-up of the program.

I crunched the numbers that night and did something I thought I would never ever do. I printed off my bank statement and current transactions so Sam could see my financial situation as it truly was. If I closed my business, I still had the business line of credit to pay off and so I would need to be able to draw enough to cover all that expense right away.

You'll recall that the computer company paid me less than I needed and I took the position anyway confident that I'd commission before it became a real issue. And providing they paid me my fourteen thousand dollar commission, I'd just break even for that segment of time.

Moving forward, however, I needed cash flow. I was not interested in investing in growing someone else's business and starving while doing so.

We met the next afternoon and I presented all my paperwork, including the research I'd done on their company. I demonstrated how the numbers would all balance out over the first year. I projected my sales to be in commission quota by eighteen months maximum; and suggested that it could even happen within the first six months depending upon the companies I viewed as my warm market.

If my warm market companies were in a position to just switch suppliers, I'd commission within the first six to eight months. I said to be sure, I'd spend one week the last week of March visiting and/or calling some of my warm market companies to get a sense of how long it would take to win them over to a new office supplies provider. I suggested that if he and I were happy with the results of that small initial market research, I could start officially on April 1, 2015.

By the third day of my efforts to contact my warm market, I was convinced that *now this* was the job all of my previous experience had prepared me for. Office supplies was a perfect product for my program. Every office uses some office supplies meaning that the numbers, and the potential, was definitely there even at an average sale of twenty-five dollars as opposed to twenty-five thousand dollars.

Truth be told, I hated running my own business. And I know I've mentioned this before. I went into my own business because, at the time, there were no other options for me. And now, if all I had to do was sell and not worry about anything else, I'd be happy; especially at this ripe old age of 61; soon to be 62.

I reported to Sam's office as we'd agreed to inform him of my findings and to say that I'd accept the job if he would provide the remuneration demonstrated as necessary for me to accept the job. He agreed.

Keep in mind that I still look twenty years younger than I am; which is not so unusual these days. However, for the first time since 1980 I had to fill out the forms for taxes and benefits as an employee; which meant Sam and Priscilla would see how old I really was…! That made me a bit nervous for sure. Yet, since her dad was there and probably my same age, I felt that they would not mind.

Time out... So now you need to know that; while all of my job searching was going on, my daughter had recognized my need for psycho-therapy after the computer company fired me. And she had approached me with the possibility of going to a therapist together and by doing so, she could put the cost through her benefit program (which was, and still is, fantastic).

I had agreed to this and, after some searching for a therapist we both felt comfortable with, we were to start in May with a therapist who specialized in trauma and PTSD.

So, I started officially with the office supplies company in April 2015. Of course the first three months of anything is considered the 'probation period'. And one other thing my PTSD allowed me to do was to focus on the task at hand and just block everything else out.

What I was blocking out at this point was the complete and utter terror of working in an office with all women. And along with blocking out the feelings, so goes the awareness needed to recognize social situations that need certain appropriate responses... most call it 'office politics'.

Judy was the life of the party for sure. She had an incredible quick wit and sense of humor. Miss Muffet, on the other hand, remained aloof. It's like having two cats. One cat will be the people cat and the other one will be more distant. Priscilla was the other owner of the company, and as the mother of three she now had the perfect scenario in the office, me being the third. And while the red lights flashed in the back of my mind, there was no way I could focus on that. I was too busy blocking out the sheer terror of having to report to an open concept office every day after a forty-five minute commute.

I do have to say here that this was, in reality, the best commute in the world. A three-lane open freeway that actually accommodates the traffic on it. No congestion. No creeping along at speeds that you could walk faster, and even the occasional accident did not disrupt the traffic flow much.

Hey, I lived and worked in Los Angeles, California and it took me forty-five minutes to get ten miles in those days. Even within Calgary there are some main arteries for traffic that are just a parking lot at rush hour. But not the new Stoney Ring Road North; it's open road all the way.

The office supplies company was a twenty-thousand square foot distribution warehouse in an industrial setting with a second floor built on one side to house two offices, a large open room with three cubicle-type offices with two small washrooms, and the computer hard drive room. Three more offices; a kitchen; two more washrooms, and a boardroom were built in downstairs. However, it was still a warehouse and very unevenly heated and cooled.

Fortunately I was given a desk in the separate office area just outside of the computer hard drive room. I had a window to my left, which was perfect as I really need natural light to maintain the energy level necessary to perform my duties. While I do take light therapy and have for several years now, which has made a tremendous difference for me, I still have to have natural light coming into my office to keep my energy high.

As time went on it became clear that the company was taking legal action against this sales person that skimmed off clients to the competition while she remained employed by Sam and Priscilla. I certainly didn't blame them; however, it was not for me to judge, or even to know about for that matter.

Priscilla was very distraught over this legal issue (and understandably so) and she did not mind expressing her frustration over it every day. She, Barry and Judy took regular cigarette breaks and discussed the issue at length. Their lawyer suggested that Priscilla make copies of all the invoices from the companies prior to their departure to the competitor to demonstrate that they had been long-term clients who had been brought to the company by Priscilla, and prior to any other sales people being hired. It seemed to be an endless task. I really felt their pain, and I say that with great compassion having experienced my whole business being taken away from me. I was glad for them if they could do something about it and recover some losses.

Meantime I was keeping my nose to the grindstone and contacting companies as fast as I could to bring in new business. It was going really well too. In June I happened to call an acquaintance in one of the larger engineering companies who gave me the name of the person in charge of ordering office supplies for the company. And it happened to be excellent timing as this buyer was looking for some very specific boardroom tables for the new building they were about to move into, and her current supplier was unable to provide them. Low and behold, those tables were in our catalogue and in stock in our main warehouse!

That one sale in June 2015 brought in more gross margin than all the sales combined for the last week of the month. Barry was thrilled and definitely recognized the great results I was producing. Being from my generation, he was well aware of the benefits of someone bringing in a warm market of their own to boost sales immediately. Sam and Priscilla were away at the time and not back until the following Monday. By then the glitter had settled and nothing more was mentioned about my June sales triumph. Sam and Priscilla never seemed to be that impressed about anything; and especially not about my warm market contribution to their bottom line.

We met every month to review the results and compare them to the forecast I'd produced; which they paid very little attention to while they kept telling me to do exactly what I was doing, yet saying it as if I wasn't doing it?

At the time I just wrote it off to the stress that legal proceedings were producing in their lives. I thought that they probably felt the universe owed them one for the bad wrap their original sales person had dished out to them. And at the point in my life that I was in at the time, I was just so happy to have benefits and to be able to finally get the therapy I really needed, I did not care if they ever gave me a pat on the back. All I needed from them was my paycheck.

In May; not only did I receive my commission check from the computer company, I had also begun the sessions with the therapist and my daughter. We had six sessions completely covered by my daughters benefit plan and I immediately booked for more sessions for myself, individually, for the EMDR that the therapist had suggested regarding my PTSD.

My therapist was most impressed when I arrived for my first session armed with my memoirs written in 1994. The work I gave her was the first seven chapters of this book. And with that, she could really get to know me very quickly. It enabled her to direct my therapy for the fastest healing and recovery.

I cannot tell you how wonderful it is to finally receive proper treatment for a problem that has been plaguing you for so long. I was beginning to recognize the 'triggers' that would throw me into my PTSD persona; which consisted of behaviors that were very destructive.

I could get very angry and say anything and everything that came to mind. And I do believe that, given the opportunity, I would have gladly engaged in a fistfight when I was pushed into the angry persona.

Or; the other, and more frequent, option was that I would begin to quiver inside and my legs would get weak while my hands would shake. I'd crumble inside into the beaten child and on the outside I'd just withdraw completely and not say anything. It would be one extreme or the other; both of which controlled me and both of which did not ever prove helpful.

Even as it was happening I would have feelings of remorse deep inside and I'd want to stop, but just could not stop it. I was merely there for the ride to where ever it was going to take me. All I could do was hang on and hope for the best.

Meantime, it was now July and the Calgary Stampede was getting under way. And I know I've mentioned it before; but I just love this event. If you ever have an opportunity to visit it; do not hesitate!

This year was no different than any other year for me. I was attending company Stampede parties and rubbing shoulders with people in companies I still had to entice to my newest product.

One afternoon while my daughter and I were on the grounds I became completely disoriented. I felt nauseated and slightly dizzy. We sat down for a while and it finally passed and we carried on. I didn't think about that again until the last Friday of Stampede.

I was able to leave work early and I had an errand to run on my way to the grounds to meet my daughter. That year she was in the Purina Super Dogs show with her little miniature dachshund. She trained that dog to do everything but the dishes. And being so cute, that little dog and her counterpart (there were two doxies in the show) were usually the stars of the show. However, I digress…

As I approached the intersection to turn left, all the traffic was very backed up due to the red light now one block behind

187

me. I looked at the far turning lane three times before I made my turn; and yet I had just entered that lane when suddenly all my air bags deployed and I could not see out of my windows at all. I really did not know what happened. All I knew was that I was stopped and I could not see out of my windows.

Upon exiting the vehicle I discovered that a very young woman was in that far lane speeding towards the intersection because that lane was clear all the way to the traffic light that one block behind me. She had hit my front passengers side quarter panel, headlight, and enough of that wheel to push it inwards. I was immobilized and considering that the vehicle was a 2008 Nissan Rouge; top of the line for its time, I might add; however, too old to bear repairs of this nature in 2015.

What I will say is that car was really there for me. I never felt a thing. Of course, we have to take into consideration the nature of the collision too. Had I been two seconds slower, I would have never been hit. She hit me initially and the tire made her car bounce off and hit me again, so she was pushing in that quarter panel where the door meets it. She was in an older model Toyota Sequoia; and it was there for her too! And her airbags deployed as well.

Fortunately we were both alone in the cars; so no one else was involved. Her dad arrived very quickly on a bicycle, as her home was only three blocks from where we were; hence the hurry she was in, I suspect. It was the last Friday of Stampede and she and I were both dressed for the occasion.

The police were less than friendly. They too want to enjoy the last Friday of Stampede rather than assist two stupid women in a stupid car accident that could have easily been avoided in their opinion.

There was no other way around it, I was charged for the mishap. Several people came forward to say that the Toyota was travelling at a very high speed. They all insisted that if she had been driving properly she would have slowed down at the intersection to make sure no one was turning since all the other traffic was stopped. But the cops didn't want to hear it. They wanted to follow easy protocol, blame the left-hand-turn driver and done with it.

I called my son-in-law to come pick me up and he refused! I said, "What?" He said it was 4:30 on the last Friday of the

Stampede and he lives twenty minutes from the city limits. He said by the time he got there I could (almost) walk home. Well, that was a bit exaggerated. But I was just too shocked to argue with him. We hung up and I just sat down there on the grass and watched as the tow trucks came to pick up the cars.

The other driver went to the hospital in an ambulance at her father's instruction. I suspected they were going to milk this thing for all it was worth. Finally there was only one police car left and the woman from it came over to me and asked me if I did not have anyone to come pick me up. I just looked up at her and said no, and explained that my daughter was working the Stampede and cannot get away and my son-in-law refused to come this far at this time of day. She just blinked at me twice and went back to her car and her partner who was in the driver's seat.

They got on the radio and another police car arrived. She told me to go to her car and that the fellow would drive me home. She left in the other police car.

He made me sit in the back like a criminal. The passenger seat was back as far as it could go so I barely had room for my legs. I told him that I didn't know the police would take a crash victim home; and he said that only the rookies get to do that; and you could tell he was annoyed.

Being the last weekend of Stampede, I was not going to deal with chasing a car accident. All I wanted was a rental so I could get back down to the grounds. And that is what I did.

If I did nothing else right financially, I did have a great insurance plan. Of course my premiums went up; but they took really good care of me even though I was deemed at fault.

So, that Monday morning I had to deal with all of this and it was no secret to my place of employment. There was a car repair shop just two doors down from us. The owner had taken care of my oil change and tire rotation for the spring when I started in April. So I had the car towed to the parking lot where I worked.

It was a hassle and an annoyance to get the assessment. It was written off, which was no surprise to me; and it paid off enough for me to put a down payment on another 2015 Rogue.

And through all this Priscilla was all out of sorts with me. She said I was taking up too much work time to deal with something that was personal... I told her I had to do it during work hours because that's when everyone I need to contact is open and available. At that she just pursed her lips and stiffened her back to project annoyance. And I thought 'whatever' and went back to work.

Interestingly enough, a couple of weeks later Priscilla's car was stolen right out of her garage! Apparently she'd raced home from work to get the kids off to some sporting event. She pulled into her garage, but left the garage door open, and the car running, as she went into the house to get the kids. She'd left her purse in the car as well.

When she returned with her brood in tow, her Mercedes SUV was gone. Can you imagine? Right out of her garage? So she had the direct experience of trying to get proper assistance over a weekend regarding vehicle mishaps. Not to mention cancelling all of her credit cards, including the company credit card. Interesting turn of events…

The authorities did eventually find the vehicle unharmed in a little town about thirty minutes northwest of Calgary. But her designer purse and all her ID and credit cards were never recovered. She ended up spending a great deal of work time replacing all that. Of course, I never said a word. I did not even acknowledge any of it was going on.

I also realized that I needed to extend my light therapy into the summer months. In Calgary our longest day is the twenty-first of June. The sun does not set until eleven o'clock in the evening. And it comes up around five AM.

I'd started the light therapy through the winter months a year or so before; because, by December twenty-first the sun does not come up until after eight o'clock in the morning; and it sets around four-thirty in the afternoon. I was definitely suffering from Seasonal Affective Disorder; and the light therapy made all the difference.

Looking back on the disorientation I experienced that year on the Stampede grounds, I am convinced that I was less alert as I was driving the day of that accident because I'd discontinued my light therapy in June thinking that the natural extended daylight was enough for me. Needless to say, I do my light therapy all year now.

By September most of my warm market was in and my revised projections (accordingly) where that by December, or January at the latest, I'd be in a commissioning position. I was so happy you cannot imagine. My program had never failed me. It has always brought in the sales I projected based upon my Excel Formula.

It was towards the end of September when I attracted a very large oil company to the table. You have to appreciate that in this day and age of technology, office supplies are not nearly as important as they were even ten years ago. So most companies I brought in would spend an average of between two hundred and one thousand dollars a month.

However, this particular big company averaged two hundred and fifty thousand dollars a year on office supplies; including break-room and facility items like paper towels and dishwasher detergent. And you have to appreciate, as well, that there are not many companies that size who would be willing to consider purchasing from a small local competitor like us. Most big companies want to work with other big companies to maintain the status quo. The bigger suppliers can afford box seats at the sporting events. The smaller competitors do keep their margins so small that there is very little left over to maintain the lifestyle that the owners become accustomed to. Therefore, there is *NO* budget for promotions at the level of box seats at the sporting, or Stampede, events.

I knew that company alone would keep me in commissions from then on. I was so enthused I could barely contain myself. But I did contain myself. No one likes a bragger; so I just rolled with it. The deal had not been solidified yet, they were just testing us out first. So I was watching every order to make sure it was correct.

So, now I have to lay some groundwork for the next thing that happened. I was in a room that shared a wall with Priscilla's office (behind me based upon the way the room was set up). The fax machine, printers, and everything else was in the main room that you entered as you came up the stairs.

Miss Muffet and Judy sat facing each other; however, there were hutches on their desks to give the 'cubicle' effect and so they did not see each other. Judy faced into the room while Miss Muffet faced the back wall that led into the warehouse. The two washrooms were to the right as you approached their desks.

It was a Thursday afternoon and the phones were very quiet. When no calls or orders are coming in the customer service department starts to get antsy. So Priscilla and Sam decided that Judy and Miss Muffet could spend that down time calling past companies who were no longer buying from us and try to get them back. Of course they hated it.

It always frustrated me so much that everyone I worked for seemed to think that anyone can sell. Again thanks to Tupperware and Mary Kay everyone thinks there is no talent; and even less skill involved. And the fact that they were calling past clients, it did set them up to win. However, very few (if any) customer service personnel want to do outbound calling.

Meantime, I'm busy all the time. I never have down time. There are always more calls to do no matter what the day or time of year. And at this particular time I had decided to do a fax campaign to a number of people who had been skillfully avoiding me.

I was calling and leaving messages saying that I was sending a fax; and then I'd send it. I had to maintain that order of effort so that the fax would arrive on their desk very soon after they picked up the voice mail message. So I was running back and forth to the fax machine, (that sat facing the wall right outside of Priscilla's office) while Priscilla had her head down on her desk; and the other two were struggling through a few calls themselves.

Finally Judy said she was feeling sick and wanted to go home early. She did that often when things were quiet because there was nothing she hated more than outbound calling. Priscilla tried to call her on it, but Judy was very convincing, so Priscilla dismissed her.

Soon after Judy left I accidently hit a wrong key on the fax machine and it started this loud beeping and would not work. I tried everything short of unplugging it; which I intended to do next when Miss Muffet bellows from her desk (not even turning around) saying I should just press the 'cancel' button.

To that I replied, "I am," and of course my frustration with the machine reflected in my voice; plus I raised my voice to respond to someone who was bellowing to me from well across the room while the fax machine was loudly beeping.

To that Priscilla snaps, from behind the wall, that Miss Muffet was just trying to help and I should not be snapping back at her.

To which I replied; "And I'm just telling her that I am pressing the cancel button." and the machine finally shut up. I completed that transmission and went back to my desk to do several more calls and several more faxes before I left for the day.

Neither one of them ever got up off their butts to come help me. Rather than sympathize with my plight, they criticized me and just left me there to struggle. Priscilla was in a position to direct the scene and she chose to make me look bad instead of being helpful. Some team unity, hey?

However, during those last calls and faxes I started to get that quivering inside. My legs were going weak and my hands were shaking. As I left I saw Priscilla had gone to Judy's desk and Miss Muffet had her chair pulled up to Judy's desk and they were half whispering.

I got in my car and the more I drove the angrier I became. My commute was forty-five minutes one way on an open freeway, so I had lots of time to work up a frenzy by the time I got home.

My therapy sessions had brought me to the point where I could finally recognize the triggers that would start my PTSD. And this time I consciously realized that I was being bullied by Priscilla! She was a domestic raising three children that she could probably just bully to discipline.

And I'd met her kids once by then and they were (are still) so wonderful and full of life. Not only beautiful as a perfect combination of the both of them; but just wholesome and they had depth.

Truly the balance Sam brings to the mix makes the difference with the children. Barry had confided in me on more than one occasion that Pricilla's mother was pretty violent with his girls. Apparently she resorted to severe spankings on more than one occasion; and for very minor misbehaviors.

So, while I could understand and relate to Priscilla; I also recognized she was not going to allow us to have any type of relationship with each other. Not even a professional one.

Therefore, by the time I got home I was in full-blown beaten child. I curled up on the couch and just quaked and cried and quaked and cried some more. What was I going to do? This time I see the firing coming. All my work that I'd done would be lost again. And this time it was way too soon to go back to my contacts with yet another product or service. Plus I had no energy to do another start up. I was now sixty-two years old and I just could not do another run just to be robbed yet again.

Time ticked on and I could not sleep. I just paced like a caged animal. All the thoughts of suicide came back. I could hear my mother's voice in my head saying I was a farmer's daughter and I'd never be anything else. And my mom's favorite, "You're so stoooo-ped; you think so much of yourself and you fool your teachers; but you don't fool me. You are nothing and you'll always be nothing."

I couldn't eat, I couldn't sleep and it was soon time for me to leave for work. So I called in sick. I wrote an email to Sam saying I was sick and could not come in. And for some reason that email made me feel much better. I made some coffee and had my breakfast and calmly sat down at my computer.

The first thing I did was Google 'bullying in the workplace' and selected several really good articles that I could use to demonstrate the issue. I also went to the Alberta Human Rights website to see where the government was by now on the subject. I knew there was increased awareness of the bullying issue for schools, and on line; but not sure about the workplace. However, to my relief; there was plenty of recent articles right there on the subject. So I decided I was going to hit this head on and not be robbed again. Not this time!

I called my therapist and made an appointment to see her first thing Monday morning. That was the soonest she could see me. Next I called my family doctor and I was able to get in right away that day at 1:30 because she had a cancellation. I wanted to get a note from her regarding my PTSD diagnosis that and said I rightfully needed the day to cope.

Next I started typing. I typed and typed and typed some more until the entire scenario that I'd experienced was down on paper in chronological order.

Then I got an email from Priscilla asking me why I was not at work. I didn't reply right away because I was supposed to be 'sick'. I thought I'd reply when I got back from my doctor.

Keep in mind that both Sam and Priscilla were aware that I was going to therapy; and, I had been completely open about my issues with the computer company. While I had not gone into detail that I'd broken down and cried uncontrollably when #1 fired me; I had explained that it was the third experience in a row where I was not properly rewarded for my outstanding sales accomplishments. And, I'd explained that I suffered from PTSD that was just diagnosed, officially, a year or so prior to my starting work for them.

The doctor gave me a note saying that I'd had a break-through regarding my PTSD and; while that was a positive thing, the actual experience can be draining a somewhat traumatic for the sufferer. I told my doctor that I was preparing a presentation to disclose my condition in more detail out of respect for them. I was hopeful that it would allow for clarity and understanding and we could work better together if we all understood the situation accordingly. My doctor thought that was a great idea.

I got back from that appointment and emailed Priscilla that I'd be in after lunch on Monday because I had an appointment with my therapist at ten o'clock that same morning; and that I'd just returned from a visit to my family doctor that day. I told her I had a note from my family doctor and that I'd obtain one from my therapist as well.

I worked on the presentation all weekend. Finally it was ready and just in time to share it with my therapist. I presented it to her and she hesitated a bit. She said it was very forthcoming and asked me if I was sure it would be well received. She expressed concern that perhaps I was revealing way too much about a very personal condition. Although, she did say that it was an excellent presentation for someone like herself who was very familiar with the condition. However, for the layman, perhaps it was a bit much.

To that I sat back in my chair and said that I didn't know how else to approach it. I told her I feared that if I didn't bring this out I'd end up losing the job. Priscilla was trying to compete with me instead of working with me. That was clear. And my therapist agreed to my assessment of Priscilla's attitude towards me for sure.

So I asked my therapist how I should handle it and she said that she could not instruct me on how to exactly handle it. All she could do was give me advice and feedback as she had just done so.

Well, I was due back at work at one o'clock and it was nearing eleven as my appointment time with my therapist neared its end. I did not have time to change any of my presentation. I just had to go with it and hope for the best.

I arrived at work on time and Sam was in his office. He said I could wait in the boardroom and he called Priscilla to come down for the meeting. I was getting that quivery feeling as I waited and my throat was really dry. Luckily I had my water bottle with me.

They came in and sat down and asked me what was going on. What I wanted to do was explain about the fax machine going off and how no one helped me; but rather just barked at me from a distance and then I was deemed the bad guy when I said two words, "I am". But that's not what I said.

Rather, I was feeling like I couldn't breathe. My ears started to sizzle and I felt light headed. All I could do was hand them the copy of the presentation I'd made for them and I said perhaps I could just read this and we could discuss it as we go?

Sam is always so open and willing to discuss anything. But Priscilla was sitting there with her legs and arms crossed, lips pursed and back ridged.

So I start reading the presentation and referring to bullying in the workplace when Priscilla puts her hand up and says, "Wait just a minute… who do you think you are? You're sitting there like you're the owner of the company and we are the employees. Am I supposed to believe that you have PTSD? The same affliction a soldier gets because of dodging bombs and gunfire? Really? You have PTSD? And because of this PTSD you should be allowed to speak to your coworkers in any tone you please? Is that what all this paperwork boils down to?"

And for the first time I saw Sam offended and almost angry. He said that this was totally inappropriate. So I said, "Okay, sorry…" and handed them the two doctor's notes; which were not part of the presentation. And then I asked, "So, what should I do now?"

Priscilla wasted no time in responding to my question with: "Well, I do not see how you can possibly work here if you feel bullied. If our management style is too harsh for your PTSD, I think that pretty much says it all, doesn't it?" And she looked over to Sam for his confirmation.

As I was hearing what she was saying, I also realized that they were probably very emotionally raw from the legal proceedings that were still under way. I also recognized that I was nose-diving very quickly and I could not stop it. I was beyond the outburst of tears that occurred at the computer company. This time I could not breathe and that led to panic; which led to me gasping for breath as my heart pounded in my ears that were already sizzling. Everything started getting dark from the outside in.

Priscilla got up and I could hear her in a muffled tone say, "Oh my god, what's happening to her?" She came around the boardroom table and got behind me grasping my shoulders with both of her hands, one on either side of my shoulders and said, "Deborah, no one here is out to get you."

Looking back on it later then, and even now, I find that to be a most bizarre reaction from her. Of all the things she could have said at that moment, why did she say that; especially since she was in the midst of firing me at the time.

Sam had left the room and returned very quickly with a glass of water; however, by that time I'd reached for my water bottle and started calming down.

Priscilla then scooped up all the papers I'd prepared for them and told Sam to handle this as she left the room. We just sat there for what felt like the longest time until he said that it might be best for me to take the rest of the day off and return tomorrow morning, as per normal, and start work. He said that we'd reconvene as soon as they arrived and finish the meeting.

I looked at Sam and said that Priscilla had just fired me. But he said that he wanted to read over my presentation and discuss it with Priscilla in private. He said that he wished they'd done that to begin with. Then he got up to leave and said I could stay there as long as I needed to in order to be able to drive home safely.

After he left I sat there and thought that this time I really had a direct hand in getting fired. I realized that I should have just handed in the doctor's notes and simply explained that I'd had a rough night and left it at that. But no, I had to come swinging in there with all this information that is not common knowledge to anyone who isn't involved in psycho-therapy. My therapist tried to stop me, but I just didn't get it.

And yet, I felt a sense of calm. I felt that perhaps it would be okay tomorrow, after they had time to really discuss the matter. After all, they'd been blindsided by all this. It's a lot to take in at the best of times. Never mind having that type of information come in on top of the legal proceedings they were embroiled in for over a year at that time.

I went home and allowed myself to rest. I had a great dinner and went to bed early and slept like a rock. The next morning I was optimistic. I felt grounded and ready for anything. I even considered the possibility that they'd fire me and feel totally justified at doing so. However, I thought back to the Alberta Human Rights website and all the information they had there on workplace bullying. I thought to myself that; if they did fire me, I was not going to go quietly this time. Not this time!

I got to work and went to my desk. I looked up my most recent conquest; the large oil company that was considering us, and testing us, with orders no less than five hundred dollars at a time. I called the contact and she was very happy to hear from me.

She told me that they were very pleased with the service and quality. In fact, she wanted to schedule an appointment to develop a plan that might include on-site product management for them. However, she felt that she would not have time until mid-November; and they would be looking to switch to us officially for the New Year.

And suddenly a bell went off in my head... of course; October was my sixth month; and, I'd managed to bring in most of the companies I had on my list. Plus this one was the icing on the cake. Really, this one alone was enough to cover my draw and the rest was now the gravy I'd be earning commissions by month after month.

Would they dare fire me now? And the answer was... yes they sure did!

I reported to the boardroom when they called me at ten o'clock. I usually arrived at seven thirty, at the latest. So by the time Sam and Priscilla arrived around ten every day I was well into my day.

We resumed our positions around the boardroom table, as established the day before; and Priscilla started the meeting. She said that she and Sam had discussed this well into the evening last night. She said that even if I could continue to work under these accusations; she could not.

She felt that trust was broken and that the company is too small to have attitudes like the ones demonstrated by my presentation permeating the overall team feeling that they, as the management, were trying to rebuild at this time.

She said that Sam would accompany me to my desk to retrieve my personal belongings and then escort me to my car and that would be it. My final check would be mailed to me.

I just sat there. I was not panicking. I was not even upset. Rather, I was expecting it; and I was prepared for it! I said nothing. I got up and went upstairs, Sam close behind me. There were boxes available that I packed up very efficiently and then came the issue of my chair. It was my own chair that I brought from home.

While I did have a vehicle fully capable of taking it; Sam said he'd put it in his pick up and drop it off the next day along with my final check and separation papers. Since we both lived in the same suburb; it was only blocks from his own home, so he thought that would be in the best interest of everyone involved.

As I drove home I decided that I was totally done with sales. If I learned nothing else from my therapy, I learned that I had been treated badly, inappropriately, and even illegally at times; and yet, my perpetrators always got away with it.

Well, not this time! As soon as I got home I got onto my computer and looked up the local colleges that were offering courses in Health Care Aide. Several of my friends in my congregation had started working as a Health Care Aide and loved it.

Finally something worked out in my favor. There was an open house at Robertson College the very next day for that very course. I attended the open house and afterwards I met with one of the counselors.

We made arrangements for a student loan and I was scheduled to start with the November 9th class. So, I got fired, officially on October 20th, 2015; and I started classes November 9th, 2015. That gave me a little over two weeks to begin my action against Sam and Priscilla.

On one hand I felt bad because they were going through the other legal thing; however, I had just as much loss recently and they had no sympathy for me. Plus, now they conveniently had all my new business that they would never have to pay commissions on. I was sure they felt they were owed that considering that the rep before me robbed them of quite a bit of business.

Between July and October Judy had confided some inside information to me. She'd told me that there had been several reps hired since the 'robber' had left early in 2013. And I recalled that Sam had commented about that in passing once. I remembered that he said that there were a number of clients he wanted me to follow up on, after I concluded my warm market list for them. He said that they were approached and then forgotten as sales people came and went over the years… And I remember thinking it was a strange comment at the time.

So, it made sense to me, now that I was fired, that they would have taken the attitude of 'get the salesman before the salesman gets us again'.

However, whatever they were thinking, I was not going away. Not this time!

I also reflected on the uncanny similarities with all the mom and pop companies I worked for over the years. Each and every one of them ran their company like a dysfunctional family.

Rather than professional behaviors, you were subjected to their autocratic and superior attitudes.

Perhaps you've see the five stages of development? They are: 1) You don't know; but you don't know that you don't know: babies don't know that they don't know. 2) You don't know; and you know you don't know: Children asking why all the time. 3) You still don't know; but you think you do know: this starts in our teenage years and can carry on throughout our entire lives! 4) You know; but you don't know you know: which is intuitive behavior, you do the right thing without thinking about it; and finally 5) You know and you know you know… you've mastered a subject; career; or a goal in life like an Olympic gold medalist; a sports superstar; or a research scientist.

Mom and pop companies are very vulnerable to the third level of development. They are doing a lot of things right and they are succeeding; therefore they think they have nothing further to learn. Why argue with success, right?

Well, having worked for dozens of mom and pop companies, my strongest advice is that you will have a measure of success based on intuition and luck. However, if you do not consciously know and record what is working, you will suddenly find yourself in a slight downward spiral. Or, if you're really lucky, you'll stall and just keep going around in the same circle.

Now, if that same circle is earning you enough money to live the dream, perhaps further development is not necessary. The danger in that is the fact that nothing stays stationary in this world and lives. If it's alive, it is subject to natural laws that were in place long before you and I were ever born.

I have seen family run businesses where the owners just milk the company for all it's worth on an ongoing basis. They put no money back into the business to upgrade computer programs, for example.

When the economy presents a challenge and business falls off a bit, they cut back on cleaning the offices. And let me tell you that the office supplies company was a pigsty. I'd suffer using that rest room until it was so gross I'd come in with a full hazmat suit, goggles and all, and just clean it and disinfect. I also kept up with the kitchen on a daily basis.

We all understand the cycles of life: the water cycle, the wind currents and the jet stream. We know what goes around comes around; and you are spiraling along with the world as it goes around the sun and around on its axis at the same time. And the way this applies to business in that, either you are spiraling up with steady growth, regardless of how slight. Or, you are spiraling down, again perhaps ever so slightly. However, either way, you will not remain stationary for long if you perceive that you are on a plateau.

In most cases mom and pop businesses will sustain the family until the founders either pass it along to their progeny or; they retire and just close it down like my dad did.

And really, if the business survives long enough to support the lifestyle the owners choose, who am I go judge? More power to them. I personally could not live that way, and that's on me. To each his own. The thing is, it often takes very little adjustment in management and marketing to maintain a slight and steady growth. It's a shame to see someone's lifelong hard work just die off due to inexperience and lack of knowledge.

Chapter Eleven
Play It Again, Sam…

You may recall that in spring of 2015, Alberta had a provincial election and the NDP won that election. The NDP are known for being the 'people's' government. They increase minimum wage and force corporations to own up to the taxes they owe.

My counselor at Alberta Human Rights took a very keen interest in my case; as she confirmed that I definitely had a case. She was also quite impressed with the binder that I'd created to track the bullying I'd experienced; and the discrimination I felt I'd endured due to my PTSD.

The binder was set up much the same as a business plan would be set up. All the supporting documentation was clearly marked so the reader could view the email sent to me the day I called in sick; as well as the two doctors notes I'd produced the day of the initial presentation regarding my condition and how the management style they employed was triggering me in a very negative way.

I'd followed the form provided by the Alberta Human Rights to describe the circumstances in chronological order. Of course my presentation along with all the articles I'd taken from the Alberta Human Rights website were included in a separate section of the binder.

True to government procedure, which I was very familiar with; I'd prepared three copies of this binder *besides* the original, which I retained as my own copy.

I asked the AB HR counselor if I should have a lawyer; and she said that was up to me. However it was not expected. She said that my case was pretty clear and very well represented by the binder alone.

The amount of photocopying that those binders required was significant. And I recall thinking how sad it was that I was spending time preparing a case against Sam and Priscilla, when I just as easily could have been preparing a full marketing plan for them to continue to grow their business.

What a waste of talent, if I have to say so myself. Had I not proven to them that I really knew what I was doing when it came to bringing in sales? And yet every time I performed, and performed well, I was punished for it. I remember thinking that; if I had not lived it, I would not believe that any one person could maintain a pattern of boom and bust like I had.

It was as if every company I worked for took notes from the one before and simply followed suit to fire me. So, let's count it down. In 2012 I lost my main contract that I'd had for six years. In 2014 I was fired from the media company after two years. In 2015 I was fired from the computer company after only nine months. And now, again, in 2015 I was fired after only six months. Well, at least the time was getting shorter in between the firings. If these were actual labor pains, I'd be crowning by now!

To withstand all this I would picture the situation like a muppet show. The companies I'd worked for I'd see as grinches. And just as we recognize different behaviors as specific to a particular animal; like a leopard for example; so did all of these companies resemble each other, and so perfectly, I might add.

And speaking of leopards, a little side note is that leopards are the most ferocious of predators. When they are injured, they become more aggressive rather than slinking off into the forest to lick their wounds.

Leopards are also extremely strong. They can and do drag a full-grown adult antelope up a tree to protect the kill from other predators. So, being raised by people like that has to leave some survival talent behind as one small glimmer of positive return for anyone who had the misfortune to be subjected to such.

I did report by email to my therapist that I'd been fired and had to stop treatment for the time being. She replied to that email saying that I should definitely follow up with Alberta Human Rights and that she'd be available as soon as I was ready to resume the treatments.

AB HR did send a letter to Sam that required a response by December 31, 2015. I knew he'd ignore it. And that was to my advantage. If they did not reply, AB HR could launch an investigation. And trust me when I tell you that you do *NOT* want the government investigating you for anything, let alone a case of bullying when you are already involved in legal proceedings regarding an employee's departure and theft of clientele.

That kind of behavior by a person who had been with a company from its inception; and who had experienced so much success, indicates an obvious resentment on the part of the departing employee. From what I'd heard through Judy, the company was a real cesspool of 'mean-girls' led by Priscilla herself just prior to the 'robbery' and to the sales person's departure.

It was brutally obvious that Priscilla just wanted to milk the company for every dime they could get out of it and they provided no upgrades, not even proper chairs, for the customer service reps. At the time of the 'robbery' there were three customer service reps and the one was on maternity leave when I started.

In fact, she'd brought her baby in to visit in May or June; I can't recall which month it was. However I know it was before my car accident. At the time Priscilla was out on a cigarette break and Judy had just returned from her smoke break, and was coming upstairs with the new mom.

I could hear her commenting on the new chairs, the radio they had now, and the little bar fridge for water and their lunches. So, I could surmise that these things were just added before I started.

Judy and Miss Muffet were all but begging this new mom to come back after her maternity leave was finished; but she insisted she was not interested. I heard her say that it was too much before and that now, with even fewer employees, the pressure would just be worse. I thought that was an interesting comment. I never asked Judy what that was all about.

Meantime, my classes got started right on time November 9, 2015. It was such an amazing experience too. I was, of course, the oldest one in the class. I was even twelve years older than the instructor. In addition to myself there was only one other young girl who had English-as-a-first-language out of eighteen of us total. And the woman I sat next to was the worst at English; which worked out great for both of us. .

I ended up staying with her for an hour or so after class almost every day to make sure she understood what we learned that day. It was wonderful for me to do the class twice; because at sixty-two one does not learn new tricks too quickly.

The other English-speaking student and I used to compete for highest scores on our tests. We got small tests every couple of days; and by the third one everyone was striving for one hundred percent.

It became the motivation that inspired everyone in the class. I also asked a lot of questions in class as I could tell when the other students were failing to get it; and they did not know what questions to ask.

I sat smack dab in the middle of the room and had a clear view of the instructor at her desk. At my age; and with my life experience, it was so easy to see what needed to be reviewed just by the look on the other student's faces.

The instructor appreciated me too; especially for staying after with my table partner. Otherwise, she would have had to do it. But that daily review was as much for my own benefit as it was for the other student's benefit. So it worked out perfectly.

I will mention here that later, when I did resume my sessions with my therapist, she was astounded that I went back to school and had a wonderful experience doing so. She'd read my story and she knew how I was treated in school and how my parents had stifled my learning. It turns out that I took no break in my therapy at all. That course was as much therapeutic for me as it educational.

Also, when we had our last in-class test; before the final exam, everyone got one hundred percent on that test! The instructor could not believe it. The president of the college came in to congratulate us, as it had never been done before in any class. I do wonder how those classes are going now.

Then came the final, and I wanted to ace that test so bad. And I got so close. I got a ninety-nine. I lost a point because I answered a question with an argument for two answers. Had I just answered the question and not tried for a one hundred and one percent, I would have had my one hundred percent. The other English-speaking student got the one hundred percent. And I was truly happy for her. Her life was just beginning while mine was kind of at a standstill at the time.

While the theory segment of the course went so very well, the practicum was another story. Book learning and the corresponding application of that book learning are two very different things.

Had my instructor from the theory been my practicum instructor I am sure I would have done just as well. However, I got the worst of the worst for my practicum. She had a reputation for being miserable, and she did not disappoint. Wow, what a bag.

Suffice it to say that as well as I did in theory; that's how bad I was on the floor. I was just a ball of nerves and I could not keep up. By the end of it I was finally getting the hang of it; and I did pass, but it was an uphill battle the whole time. I was so glad when it was over.

At the same time, I handled it without getting triggered into either of my PTSD personas! That was the most encouraging aspect of the whole experience. My ability to focus on the job at hand; and that job being taking care of elderly ones who are dependent upon the Health Care Aides, kept me grounded.

The residents of the care facility where we were fulfilling our practicum were my priority. And my first duty was to care for them. So I was not worried about anything else going on around me; or being done to me. As there were times when that instructor was blatantly abusive and I just shrugged it off.

Perhaps the fact that I knew I could not be fired played a large part in my ability to perform; and roll with the punches that instructor dished out. I never discussed that with my therapist; but it makes sense to me.

PTSD will block out a great deal when it wants to; that is until nighttime, when it's time to sleep. That's when all the stress of the realities come flooding back. While I was doing great; I was spending student loan money to survive. The only way I could keep the panic at bay was to picture myself climbing into God's lap and resting my head on his chest.

I'd pack the two extra pillows, one behind me and the other I'd cuddle into my chest so it felt like his arms were holding me on his lap. And that's how I got to sleep the entire time I was back to school.

Because I did score so high in my theory, and my practicum instructor was floored when we had our final interview and I told her I was sixty-two years old, so she gave me a good score after all; I was one of the first in our class to get a job.

My course was officially finished the 31st of March 2016; and I started work April 15th for an in-home care provider. That meant I had to drive from house to house to provide the various services the elderly in this particular program required.

Meantime, by the beginning of March Sam had not yet responded to the second letter sent by Alberta Human Rights either; and apparently the representative showed up on the warehouse doorstep! At that point Sam reached out to their lawyer, who was already helping them on the other issue, which was still in play, by the way. And so AB HR notified me that Sam and Priscilla had now included their lawyer. With that bit of news I thought I should probably find one for myself.

After an extensive search I finally found one and took my binder to meet with him one day after practicum the middle of March. He was quite impressed with my binder and asked me who the lawyer was for the other party. When I told him he responded very confidently. He said he knew this fellow lawyer and would definitely work with me on this case.

Well, it was about one week later when I received an email from my lawyer suggesting that I take the settlement offer of five thousand dollars and fully paid career counseling to reset my career. He told me that he'd seen issues like this in the past and the departed employee has no chance of obtaining any compensation; especially since my time with them had been only six months.

So I replied, by email, to this lawyer, the one that was supposed to be on my side; and I asked him why Sam and Priscilla had two lawyers and I had none? I told him now *HE* was fired and that I'd be by his office the next day to retrieve my binder. And, I added that I'd better not see a bill for this. He had my retainer and he didn't even deserve that for what he did for me.

I decided right then and there that I'd wait to see what AB HR would do with the case. I had confidence that the NDP were the people's government and they'd do right by me.

A couple of days later I got an email from Sam and Priscilla's lawyer. He said that he'd been trying to get in touch with my lawyer and learned that he was not representing me anymore. He asked if I'd seen the offer that Sam and Priscilla had put forth to my lawyer.

I replied that I had seen the offer and that's why my lawyer is no longer representing me. I told him that I'd decided to leave the case in the hands of the AB HR and reiterated my confidence in the NDP government to do right by me.

So, the next day I got another email from Sam and Priscilla's lawyer saying that he needed to talk to me. I replied and said that anything he had to say, he could say in an email.

He replied to that and said that what he had to say needed to be said in person; at least over the phone. He added that it would not interfere with anything I have going with the AB HR. However, he insisted that it was information he needed to disclose to me directly.

I replied to that saying that; if I agree to this conversation, will he guarantee to leave me alone afterwards. And he wrote back saying that he would indeed leave the issue to work itself out as it may.

So I told him to call me the next day at two o'clock in the afternoon; which he did, promptly at two o'clock the phone rang. I picked it up to hear him say that he was going to get right to the point…

Then he said that Sam and Priscilla realize now that this whole thing was just a big misunderstanding. He told me that Sam and Priscilla thought I was so unhappy there that I wanted to leave the company. And so, they now wanted to offer me my job back! Yes, they wanted to offer me my job back!

I must say that I did not breathe for a very long time when he said that. My mind dashed in every direction. Then I recalled that the first thing the AB HR counselor asked me when she finished paging through my binder. She asked whether it was possible to get the job back.

At the time I told them that it was a small mom and pop company. There was no Human Resources department at this company. There were no other managers to work for there. I'd have to work for Priscilla again and I doubted very much that she'd be willing to work with me ever again.

But now they were offering me the job back. When I tuned back into what this lawyer was saying, he was saying that he could send the offer to me by email and I could get back to them. However, the offer was good for only ten business days; to give me time to get another lawyer if I deemed it necessary.

Well, fortunately it was a Tuesday, April 12th. And I did get another lawyer. I don't even recall how I found this guy. However, I met with him on April 21 and we replied to the first offer asking for more money to compensate for the student loan I had to get.

Otherwise, they were offering me the same job and they would treat the re-employment as if I'd never left, which meant I'd reach my five-year mark sooner to gain extra vacation time. However, I did not get my clients back! And that was the screw-me-to-the-wall that they held in their own favor. The deck is always stacked in favor of the house.

My lawyer said that; first of all, they never expected me to even consider the offer. They were hoping I'd just brush it off. And then when AB HR heard that I rejected a reasonable offer, I'd lose the case completely and get nothing, not even the measly five thousand dollars they were offering after I closed my business and became their employee at age sixty-two; and I might add, brought in over one hundred new clients that included that huge oil company.

My lawyer said that I was really between a rock and a hard place with this situation. To him neither option seemed viable.

Yet, I already had another job. In fact, I was starting a whole new career. However, I'd done some number crunching and the money available to me, starting this Health Care Aide whole new career, was barely enough to cover my student loan.

On top of the student loan, I still had my line of credit I had to pay down; and I was leasing the new car I got after my accident in July 2015. My insurance premiums had already gone up… and the base Sam and Priscilla were giving me would cover everything. Mind you, there was nothing left over; but maybe, just maybe I could do it again and reach the commission quota.

It would take at least eighteen months starting from scratch. I had *NO* warm market to bring in this time. But it was a far better opportunity than the Health Care Aide had to offer at the time.

I turned to my lawyer and said, "I'll take it. I'll take the job back!" He looked at me and asked me if I was sure. He asked me if I'd be able to work with someone who had proven a primitive management style at best. And I said I had to try. My lawyer also knew that we could not reject the offer again. If I did they could just say that the offer was off the table and I'd be left with nothing because I refused a reasonable offer.

I'll never know if I could have pushed it further; and I really don't care.

Now, consider this. At this time in history in Calgary companies were downsizing everywhere and anywhere. People were being laid off. The price of oil was at its lowest; and I had not one, but two jobs.

I had already established a route of elderly that I was responsible for according to a schedule. I could not just walk away from that. The company I was working for had to find a replacement for me.

So, I was working days at Sam and Priscilla's company, and evenings for the In-Home Health Care Aide company; and I was about to turn sixty three. And this went on for two weeks from May 16 to the 31st.

When I met with Sam to get set up again I played it very respectful and grateful. While most people would have gone in there all puffed up saying, "Yeah, I got my lawyer on speed dial. You better watch yourself." And I am sure they had reservations about how I was going to be coming back. They had to be aware that I knew full well that they did not think this was a big misunderstanding.

What I think really happened is that my first lawyer was still thinking along the lines of the PC days in Calgary when intimidation was the name of the game. Sam and Priscilla's lawyer just puffed himself up and noted that I'd been fired from my three previous jobs and it would go nowhere in court. And I was not interested in finding out either… So I was truly grateful to take another run at this opportunity.

Therefore, I approached it with gratitude. They gave me a private corner office. It's an inside office, so no windows. But I put up a mirror to trick my brain into thinking I did have a window as it reflected the window in my office door.

They got me a sit-to-stand desk, so I could stand up for part of the day. And that was perfect for me. Sitting too much ties up my back. Being able to stand really allows me to enjoy my work too.

I kept my head down and did the job. Judy came into my office a number of times, as she travelled to and from the kitchen, and tried to goad me into telling her what happened. But I never took the bait. I never said one word to anyone about what really happened.

The best part for everyone is that Priscilla no longer came into the office. I'd never seen Sam so happy. However, I discovered some anomalies in the computer program we work with. My files were being changed and so I started taking pictures (print screen) of my files when I'd set them up.

Then, when I'd find things changed; I'd go to Sam and show him my pictures of the files from a couple weeks ago (the date is automatically shown on the file and is unable to be tampered with); compared to the file at the time. I pretended I didn't know that Priscilla was accessing the files remotely to cause me frustration.

That went on for months until it finally stopped. A couple days after it stopped Barry mentioned to me that they'd discovered that Priscilla doesn't separate family and business very well and that's why she was not coming in anymore.

There were a few other little sabotages too that I just rode the wave on. I did get triggered a time or two; but we all survived it. I started my therapy again to exhaust the 2016 and the 2017 benefit budget for it. And will be back to it again in January 2018.

As I write this the second last week of December 2017 I have to say it's been quite a ride. As of May 16, 2017 I was back working for Sam a full year. In the middle of October they removed all the customer service from my efforts. And wow, what a difference.

While very few customer service personnel want to do outbound calls; outbound calling sales people do *NOT* want to do customer service. That's like taking a prize racehorse and putting them on a milk wagon; and then wondering why there's spilled milk!

To me customer service is like having to babysit these people. So now, as soon as the prospect has placed their first order, they are assigned to a customer service rep to follow up and make sure they keep ordering.

Judy left the company in September 2017 and Sam hired two fantastic guys who each have over ten years in the stationery industry. They know the products and the industry at a depth I'll never have. Nor do I want to.

I also have my energy back. There for a while I was just dragging myself home so drained and exhausted. But now I look forward to going to work every day because I can just do what I am the best at; sales!

Sam even admitted that he recalls that I explained this assembly-line-type structure the day we interviewed in person just before I started with them the first time. I'd suggested to him then to just let me bring in the sales and pass them on to customer service. However, he wanted to hire salespeople to build a business within a business, as he called it; which meant I would develop a clientele that I would nurture and keep for all time.

But he said, and I agree, that they were just not in the position to structure the company that way at that time. However, with Judy gone and her replacement of two fellows who had a great deal of experience, now they were in a position to give the assembly-line approach a try. They have the right people in the right positions. And you know what, I am truly glad for them.

We all live and learn. And if any two people deserve to have the tides turn in their favor, it's Sam and Priscilla. Yes, Priscilla and I won't be going for coffee any time soon. But she's a really good person deep down... really deep down perhaps. And I'm talking waaaaaaay down...

Sam restructured the commission quota and I should be there by the end of January 2018. And that was from scratch, ladies and gentlemen! *Oh yeah, end zone victory dance yet again...!*

Would you like to know what happened to some of my other abusers?

The owner of the marketing company that was stolen from me in 2012 died of cancer in the summer of 2014; when I was with the computer company. The marketing company was reduced to three employees and Lizah was not one of them.

The last time I spoke to Dominick he had been doing the phoning (as per my program) for another company; who was referred to him by the owner of the marketing company, but that project was coming to a close. I have no idea what he's doing now.

Lizah's husband died of complications associated with diabetes and no one knows where she is now.

The woman at the media company left that company and I caught up with her recently on LinkedIn. She told me that the fellow they fired me for never brought in any business. She admitted that my program produced the most sales for their company in comparison to any other advertising or marketing that they ever did. And to that I responded, "That's interesting".

But the best one of all was when the computer company called me one day *'by accident'*. I was driving home from work just this past September (2017). My cell phone rang through the Bluetooth in my car just as I'd tried to voice-dial my daughter, as we often keep each other company on our commute. So I was a bit flustered that it was ringing back to me as I was trying to dial out. Well, to my surprise whose voice do I hear but the head accountant at the computer company.

She asked who she was talking to; and I said I was so sorry that I must have dialed her by accident. I said that I still had her number in my phone. To which she said, "Oh, Deborah? How are you? I am so glad to hear from you."

So I said I was fine and asked her how she was doing. And she replied that #1 had just retired and one of the original programmers had died just over six months ago. It was quite a shock. He was older and had been suffering with several health issues; but he seemed to be handling it all just fine. And then suddenly he passed away in his sleep.

I remarked that having #1 gone is probably wonderful for everyone. I commented that he was so stiff and a real a-hole to work with from the position I was in at the time. I told her that I suspected that he fired me because I proved him wrong by making a sale long before he said I would.

To that she just laughed. Then she asked me if I was happy where I was working; and asked, "And where are you working?"

Well, I must say, I have never enjoyed gushing over how happy I am to be where I am more in my life than I did at that moment. What I didn't tell her is that I would not work for them again, even if they were the last sales opportunity on earth. And if that were the case, I'd pursue the Health Care Aide option.

I know they will never find anyone to sell for them the way I did. No one sells anymore the way I do. I'm a dying breed and I know it. Last of the dinosaurs I suppose. And that's okay.

I'm just so happy to live a 'normal' life for the first time in my life.

Every time I hear of suicide in the news; read it on line; or hear of it from associates it just tears me apart inside because I know that pull. I know that black hole with no light anywhere; and I suspect not even a pinhole of light for them.

I know the sheer and utter hopelessness that envelops your entire being until there is no air to breathe.

There were times when I'd lay on my back in bed and just let that hopelessness press down on me thinking that, if I could just let it stay there, I'd just fall asleep and never wake up as I'd have no strength to fight the weight to take another breath.

And to that I say – write. You have to take time in between the temptations to end it all and write. It does not have to make sense to anyone else. It does not even have to be complete sentences; just write down words that come to your mind. Write down feelings. Draw pictures if you don't have the words. Or take crayons and color on a blank piece of paper with the colors you are attracted to in the box of crayons.

Make sweeping lines like a rainbow with the colors you see and feel. But do this one thing for sure:

Write these words: "WAIT ONE MORE DAY in all capital letters, just like that *'wait one more day'* on a piece of paper, or on a file card, and put it where you will see it every day. And find help. There are programs in every city. There are shelters and suicide hot lines in every city. There are doctor's offices in every city. Be your own best friend and be determined to help you. If you are all you have, why would you use that opportunity to hurt yourself even more?

If you cannot afford to go to therapy just yet, Google 'EMDR Therapy' and you can even see videos demonstrating how the procedure is administered.

Those spots were never yours to begin with! If I could change mine; you can surely change yours!

Chapter Twelve
Journey to Healing

When I learned that a book takes the better part of a full year to reach the bookstores, I thought perhaps it would be interesting to record part of that year and include it as the last chapter. Those of us who suffer scars (spots) from abusive, neglectful, and traumatic childhoods will often abuse ourselves when there is no one else to do so. And to this I say, "Time is up!" This is not to minimize the injustice we've suffered, not by any means; please understand that. Rather, I want to share with you the journey of healing.

The EMDR therapy is one of healing. It does not require you to relive the trauma! And after so many years of bouncing from one therapist to another to just regurgitate the painful, humiliating, and demoralizing events, only to find myself no closer to healing each time, served to make the positive benefits of this therapy that much more obvious.

So, time is definitely up for the spots, scars, and wounds that persisted in robbing me (and you) of the full potential in finding joy, peace, and happiness in this life. So, please do join me in the recovery...

The first challenge for me was money, of course. Having been fired so many times in the most recent past, I was living paycheck to paycheck like a student just out of university. And I even had a student loan now, as well, on top of the business credit line I was still paying down. I had to budget absolutely everything to the dime. In fact, there was no money for entertainment or clothes! I had not purchased new clothes for at least five years by the time I started my EMDR therapy.

You should also know that the mouse for my computer desisted and ceased operation just before I wrote the last five chapters. And having to use the touch-pad on my laptop has been so annoying… and I'm not getting used to it either.

This is probably a perfect time in the story to mention that the publisher I did decide on was obviously the best one. Austin Macauley of New York was so accommodating. You see, an unknown publisher has to pay for part of the expenses of publishing the book. The amount I was charged was so reasonable in comparison to the opportunity they were providing for me; and in comparison to other publishers. And the shared remuneration on book sales is also most generous. I will be forever grateful for their professional support.

However, even though the amount of money they were charging me was just a little more than one month's pay for me; there was NO extra money anywhere. I did not even have that much room on the one credit card I still kept so I could remain somewhat in the flow of modern financial management.

Austin Macauley actually put me on a payment plan that abled me to squeeze enough money out of my grocery budget every month to put on my credit card to just cover each month's payment to them. The only place I could skim off extra money was from my grocery budget. I needed to lose weight anyway; so I used this opportunity to do so.

Every time I felt hungry, my first thought was that I had not yet graduated from the University of Hard Knocks. I'd see myself as still being that starving student and feelings of hopelessness would wash over me. However, I'd immediately shake that off and apply my butterfly hugs (a coping procedure that I'll explain later) to shift my thinking to the fact that this time I was going to cross the finish line. This time I was going to succeed in spite of all the elements against me, including my age and my lack of a formal university education.

And speaking of age; I did not enter my sixties gracefully. My hands have become gnarled with arthritis. For example, I can hardly do the simplest mending, whereas, before I was a skilled seamstress. Even putting on earrings is a challenge because my hands are so stiff. My hearing started to become a challenge in my forties already because I was a disco-duck in my younger years. Spending so much time in the clubs of Philadelphia with loud music took its toll on my ability to distinguish different tones. This has resulted in being totally useless if I am confronted by someone with a foreign accent. Some of the tones they use and the way they accent their words is just lost to my ears. Wearing four-inch spike heels to the disco clubs, and for work every day, just wrecked my back and hips. I was in orthotics by my late-fifties. And I thankfully I met a fantastic doctor who assessed me correctly. He bought me more time before a hip replacement. So far, so good; and here's hoping I go before hip surgery becomes absolutely necessary.

The other challenge regarding money was that I was paying US dollars to Austin Macauley and earning Canadian dollars. Yes, that hurt! And yet, I did it. I made that payment every month until the entire bill was paid off. It took all of seven months.

I've been keeping a bottle of Champaign in my fridge since 1996 when I started to promote my gift line. I was convinced that it would just take off; and of course when it did, I wanted to pop that cork to celebrate. Well, needless to say, that never happened. And as I approached the final payment to publish this book, it crossed my mind to finally pop that cork. But I didn't because the book was nowhere near the bookstore shelves yet. And I probably won't celebrate until the book has been on the shelves for a full year.

Getting back to my story; returning to work in January 2018 after spending the better part of my two weeks off writing chapters eight through eleven, I was feeling pretty confident.

At this point in my journey, and with each stage of healing, I tended to want to believe that I was all better now and could move on and experience no real setbacks anymore. I expected that I'd see the crash coming and be able to avoid it by using the various techniques that I was taught in therapy. And up to this point, I was doing just that; and very successfully I might add.

However, I was about to realize a whole new level of self-awareness. I was about to learn how fast a trigger could set me reeling and set me back! With this coming episode I was about to realize just how strong the PTSD had a hold of my perceptions of the world around me and, consequently, my ability to cope with those perceptions.

It was mid-January and we were still battling severe snowstorms. Our main warehouse where all the product arrives for Alberta is in Edmonton, which is a three-hour drive north on some of the most open highway in Canada. When the wind blows snow across the prairies, it is definitely a force to be reckoned with and respected.

Yet, in spite of our consistent bad weather, it did not happen very often that our truck from Edmonton arrived late, or not at all. I certainly developed a deeper appreciation for the people that drive trucks for a living. They are truly super heroes; and yet totally unsung among our first world problems and solutions. Technology is constantly in the spotlight as being praiseworthy in spite of the enormous problems it causes. Yet these men and women that battle traffic to perform local deliveries, as well as the long-haul drivers, are rarely acknowledged, let alone rewarded for their talent and expertise.

Well, as it happened that morning in mid-January, the truck was late. It had not even arrived yet by ten o'clock, which was our boss's regular arrival as he usually stayed well past closing.

I always needed help getting our product catalogues from our warehouse into the office area so I could construct the promotional catalogue packages we offered new prospective clients. These books are two inches thick and packed ten to a carton.

Our senior driver was just coming in from the warehouse with one of the customer service reps; so I asked him for help. They were not loading trucks, so they had little else to do.

The senior driver suggested that the customer service rep should help me; so he and I proceeded to perform the task just as my boss was arriving

I remember seeing him come around the corner from the front door and head straight for us. He smirked with a look that seemed to say 'got ya' and asked what we were doing.

When I started to explain, he interrupted me and said I was to ask *HIM* for help and not interrupt the other staff from their duties.

In my mind, I was yelling, *"What? Did I not ask you THREE times for these catalogues? I was out of catalogues a full week ago and I cannot do my job without them. You never bothered to get them for me and now you publically reprimand me for asking for help in a perfectly legitimate manner?"* However, on the outside I just froze in place while the customer service rep walked away with my boss trailing close behind as he headed to his office. My head was spinning, my heart was pounding and I just wanted to run, run, run, and run some more. Suddenly, I was right back in that grocery store checkout line when I begged my mother to take me to the potty. She just kept saying, "You can wait, stop pesting." And I did try so hard to hold it; but when failure came, it came fast and hard. I'd never seen myself pee that hard before. Considering that I was about three years old at the time, that makes perfect sense.

I remember screaming as it burst forth and my mom slapping me over and over, saying, "I told you to wait, now look at the mess you've made."

The faces around me were all looking on in distaste and disbelief. Looking back through adult eyes, I now realize that their reaction was to my mother's behavior, not mine. What mother slaps their three-year-old because they'd had an accident of that nature? Yet, no one said a word. In those days, in that part of the world, that kind of behavior was most common. And might very well be so even today in that part of the world.

The check-out clerk used the intercom to call for a 'wet clean up' and my mom was now saying that the discomfort I was about to experience driving home with wet pants was well deserved. To that, my dad scooped me up; took me to the car to put me in the back seat; and his gestures were not gentle.

As all that was going on in the back of my mind, I went to my office and applied the process for calming myself down. It consists of 'butterfly hugs' and I add rocking back and forth to that. A butterfly hug is administered to oneself by crossing your arms in front of you and placing your right palm just below your left shoulder; and the left palm just below the right shoulder and then patting yourself alternately, taking deep breaths and bringing yourself back to the reality that while a public reprimand was inappropriate, embarrassing, and unfair, it was not as severe as my PTSD wanted me to believe.

The scene from the grocery store faded and the next thing that came to my mind was a clear vision of me tearing the place apart. I wanted to throw the computer up against the wall. I wanted to throw my chair through the window in my office door. In my mind, I was the hulk throwing a huge temper tantrum. And all the while yet in another compartment of my mind, I was shocked that I was having such a severe reaction. I thought I was past this… but apparently not!

It took about twenty minutes until I could get back to work and just forget the incident. It was not worth fighting with my boss over it. Once I was back to reality and in the present moment, I was able to decide to just let it go; and so I did. And I gave myself a huge pat on the back for not only surviving that PTSD episode, but for controlling it flawlessly as well.

In addition to this type of reaction, especially if caught off guard, my PTSD came with a very strong dose of paranoia. Suffice to say that if anyone could come up with a conspiracy theory, it would be me.

I could think of ways others could sabotage me that would amaze Alfred Hitchcock, if he were still with us.

So as I gleefully reported to work every day to do what I loved, I became very suspicious when my 'direct marketing program', the one that had never failed to bring in new business, began to return meager results at best. And considering the actual sabotage I experienced when I initially returned to work, my suspicions were always ready to demand my attention.

January is traditionally a very good month for sales of most things business-oriented. That's because everyone flakes off in December one way or another. If they are not off on vacation, as I am for the last two weeks of December every year, they are partying their butts off by attending one holiday event after another.

Therefore, when January produced six, yes I said six, new clients when my target was thirty minimum; you can imagine the bells, whistles, and red flags that went off in my head! As any normal person would be alarmed, add my previous experience with the program that 'never' failed fueled by an oversized dose of paranoia, and we are talking sleepless nights.

I started to be more attentive to details and noticed that it appeared as if company names and notes were disappearing off the Excel spreadsheet that I used to keep track of my 'prospecting' efforts. Spending some extra time with the copies I made of my work, I could see that information was being lost when actually saving the file at the end of the workday. I decided to stay focused and really put the pedal to the metal for the first quarter and see how it went by the end of March. Meantime, I did talk to a number of other sales people, who are friends of mine and who I trust to give me an honest answer to the question: 'Are sales this bad everywhere?' And indeed they were. I was hearing that six new customers in a month would be most appreciated by the majority of my fellow sales people.

At the end of March, I printed off all of the computer reports for daily sales for all three months; January, February, and March. I was convinced that my sales were being confiscated before the computer could record them under my sales number. So, therefore, someone else was taking credit for my sales! And please understand that there are fifty-three companies listed per page and there are ten to twelve pages PER DAY recorded. And yes, I printed them ALL. Sixty working days times just ten pages per day would produce six hundred pieces of paper.

Over the Easter long weekend of March 30, 31, and April 1, 2018 I spent just under twelve hours (three to four hours a day) combing through all that paper work comparing each day to the day before and sure enough, I found companies missing from my sales report. Nearly four dozen companies were unaccounted for within my scope of research. This was most concerning and I had to wait until I was back at work to search the customer files to see who had claimed these (possible) sales.

You can bet I was at work very early that morning and one by one I checked in on these missing companies. And to my surprise; they were all accounted for! Each and every one had been either removed from the prospecting effort (by myself) because they asked to be removed; or the company no longer existed; or it was a duplicate account for a company already in my follow-up process. However, what I did uncover was that there were five companies I'd brought in that had been put back into my area. This was most curious because customer service is supposed to assign all new clients to a customer service representative upon the delivery of the first order. And from that point onward, the client's file bears the customer service rep's code number rather than mine. Further research revealed that these five companies came in at a low margin for their first order. So, because the customer service reps receive a commission based upon the margins they maintain; they removed these specific clients so their margins were not dragged down by these particular sales. That way they got paid more! Needless to say,

Sam was *NOT* amused by my findings; and appreciated my efforts, as I showed him the mound of paper with all the little sticky arrows pointing to the discrepancies as they were found. While the discovery rendered my concerns that something was going on as justified, it was not nearly as gratifying as having found the infraction that I was expecting. Therefore, alas, I carried on my prospecting efforts, fully aware that the market was really as bad as my program was demonstrating it to be, and no one else was to blame. The entire issue and the effort necessary to carry out the research proved to me that I could control my emotions and truly channel the negative energy into productive activity. After I got over the disappointment, I congratulated myself for a job well done.

So, into second quarter we go. At the time I was feeling very grounded and I had put my paranoia to rest. All was quiet and peaceful in my little corner of the world and I am happily doing the job I love. And to my sheer delight, a company that I've chased with every line I'd ever carried in Calgary called me to place their first order.

This felt like a reward from the great beyond for my good behavior and for keeping control of things. I took the order and did the data entry as I'd done so often before; however as Murphy's Law would have it, I made a mistake.

The computer system we use is very basic, and for what we do it is quite sufficient. I am not complaining about the system. However, when you do have to correct a mistake, it takes a minimum of three very specific, and multifaceted, steps to do so. And because this was a very important new client for me, I really wanted this to go perfectly.

After I corrected the mistake, I took the order to Sam. I demonstrated how I corrected the mistake I'd made and asked him to look it all over to make sure it was all correct and told him why this was so important to me. He acknowledged my win with all the appropriate commendations and verified that the order was correct, and they would receive their delivery the next day as per our usual service.

At this point I have to interject that I always loved working for Sam. He is one of these 'really nice guys' that gets caught by a manipulative witchy woman who drives the guy to his fullest

*potential in strength and energy. Yet, somehow he remains just
a really nice guy.*

I drove in the next morning with wings on my shoes only to
be met by our senior delivery driver who informed me that *NO*
product arrived for my new client... not *ONE* of the ten items
they'd ordered was on the truck from Edmonton that morning.

The first thing that hit me was wondering if I was dreaming
this... because this could not be happening. I'd made double and
triple sure that the order was correct... I went to my computer
and checked the order again and the correct address was on it.
Everything was right... so my mind was screaming, *WHAT
HAPPENED?*

I immediately wrote an email to Sam, as he'd get it on his
phone... and then I called Edmonton and caught up with our
driver there. I asked her if she'd seen an order for this company.
At first she said no, but then she caught herself and said yes, she
had. And because it had a Calgary address, she'd sent it back.

Up to this point, I was keeping it together. I was dealing with
the issue and seeking a solution. But the fact that our driver sent
the order 'back' meant that it would be two days before it was
rerouted back to Calgary. I knew I might be able to avoid the
two-day delay; but first I had to call the client and let them know
that the order was delayed and not being delivered today as they
expected.

I find it is always better to be the one to tell them that
something went wrong rather than having them call us to say the
order did not arrive. Fortunately, the buyer was most
understanding about it and said there was no rush on any of the
items. And while that is reassuring; we still had not performed to
our best potential on their *FIRST* order. You get only *ONE*
chance to make a *FIRST* impression; and this was on me. It was
my face on this mishap with a company I'd been chasing for
thirty years... Greaaaaaaat!

As I was wallowing in some very well deserved self-pity, the
senior accountant came in and started offering me solutions that
I'd already administered and was well past. So he was only
serving to frustrate me and that triggered the anger. Up until this
point, I was holding my own. I was dealing with it. But now this
guy; who was otherwise my best friend at work, mostly because

223

we were the same age, was not helping me, but was serving to make matters worse while my next challenge was getting that order to Calgary the next day. Meantime, I got a reply email from Sam saying he'd look into it as soon as he arrived; which was nearly two hours in the future and too late to get that order off the return pile and onto the pallet that would be delivered to Calgary the next morning.

Well, after my buddy (the senior accountant) made me retrace my steps, he said he knew how to get the order redirected to ensure its arrival for the next morning. I went with him to his office and sure enough, he was able to contact the right people just in time to have that order redirected to the pallet scheduled for us the next day.

We also uncovered the reason for the mistake. Apparently the file had a code in it to deliver the product for this company's Calgary address to Edmonton. Once upon a time, this company did all of its ordering in Edmonton and had trucks of their own to bring the product to Calgary. We corrected the code in the system and, breathing a sigh of relief, I went into the break room to construct some catalogue packages. Yet, to my surprise the more I tried to put the issue behind me, the angrier I got. The butterfly hugs were doing nothing for me. All I could think about was how diligent I'd been to ensure that the order would deliver properly. I'd even asked Sam to look it over to make sure it was correct. How did he miss the delivery code being wrong? My ears were sizzling and my head was beginning to pound.

I'd been back at my job one month short of two years by this time and it was the first time that I had to just get out of there before I did something drastic and something I'd surely regret. The catalogues and samples set up for the packages were left on the table; I went to my computer and wrote an email to Sam saying I was sorry, but I had to leave. I just could not be there. He emailed right back saying it was okay and that I should just go.

I got in my car and started for home; and the minute I got onto the freeway, the anger subsided. I was home by nine o'clock in the morning and I went to my computer and began typing it all out for my next session with my therapist.

As little as six months before this episode, if the same thing would have happened, I would have been on a downward spiral for days. I would have beat myself up and felt like I wanted to die. I would have been feeling hopeless and useless and seeing my entire life as a complete failure. That was the process I called 'going down the rabbit hole'. I would have been writing out my suicide note and making my plans; and then I'd wait one more day.

But not this time! This time I bounced back as soon as I put distance between myself and the issue. And you might say it was ridiculous for me to be so overwhelmed by failing to deliver office supplies. 'Really? This is not like brain surgery. This is not a life and death service we provide. It's office supplies for goodness' sake… get over it.'

But, I come from not only PTSD, but also from a generation that took pride in their work. Whether cleaning floors, driving a truck, or delivering office supplies, my generation took pride in their work. We were passionate about what we did for a living. Because each and every one of us is not just another brick in the wall; each and every one of us mattered. And what we did mattered regardless of how small the task may have seemed; because it was (and still is) all necessary to keep the world turning, growing, and productive.

And that brings me to the next thing for which time is definitely up: rudeness on a *business* telephone!

Most of my business life I have had to use the telephone to find people who could benefit from whatever product or service I was representing at the time. And yes, it is a 'soliciting' call… *insert gasping and shock expressed by an excessive intake of air here*. I agree that if someone calls your private home (if you still have a 'land-line' like I still do); or if someone calls your cell phone, go ahead and be as rude as you want to because you are representing you and only you.

However, if you are answering the phone for a company; if you are a buyer of the product or service for a company, is it not your job to respond to such opportunities? If you are being paid to do a job that might include phone calls accordingly, why does that give you license to be rude to the caller?

In fact, that rudeness is actually a form of prejudice and bullying! It is certainly not an act of professional interaction, or even intellectual communication. It is just pure prejudice because you have *NOT* taken time to know who you are talking to in order to make a sound, informed business decision. It is bullying because you are treating that person in a manner I am very confident that you would not appreciate if you were on the receiving end of the behavior.

For years upon years, and upon more years, I just took the behavior as part of the job. I'd been conditioned to accept this harsh treatment as if I deserved it for being so presumptuous to expect the person on the other end of the line would love and enjoy their job as much as I did and who, therefore, would want to do their job the best that they could.

Then again, I expect that some of those rude receptionists and buyers felt good when they beat someone down for daring to contact them for an aspect of business that they were being paid to do.

As well, perhaps they were told by their management to be as obnoxious and as demoralizing as possible if a solicitation call came in. Or was it just their interpretation of their job that was amiss?

I decided to start checking into it. I started going on the websites of companies where I experienced this distasteful behavior and I would send an email, if I could; or I'd send a letter by snail mail to the management of the company.

This went on for months and months and I never heard back from anyone, until one day I did! Of course I cannot mention any names, and here I won't even mention the industry to ensure privacy for this company. However, the action this gentleman took to my disclosing email made all the non-responses worth the wait.

When he got back to me to tell me that the story from the receptionist was very different than the version I voiced, it finally dawned on me. Not one of those receptionists would ever admit how they really treated me. And without a recording, it was a matter of 'he said; she said'.

If anyone tells me, someone who has been on the phone for forty-one years, that they have an 'approved vendor list', of course I am going to thank them and be gone. I don't want to waste time even chatting niceties to someone where there is no potential for new business. What astounded me most was the fact that I *NEVER* once suspected that the receptionist would paint herself so innocent. How naive could I possibly be? And of course the management will side with them against the big bad telephone solicitor. From the management's perspective, there is no way that the evil telephone solicitor could have been polite, professional, and respectful; and the actual offense was initiated by their own employee.

At the same time, the receptionist herself knows full well how the call *REALLY* went. And hopefully the inquiry by a member of the executive population in her company will have instilled a more respectful approach to the issue next time.

Needless to say, to record the conversations without first mentioning the fact is illegal. To mention it will probably incite immediate disconnects as the recipient will just hang up. On the other hand, it might initiate a more respectful response... In any case, I am in no way equipped to record the calls whether I mention it or not. So, I have to just let it rest.

In the meantime, however, the experience provided the opportunity to meet the most wonderful man. He was just a real warm human being. Someone anyone would love to work for. I never met him in person. In fact, I never spoke to him over the phone. The entire encounter was a series of emails. I missed his emails starting the very next day after the matter was settled. I told him I would miss them and his last email to me was full of encouragement and I quote:

"Keep your chin up, your eye on the prize, don't sweat the small stuff (and it is all small stuff) and dance like no one is watching... everything will be great!"

I could go on and on about my individual experiences and my recovery journey. However, I think it much more beneficial for you now if I were to share (and recap those worth repeating) some of the aspects of my therapy that were, not only unique to the EMDR process, but also effective and healing.

This technique is so more effective, more quickly, than any other therapy I've tried before EMDR.

The entire purpose of this publication is to encourage those of us who are functioning and somewhat productive in their lives; yet know that they have much greater potential. I'm speaking of feelings that go beyond feelings of inadequacy and unfulfilled potential that we all feel before we achieve 'living the dream'.

I'm talking about realizing that you are sabotaging yourself. You are stuck and cannot seem to get past some level in life as if you are in a glass box. You can see the prize. You can see the results and the goals you want. However, they repeatedly remain just beyond reach. And this frustration will often make you feel like ending it all rather than carrying on in determination. Even if it's a fleeting thought, take note and address it sooner rather than later.

And this is something only you can know, and only for yourself. While you may recognize it in others; unless they realize it for themselves, there is no therapy that will help. That is not to say that you cannot offer this book to these people in hopes that it sheds light on their own awareness so that they can break free of the ties that bind them; whatever they may be. However, it can be just as damaging to point it out for them. Just offer the book in any case where you think a person is stuck and missing out on living their fullest potential.

All of the motivational speakers along with all of their literature and public appearances have so much to offer; and yet most of us cannot put their advice into any long-term action due to the spots we carry

While my spots ran deep, as PTSD does, most spots are more superficial in nature and therefore much more easily removed. Some might identify them as 'habitual/learned behavior patterns' or 'knee-jerk reactions' and acknowledge them as 'normal' reactions given the circumstance.

For example, some people think being rude on a business phone is justified. So, that is merely a 'learned, habitual behavior pattern', a 'Knee-jerk reaction' that simply requires an education to change it for the better. Road-rage is another behavior recently surfacing as a more frequent occurrence. Let me tell you that I firmly believe that road-rage was *invented* by PTSD. Traffic is the perfect setting to arouse the most negative, violent, and unforgiving behaviors capable of otherwise docile people. And this is definitely not gender specific. Road-rage has no preference when it comes to gender, age, socio-economical standing, or religion. In fact, have you ever seen a crowded parking lot for any place of worship empty out calmly and politely? If you have, check one more time before you let me know! And please do let me know:

support@spotsonaleopard.online.

Any behavior that 'takes over' without your consent is coming from spots created in your personality by adverse experiences. Here I strongly suggest that you watch the movie "Inside Out". It provides a very simple portrayal of how the mind and emotions work together; and at times independently of one another as if in a contest to be in charge

If anyone would like to just explore the possibilities of improving one's own ability to live their authentic self and realize their full potential; as I've mentioned before, this EMDR process does not require you to relive the circumstances, trauma, or offense that caused whatever issue you have; whether it be PTSD or something else. Rather, it *allows* healing by setting the stage for the brain to reprocess the event(s) and therefore remove the spot, which is the trigger point that ignites the inappropriate behavior.

We all recognize our different roles in this life such as: wife, husband, mother, father, daughter, son, friend, relative, professional, worker, consumer, motorist, member, official, and on it goes. And we can usually move seamlessly from one role to another; and often combining roles when necessary.

This is all very typical (as I avoid using the term 'normal') and all of these aspects are considered 'parts of self'. In addition to the aforementioned 'parts of self', we will also contain aspects of our childhood and adolescence; along with a manager part, a bystander part, a defender part, and so on. And each of these parts step to the foreground in any given situation to interact with the world around us.

When a person experiences (especially) trauma, the experience does not 'file' properly in the brain. The trauma isolates the experience in the area of the brain that houses perception and response rather than 'filing' it as a memory. And because the brain does not know time on its own, whenever something occurs that reminds the brain of the traumatic experience, the 'fight, flight, or freeze' response is *triggered* because the trauma is identified as a threat; and, it plays out as if the incident is occurring (threatening) in the present moment rather than reflecting as just an unpleasant memory.

The actual incident may not play out to the point that the person can recognize it in detail. Rather, the feeling of 'fight, flight, or freeze' will simply take over. So, which 'part-of-self' should respond to this? The answer to that question depends totally upon the individual experiencing the situation. Finding your answers to your reactions is like unraveling a tangled ball of yarn. This is why you need a therapist; a qualified, licensed therapist to guide you through it. And let me tell you, after so many experiences with therapists, and each one was affective in their time, I feel qualified to say that the EMDR process was by far the most rewarding and the most healing. And I can truthfully say that the journey was pleasant because I did not have to relive the trauma, which was severe for me, as you know.

That is not to minimize the work necessary. For example, writing has always been a very soothing and satisfying outlet for me. Yet now, finishing the last five chapters of the book in December 2017, and then continuing in 2018 with this final chapter as the book is in editing, has been real *WORK* for me. I will realize the reward of soothing satisfaction only after the book is on the shelves and available to those who can benefit from the story it contains.

While I cannot see myself as 'an author', having written only one book, and one about my direct experiences, I have great empathy when I hear other authors say that they love 'to have written' rather than describing themselves as 'loving to write'.

For me, writing the book nagged me in the back of my mind constantly, no matter what else I was doing. It took a great deal of focus to quiet it down enough to be in the moment while doing something else; and especially at work. Outings with my daughter and grandson were the only things other than watching TV that could quiet the nagging down enough to let it rest. Although, my true passion is volunteer community service and I do engage in that on a weekly basis. And when I am working in my volunteer service, nothing distracts me. In fact, that has always been my sanctuary and where I obtained the recharging necessary to carry on with the obligations of working for the almighty dollar in this world.

Meantime, on July 3rd of 2018, the Office Supply Company finally had enough evidence to fire me again. They'd given me a pile of dead wood to sift through and when the sales were minimal, they could 'discontinue the program' and me along with it. In other words, the companies they had me calling were either set in their ways, unqualified to use our services, or no longer in business at all anymore.

Had they settled with me rather than offering me the job back in April of 2016, I would have settled for one year's worth of income... the way they did it, they paid twice that plus severance... oh the wisdom of the young entrepreneurs.

I was actually glad that they finally let me go. I was tired of being where I was not welcome. In fact, I'd told my daughter only the week before that I was getting to the point where I wished they would fire me.

The severance supported me through July and August as I tried to find another job. And during that time I realized how devastating it had been to report to that job every day.

Suddenly my back was not tied in knots anymore. My digestion straightened out. I kept busy with my volunteer work and found myself happier and healthier than I'd been in years.

As I finish this final chapter, I am seeking to donate a portion of the proceeds of the book to a charity that will benefit the people most regarding the spots we all carry. You will see the outcome of that search on the back page.

I also started seeking sponsorship from a number of companies that I either have used their products for a very long time, or, I have been a faithful client of, or, I have a great deal of respect for and wanted to be a part of promoting them to others at the same time. Again, if any of the companies or organizations that I approached became a sponsor for this work, you will see them listed on the 'sponsor' page, probably following the final page of text.

Meantime, yesterday the announcement was made that a very well-known designer from New York (Kate Spade) committed suicide leaving a thirteen-year-old daughter behind. My heart just broke at this news and I cried and cried. I felt like this book may be too late. And it is too late for her; but not for others! Then Anthony Bourdain! ...what? My heart is just aching at this news.

So I am asking you now, you reading this book, get on social media ASAP and begin the outreach. Let's get the word out about the process that helped me for so many years can help anyone. And that process is as follows:

Write down all the steps you plan to take to end your life. Make sure they are in the proper order. Write down on the reasons that you have to end your life. Write the note you plan to leave behind.

Read all your notes, your letter, and your plan over to ensure you did not miss anything. Read them as often as it takes until you are sure that everything is in order.

Then put all that paper into an envelope… write the date and time on the envelope; and then WAIT ONE MORE DAY… 24 hours…

And while you are waiting, take a pillow and hold it in your arms. Get into a rocking chair, or just rock back and forth in the seat you are in and be your own best friend right now. What would *YOU* say if *YOU* came across a person who was planning to end their life; what would you say to that person?

I promise you, if you wait one more day and allow yourself to sleep, to rest, *WITHOUT* mixing drugs and alcohol, things will not look as bad in 24 hours as they do now. *PLEASE WAIT ONE MORE DAY.*

Perhaps you feel that 'time's up' and 'wait one more day' are a direct contradiction? However, time's up for all the pain and suffering. Time's up for being robbed of the joy and happiness you deserve as much as the next person. To take yourself out of the life that could be so wonderful is not the answer. Only you can stop the torture. Only you can get the assistance you need to determine why this is happening to you; and *YES,* it *IS* happening *TO* you!

Sometimes our choices put us in circumstances where we do suffer consequences. However, you can claim only part of the responsibility. The other part belongs 'out there' with the people, the systems, the circumstances, whatever is holding you down… and only *YOU* can stop it… only *YOU* can turn this around and *YOU CAN* do it…

And if you are reading this because of mere curiosity; or perhaps you know someone who has struggled the way I have and you've always wondered why they seem to always have such a hard time of it… PLEASE, tell them about this book. Plus, get on social media and talk about this book. Start tweeting, or go to your Facebook page, or whatever it is that gets the word out quickly, and let's reach out as a society, as a community, as human beings that love other human beings and let's make a difference. Let's see the suicide numbers go *DOWN* from this day forward...

Come to my blog website and share your story: https://www.spotsonaleopard.online.

WAIT ONE MORE DAY is the first step. The next step is making the appointment to see someone who can assist you in turning your life around. There are help lines in every city where this book is being distributed. Make the call! And ask for EMDR... find it online, google it, and get an appointment.

If EMDR is out of reach due to dollars... let's make that the next thing we tweet about! Let's get the therapy needed affordable please! Meantime, you can find demonstrations online.

As I finish this it is the first part of July 2018. I'm going to have to hand this last chapter into my publisher as I suspect I am holding up production. However, I am going to continue to write my experiences and my journey through healing; through seeking sponsorships; and through publishing this book and I will be sharing that information on my blog website; at my book signings; and my public appearances.

So, I do hope to see you there so we can compare notes! Until then… reach out and help someone else wait one more day…

Most Sincerely,

Deborah Susan

Deborah Susan

Suggested Reading

Homecoming & Creating Love	by Dr. John Bradshaw
The Road Less Traveled	by Dr. M. Scott Peck
I'm Okay – You're Okay	by Dr. Tomas Harris
Chicken Soup for the Soul	by Dr. Jack Canfield and Dr. Mark Victor Hansen
Celestine Prophecy	by James Redfield
Winning Through Intimidation	by Robert Ringer
You Can Heal Your Life	by Louise Hay
Lip Service	by Kate Fillion
Beyond Sex Roles	by Dr. Gilbert Bilezikian
With No Fear of Failure	by Fatjo/Miller
Your Sacred Self	by Dr. Wayne Dyer
Pulling Your Own Strings	by Dr. Wayne Dyer
Dinosaur Brains	by Bernstien/Rozen
Shadow Syndromes	by Dr. John J. Ratey

And Now a Word from Our Sponsors

Although I did approach a number of businesses, associations, and organizations prior to this book going to print stage, no one stepped forward.

And I certainly appreciate their hesitation. There are so many legitimate causes available for our monetary donations, as well as our volunteer time; how does one make a choice?

I still receive a number of calls every week in which I am solicited for a contribution of some sort. And just as I have dedicated myself to the cause of suicide prevention, so have many others committed themselves to a cause that is dear to their heart; and probably for much the same reasons as I have for my commitment. And my heart goes out to each and every one of them.

Therefore, we have to stand on our own for our cause.
We have to be determined to see suicide statistics drop within the year of mid-2019 to the end of 2020.

Give what you can. Perhaps it's time that you have to offer? Is it dollars because you have no time to allocate? Perhaps it's a little bit of both?

Yet, if all you ever do is recommend this book to one person, you have done a great thing.

If this publication rescues only one person who would have otherwise ended their own life, then all the time, effort, and dollars would have been well worth it.

I hope I see you at one of my book signings, or a meeting scheduled for readers who have questions.

My personal appearances will not consist of a lecture or discourse on even the most relevant issues. Rather, I want to hear your questions and how I can help you.

Rather, my personal appearances will be to hear from you! The following page has a few things on it that you should be prepared with if you want to attend one of my meetings.

Meantime, I look forward to seeing you there.

Feel free to write your notes on this page and bring it to the meeting (and/or write out the necessary information on a separate piece of paper and bring that along with you, please).

You will be asked to leave your questionnaire with my assistant as you enter the room.

If you would be willing to be recognized for your question or comment at the meeting, please include your name:

Name: _____

City and State: _____

Question or Comment for discussion: _____

_____
_____
_____
_____
_____
_____
_____
_____
_____
_____
_____
_____
_____

If your question or comment is urgent; please do send me an email! support@spotsonaleopard.online.